"Aykut, Foyer and Morena have produced a unique volume of rich case studies on the performative function of COP21 in Paris. It drives forward our understanding, in new and unexpected ways, of how the idea of climate change alters political, social and cultural worlds, just as importantly as a changing physical climate is altering the material world. These 200 pages are an important complement to the 3000 pages of the last IPCC report."
— **Mike Hulme,** *Professor of Climate and Culture, King's College London, UK*

"*Globalising the Climate* brings together ten fascinating and original takes on key under-discussed elements of the climate change issue and the 2015 Paris negotiations in particular. The volume also brings central Francophone debates to English language readers — an overdue and much-needed contribution."
— **J. Timmons Roberts,** *Ittleson Professor of Environmental Studies and Sociology, Brown University, USA*

"Only the ethnographic method could give us such a remarkable view of what is arguably the most important diplomatic event since the birth of the United Nations. The authors' descriptions give a vivid understanding of the conundrum of climate diplomacy: it is supposed to cover the whole globe and yet it reduces the globe to a tiny set of documents and issues inside small closed rooms and local events. This is political anthropology at its best."
— **Bruno Latour,** *Professor, Sciences Po Paris, France*

"In combining critical analysis and ethnographic fieldwork, *Globalising the Climate* provides the reader with unique insights into climate governance in-the-making and valuable examinations of the many ways in which the warming climate transforms other global debates. Thought-provoking and timely."
— **Oliver Geden,** *Stiftung Wissenschaft und Politik, Berlin, Germany*

# Globalising the Climate

Frequently presented as a historic last chance to set the world on a course to prevent catastrophic climate change, the 21st Conference of the Parties to the Climate Convention (COP21) was a global summit of exceptional proportions. Bringing together negotiators, scientists, journalists and representatives of global civil society, it also constituted a privileged vantage point for the study of global environmental governance "in the making".

This volume offers readers an original account of the current state of play in the field of global climate governance. Building upon a collaborative research project on COP21 carried out by a multidisciplinary team of twenty academics with recognised experience in the field of environmental governance, the book takes COP21 as an entry point to analyse ongoing transformations of global climate politics, and to scrutinise the impact of climate change on global debates more generally. The book has three key objectives:

1   To analyse global climate governance through a combination of long-term analysis and on-sight observation;
2   To identify and analyse the key spaces of participation in the global climate debate;
3   To examine the "climatisation" of a series of cross-cutting themes, including development, energy, security and migration.

This book will be of great interest to students, scholars and policymakers of climate politics and governance, international relations and environmental studies.

**Stefan C. Aykut** is a political scientist and sociologist at the Laboratoire Interdisciplinaire Sciences Innovations Sociétés (LISIS) at Université Paris-Est Marne-la-Vallée, France and an associated researcher at Centre Marc Bloch in Berlin, Germany.

**Jean Foyer** is a political scientist and sociologist at the CNRS-affiliated Institut des Sciences de la Communication (ISCC), France.

**Edouard Morena** is a political scientist and an associate researcher at the CNRS-affiliated Laboratoire Dynamiques Sociales et Recompositions des Espaces (LADYSS), France. He is also a part-time lecturer in French and European Studies at the University of London Institute in Paris (ULIP).

# Routledge Advances in Climate Change Research

For a full list of titles in this series, please visit www.routledge.com

# Globalising the Climate

COP21 and the Climatisation
of Global Debates

Edited by
Stefan C. Aykut, Jean Foyer
and Edouard Morena

LONDON AND NEW YORK

from Routledge

First published 2017 by Routledge

2 Park Square, Milton Park, Abingdon, Oxfordshire OX14 4RN
711 Third Avenue, New York, NY 10017

*Routledge is an imprint of the Taylor & Francis Group, an informa business*

First issued in paperback 2018

*British Library Cataloguing-in-Publication Data*
A catalogue record for this book is available from the British Library

*Library of Congress Cataloging-in-Publication Data*
A catalog record for this book has been requested

ISBN: 978-1-138-67559-9 (hbk)
ISBN: 978-0-367-02679-0 (pbk)


Typeset in Goudy
by Apex CoVantage, LLC

# Contents

# Figures

# Acknowledgements

We wish to begin by thanking the Institut Francilien Recherche Innovation Société (IFRIS) for its financial contribution towards the research project that forms the basis for the present book. Our sincere thanks also go out to the Ile de France regional council for funding a postdoctoral fellowship, and the GIS Climat for its support of the international workshop organised in Paris in July 2015.

We would also like to thank the Centre Alexandre Koyré d'Histoire des Sciences for its administrative support, and the organisers and participants in the "Changement climatique et Biosphère" research seminar for their stimulating discussions and collective wisdom. We also wish to thank the Institut des Sciences de la Communication (ISCC) for its continuous logistical, scientific and moral support.

On a more personal level, we wish to thank Kara and Paul for their fantastic work translating and editing earlier versions of the chapters contained in this book. We also wish to thank Anabella Rosemberg for taking the time to share her "insider" perspective on the international climate debate, and for facilitating our access to the Paris conference.

Last but by no means least, our deep-felt thanks go out to Amy Dahan. Amy supported us throughout the various stages of this project. Thank you, Amy, for the lively and rousing discussions, for your invaluable advice, patience and affection. The present book and associated project were a way for you to "cut the strings" with class and magnanimity.

# Acronyms

| | |
|---|---|
| ADP | Ad-hoc Group on the Durban Platform |
| AOSIS | Alliance of Small Island States |
| BECCS | Bioenergy with Carbon Capture and Storage |
| CAN | Climate Action Network |
| CBD | Convention on Biological Diversity |
| CBS | Climate Briefing Service |
| CC21 | Coalition Climat 21 |
| CCS | Carbon Capture and Storage |
| CEA | California Environmental Associates |
| CGBD | Consultative Group on Biological Diversity |
| CJA | Climate Justice Action |
| CJN | Climate Justice Now |
| COP | Conference of Parties |
| CIFF | Children's Investment Fund Foundation |
| CW | ClimateWorks Foundation |
| E3G | Third Generation Environmentalism |
| ETS | Emission Trading Scheme |
| ECF | European Climate Foundation |
| FAO | Food and Agriculture Organisation |
| GCCA | Global Call for Climate Action |
| GHG | Greenhouse Gas |
| GtC | Gigatonnes of Carbon |
| IIASA | International Institute for Applied Systems Analysis |
| IEA | International Energy Agency |
| ICC | International Chamber of Commerce |
| ICSU | International Council for Science |
| IDDRI | Institut du Développement Durable et des Relations Internationales |
| IETA | International Emissions Trading Association |
| IIED | International Institute for Environment and Development |
| IIPFCC | International Indigenous Peoples Forum on Climate Change |
| IMF | International Monetary Fund |
| IPCC | Intergovernmental Panel on Climate Change |

| | |
|---|---|
| IPPI | International Policies and Politics Initiative |
| IUCN | International Union for the Conservation of Nature |
| LARCI | Latin America Regional Climate Initiative |
| LDC | Least Developed Countries |
| LPAA | Lima-Paris Action Agenda |
| NETs | Negative Emissions Technologies |
| OECD | Organisation for Economic Co-operation and Development |
| OPEC | Organization of the Petroleum Exporting Countries |
| PC | Project Catalyst |
| PBL | Netherlands Environmental Assessment Agency |
| PIK | Postdam Institute for Climate Impact Research |
| PPM | Parts-per-million |
| PtB | Place to B |
| REDD | Reducing Emissions from Deforestation and Forest Degradation |
| SBSTA | Subsidiary Body for Scientific and Technological Advice |
| STS | *Science and Technology Studies* |
| UN | United Nations |
| UNFCCC | United Nations Framework Convention on Climate Change |
| UNESCO | United Nations Educational, Scientific and Cultural Organization |
| UNDP | United Nations Development Programme |
| UNEP | United Nations Environment Programme |
| WBCSD | World Business Council for Sustainable Development |
| WIPO | World Intellectual Property Organisation |
| WRI | World Resources Institute |
| WTO | World Trade Organisation |
| WWF | World Wide Fund for Nature |

# Biographies

**Stefan C. Aykut** is a research fellow at the Laboratoire Interdisciplinaire Sciences Innovations Sociétés (LISIS) at Université Paris-Est MLV and INRA. He has extensively written on global climate governance and on the political sociology of energy transitions, and is the co-author, with Amy Dahan, of *Gouverner le Climat? 20 ans de négociations internationales* (2015).

**Alice Baillat** is a PhD candidate in political science at Sciences Po Paris (France). Specialising in climate diplomacy, over the past six years, she has been studying the most vulnerable countries' involvement in the UNFCCC process, with particular focus on Bangladesh.

**Sarah Benabou** is a research fellow at the Institut de Recherche pour le Développement (IRD) in Paris (France). As part of a wider interest in the political economy of environmental conservation, she specialises in the study of environmental conservation in the Global South (with a focus on India). In addition to her ethnographic work in India, she has been actively following the involvement of business actors in international biodiversity and climate negotiations.

**Christophe Buffet** is a Paris-based researcher and consultant in climate change adaptation and disaster risk reduction. He studies adaptation and official development assistance, the interface between climate sciences and policies, and community-based adaptation.

**Monica Castro** is a postdoctoral researcher at the University of Pau (France). Her research focuses on international environmental policies in the Global North and South and their effects. Her most recent work looks at the social conflicts related to fossil fuel production.

**Jean-Baptiste Comby** is an associate professor at the University of Paris 2–affiliated French Press Institute (France). He has conducted and coordinated research on the social construction and perceptions of climate change as a public problem in France in the 2000s. His findings are included in his most recent book, *La question climatique: Genèse et dépolitisation d'un problème public*.

**Joost de Moor** is associate researcher at the Center for Understanding Sustainable Prosperity at Keele University (United Kingdom). His research focuses on social movements, environmental movements and more specifically on the international climate movement. He has published on these issues in *Mobilization* and the *International Journal of Urban and Regional Research*.

**David Dumoulin Kervran** is a sociologist at the Institut des Hautes Etudes de l'Amérique latine (IHEAL-CREDA) at the Sorbonne Nouvelle University in Paris (France). He has published extensively on NGOSs and transnational networks, the politics of traditional knowledge, multiculturalism and conservation policies in Latin America. His current research focuses on field biologists in tropical regions and the importance of place in science production.

**Jean Foyer** is a sociologist at the CNRS-affiliated Institut des Sciences de la Communication (ISCC) in Paris (France). His main areas of interest are global environmental governance, socio-technical controversies and indigenous and environmental mobilisations. He is the author of *Il était une fois la bio-révolution* (2010), *De la integración nacional al desarrollo sustentable* (2011) and editor of *¿Desarrollo con identidad? Governanza económica indígena* (2010) and *Regards croisés sur Rio+20* (2015).

**Hélène Guillemot** is a researcher at the Alexandre Koyré Center (CAK) in Paris, France. Her research focuses on modelling practices in the field of climate science, on climate change controversies, climate change expertise and the interactions between science and politics.

**Lucile Maertens** is a postdoctoral fellow in political science and international relations. Funded by the Swiss National Science Foundation, she is a visiting researcher at Columbia University/Earth Institute in New York (USA) and an associate researcher at CERI/SciencesPo in Paris, France. Using ethnographic methods, her work focuses on UN discourses and practices on security, environment and climate change.

**Edouard Morena** is a lecturer in French and European politics at the University of London Institute in Paris (France). Over the past five years, he has been actively monitoring non-state actors' involvement in international environmental and development processes – with particular focus on the UNCSD and UNFCCC. He recently published *The Price of Climate Action: Philanthropic Foundations in the International Climate Debate* (2016).

**Nils Moussu** is a graduate assistant and PhD candidate at the Institute of Political, Historical, and International Studies (IEPHI) at the University of Lausanne (Switzerland). His main research interests include climate and carbon market governance, business associations' political strategies and business discourses on the environment.

**Birgit Müller** (PhD Cambridge 1986) is a research director at the LAIOS, CNRS/EHESS in Paris, France. She explores global governance of food and agriculture at the FAO and agricultural practices in Canada and Nicaragua. She examines worldviews and corporate power in relation to seeds and soils. Birgit's published books include *Disenchantment with Market Economics: East Germans and Western Capitalism* (2008) and *The Gloss of Harmony: The Politics of Policy Making in Multilateral Organisations* (2013).

**Aurore Viard-Crétat** is a postdoctoral researcher at the Institute des Sciences de la Communication (CNRS/Paris Sorbonne/UPMC). Combining science and technology studies and anthropology, her work focuses on international forest and environmental politics. In particular, she studies communities of experts (researchers, NGOs, consultancy firms) inside and around the development aid system and looks at how they contribute to renewing and perpetuating it.

# Introduction: COP21 and the "climatisation" of global debates

*Jean Foyer, Stefan C. Aykut and Edouard Morena*

Frequently presented as a historic last chance to set the world on a course that prevents catastrophic climate change, the 21st Conference of the Parties to the Climate Convention (COP21), held in Paris in December 2015, was a global summit of exceptional proportions: 150 presidents and prime ministers attended the opening ceremony – a record; some 30,000 registered participants came together in the Le Bourget venue near Paris during the two weeks of the conference. An even greater number of people attended the countless civil society events scattered across the city. From large public gatherings to invitation-only and fairly low-key corporate events, Paris was, to borrow the name of a media hub created for the conference, *the* "place to be" for anyone interested – even marginally – in the climate issue. COP21 was not only a high-stakes conference with an exceptionally high turnout. By bringing together politicians, negotiators, scientists, journalists and representatives of civil society from across the globe, it also constituted a moment and a space where "the global" became local. For any researcher interested in the climate issue, the COP21 event represented a privileged vantage point – an "emblematic instance" as it were – for the study of global climate governance *in the making*.

It goes without saying that climate governance is not restricted to international climate summits or the United Nations Framework Convention on Climate Change (UNFCCC). It extends "beyond" or "outside" the UN climate regime, through the individual or combined actions of multiple stakeholders and initiatives. These range from regional and national policy actors to intergovernmental bodies, local governments, social movements and corporations, as well as public or private carbon markets and offset schemes (Okereke, Bulkeley and Schroeder 2009, Ostrom 2010, Moncel and van Asselt 2012). While centred on the UNFCCC, the Paris conference produced a "gravitational pull" on a range of actors who were, for the most part, not directly involved in the climate negotiations. In this sense, COP21 offered a unique snapshot of the current state of play in global environmental governance, and the attendant – and at times less discernible – spaces of engagement in the climate debate. The contributions to this edited volume analyse the Paris conference as a "total event";[1] as a historic moment in which multiple discourses, practices and actor networks came together for the duration of a two-week conference.

## Transnational mega-events and the making of globality

At first glance, COP21 took the form of a three-part drama combining the three classical unities of time, space and action. The space was the Le Bourget conference centre just north of Paris. The time was a two-week period in early December 2015. And the action was the negotiation of an international climate agreement that sets the world on a course to a low-carbon future. Yet, on closer scrutiny, the Paris conference – and other comparable transnational mega-events for that matter – broke away from its formal time frame, space and action agenda.

As with a number of other international processes, climate conferences are organised yearly in different host cities.[2] Like a travelling circus, the climate COP has to be rebuilt from scratch as it moves from one venue to the next. Having said this, COPs do have some basic things in common. They systematically include a "blue zone", where access is restricted to registered participants. In addition to hosting the negotiations, the "blue zone" houses an exhibition space (for countries, NGOs, IGOs and businesses), meeting rooms for side events, delegation and observer offices, a media centre and amenities, such as cafeterias and restaurants. Civil society gatherings and events that target a wider audience are organised outside of the blue zone. Infrastructures and venue capacities vary depending on the host country and the conference's importance – for the host country and the UNFCCC. In Paris for example the blue zone, the semi-official civil society space *Espaces Générations Climat* and the business forum *La Galérie* were all in Le Bourget, a city that is located in the northern and working-class Parisian suburb of Seine Saint-Denis. The conference's location on the outskirts of Paris heightened a sense of proximity between the *Espaces Générations Climat* and the official conference while simultaneously widening the gap between the conference and the countless events taking place inside Paris. These included, among others, a large gathering of climate movement actors in Montreuil, a city just east of Paris, and at the *CentQuatre*, an artistic space in the city's 19th Arrondissement district. A business event, *Solutions COP21*, was also organised in the more affluent western part of the city. As with other international summits, the Paris COP expanded outward through a series of concentric circles from the negotiations space in Le Bourget to various locations across the city and its surroundings.

These physical spaces are generally associated with social spaces – spaces that can be understood as "relatively autonomous spaces of practice and meaning within the social world, and at the heart of which mobilisations are united by relations of interdependence" (Mathieu 2007, 133). UN mega-conferences connect a wide array of more or less autonomous and homogenous spaces within which diverse actors do very different things. Although there is a high degree of interaction between them, different spaces can nevertheless be identified. These include, among others, a negotiations space, a civil society space, a business space and a media space. The existence of these spaces further challenges the three classical unities – time, space and action – mentioned earlier.

Since their beginnings, UN climate conferences' "nomadic" character generated a distinctive form of political globality that resonates with the globality of the prevailing scientific framing of the climate problem (Aykut and Dahan 2015). This aspect of climate governance reminds us of Marc Augé's (1995) notion of "non-places", which he uses to describe the ahistorical and interchangeable localities of our transport (motorways, airports, hotels) and consumption infrastructures (shopping malls, supermarkets) so characteristic of globalisation in the age of "supermodernity". For Augé, non-places signal a break with more classical sociological and anthropological representations of place as "culture localized in time and space" (Augé 1995, 34). Hence, UN conferences share some common characteristics with non-places. Like shopping malls, successive climate conferences reproduce the same delocalised spatial and organisational arrangements. Like airports, they are detached from their surroundings through physical barriers and security checks. Like hotels, they are spaces of transit that are essentially defined by the functions that they accomplish. The venues of climate conferences are the *infrastructure* of what is commonly referred to as "global governance". Akin to the "pneumatic parliaments" described by Peter Sloterdijk in his scathing account of attempts to "export" Western democracy in the George W. Bush years (Sloterdijk and Mueller von der Hagen 2005), climate conferences project the norms and principles of a UN-led global democratic order in very different local contexts. This is not without creating a series of rather paradoxical situations – one only needs to look at the debates that surrounded the Doha climate conference (COP18) in Qatar, an absolute monarchy that applies Sharia law and has the highest per capita $CO_2$ emissions in the world. The fact that the "global circus" of climate conferences can accommodate such contradictions is in itself an interesting feature of global climate governance.

That being said, climate conferences differ from Augé's non-places in various ways. Unlike shopping malls, they are not ahistorical but carry with them a particular negotiation history consisting in successive cycles, landmark conferences, breakthroughs and disillusionments. Unlike airports, they tend to attract the same group of people year upon year. Through their spatial arrangements, they also encourage interactions among participants (doorway encounters and informal exchanges over coffee or lunch). And unlike hotels, they do foster a certain level of local "colouration" depending on the conference's host city and country. COPs also convey a particular set of norms – diplomatic language and civility, formal debating rules – and procedures that are characteristic of UN settings.

Hence, repeated encounters, a common history and shared norms have contributed to the rise of a "climate community" with its own codes, practices and language; a community that not only comes together annually at climate COPs but also assembles during smaller and more low-key "intersessional" meetings at the UNFCCC's headquarters in Bonn, Germany. This community is not confined to country delegates but extends to a variety of non-state actors who are active both inside and outside of the official negotiation space. This is a consequence of multiple factors. Among them is the fact that Northern NGOs have historically provided crucial support to country delegations from the Global South. We also witness a high level of individual mobility between NGOs, think tanks, business associations and national delegations. COPs are therefore characterised by their multiple levels of historicity and protracted temporalities – those of negotiation cycles, civil society and business mobilisations, as well as the progressive emergence of what can be labelled as a global climate culture.

This historicity has a complex relationship with climate COPs as international mega-events. While COPs are all events in the organisational sense of the term, they are not all – far from it – historic events. The Paris climate conference clearly stood out when compared to the series of COPs that preceded it since Copenhagen (COP15). It was supposed to mark the conclusions of a negotiation cycle and produce an international agreement that would form the basis for climate action in the coming decades. In addition to this, the COP organisers and architects of the final agreement, with support from global media and communications outlets, construed COP21 as an international mega-event of historic proportions. Through its performative power, the Paris conference was supposed to generate "momentum" for action on climate change among state and non-state actors – and in particular to send clear signals for businesses and investors that the world was irreversibly shifting towards a low-carbon future.

The preceding paragraphs signal how transnational mega-events like the Paris climate conference cannot be simply boiled down to the international negotiation process. To fully capture what is at stake in international climate debates, research on climate governance must go beyond the negotiation process and its formal outputs – treaties, decisions or declarations. Seyfang and Jordan (2002), for instance, show how the functions of environmental mega-conferences extend beyond the legal documents that they produce: they set global agendas, connect problems, shape common principles, create spaces that allow for the emergence of global leadership, promote capacity building and contribute to legitimising global institutions. Through their ethnographic research, institutional anthropologists have also shown how international negotiations contribute to the production and diffusion of shared norms and understandings (Randeria 2003, Bendix 2012). They have also highlighted their *performative* function in that climate conferences project the idea that there does exist a "global community" that addresses the world's problems (Little 1995, Müller 2013). Building on these and other analyses, the contributions in this volume combine pragmatist approaches to the study of international relations with sociological and anthropological perspectives on climate governance. In doing so, they frame COP21 as an event that simultaneously *reflects* our global condition and *produces* a specific form of globality.

## Climatising the world, globalising the climate

In light of these debates, contributions to this edited volume examine COP21 as an arena where new framings of global problems, approaches to global governance and actor coalitions are tried and tested – framings, approaches and coalitions whose effects transcend the climate arena. Climate conferences take up an ever-growing number of issues, from debates about development, energy and forests to biodiversity, global inequality and urban planning, among others. In return, they attract a growing number of actors from very different backgrounds and who each have their own interpretations of the climate problem, its causes and possible solutions.

This points to a broader two-way shift in the global climate debate. On the one hand, we are witnessing a *globalisation of the climate* problem through the inclusion of new issues and actors into the climate regime (Aykut and Dahan 2015). This globalisation is more sectorial than spatial, as it relates to the extension of the "jurisdiction" of the climate arena, which has come to encompass an ever-growing number of problems. On the other hand, a *climatisation of the world* can be observed, whereby actors in other arenas present issues that were formerly unrelated to the climate problem through a "climatic lens" (Foyer 2016). This leads to the alignment of these topics on the climate problem, and to their treatment according to the dominant logics of the climate regime.[3]

Both processes are interwoven and dialogical since the globalisation of the climate presupposes the climatisation of new topics and vice versa. They can subsequently be viewed as forming two sides of the same coin, observed alternatively from within the climate regime or from its periphery. They are translation[4] processes that extend, on the one hand, from within the climate arena to a particular topic or area, and, on the other, from a particular topic to the climate arena. While closely related, both movements abide by distinct logics and do not always involve the same actors. Thus, the climatisation of an issue by actors outside the climate regime may or may not lead to its effective inclusion in climate talks. Inversely, the integration of a new topic in climate governance does not necessarily affect its treatment in other governance contexts. The chapters provide some examples for such processes of incomplete or partial climatisation. Having said this, the dialogical movement presented earlier can be synthesised through two questions: what does the climate regime *do* to other issue areas as it expands to and integrates an ever-increasing number of topics in international politics? And what do these other issue areas *do* to the climate regime, as they enter the global climate debate?

These questions can be supplemented by a series of more cross-cutting ones: for instance, can we distinguish different forms and intensities of climatisation? What are the driving forces behind these dynamics and how – according to which logics and social processes – do they unfold? What are the obstacles to both the climatisation of new topics and their inclusion in formal climate talks? How does climatisation affect the ways in which climate change is made "governable" in climate talks? Last but by no means least, do the two processes – the globalisation of the climate and the climatisation of the world – get us any closer to actually solving the climate problem?

## Modes and degrees of climatisation

In Paris, the dialogical process of climatisation of the world and globalisation of the climate was operating at its fullest. COP21 simultaneously represented the high point of a long-term process and acted as an extraordinary "climatising machine". Indeed, over the years and months leading up to the conference, the climate debate was expanded to include a variety of new topics, such as security, agriculture and financial regulation, while simultaneously consolidating existing links to others, such as development, fossil fuel regulation, traditional knowledge and indigenous rights. By closely monitoring the event and its preparations, we were able to further understand and describe the climatisation process, study its contours depending on the issue area and assess its wider bearing on global debates. It thus appeared that climatisation can be more or less pronounced and take on a variety of different forms over time and in different domains. Through their focus areas and methodologies, the chapters in this book set out to capture the climatisation and globalisation processes in all their complexity. They do so in three main ways.

A first group of chapters highlights the climatisation process's "selectivity" – that is its variability and unequal intensity depending on the issue area. The first chapter deals with the heart of the climate regime. Stefan Aykut analyses the climate negotiations as a collective drafting exercise, in which text-editing activities are distributed across time and space. Examined through this lens, COP21 simultaneously appears as an occasion, for a variety of actors, to lobby for the inclusion of new issues and topics into climate talks, and as a highly efficient cleansing device where climate change is rendered "governable" through the deliberate omission of certain issues and alternative approaches to the problem. Chapter 9 further elaborates on this theme by providing an in-depth analysis of the dynamics of selective climatisation in a specific policy domain: fossil fuel regulation. Stefan Aykut and Monica Castro show how debates on energy – and in particular on fossil fuels – are in many ways "hyper-climatised" but surprisingly absent from the discussions and negotiations under the UNFCCC. The analysis of this "energy paradox" reveals that institutional logics and deliberate strategies of major actors in climate governance conspired historically to keep energy issues out of negotiation texts. In Chapter 6, on security and migration, Lucile Maertens and Alice Baillat show how both issues are increasingly framed in "climatic terms" and how this, in turn, contributes to a "dramatisation" and "humanisation" of the climate crisis. The authors also contend, however, that the integration of security and migration in climate talks is incomplete and partial, as strong political and institutional obstacles prevent their treatment in one single international arena.

A second set of chapters focuses on the climatisation process's political and strategic dimensions. In Chapter 2, Hélène Guillemot explores the changing relations between science and politics in the climate regime. In her description of the process that resulted in the adoption of a 1.5°C long-term temperature goal that is deemed "necessary" from a political perspective, but already "inaccessible" from a scientific point of view, she examines how the scientific community struggles to adapt to this objective and cope with the pressure to align research agendas on the demands of global climate politics. In Chapter 8, Jean Foyer and David Dumoulin explore the process that led to the inclusion of a reference to "traditional knowledge" in the adaptation section of the Paris Agreement. They show that this inclusion is the result of a long history of mobilisation by indigenous actors. The climatisation of traditional knowledge, they claim, contributes to "re-enchant" the climate arena, but it also comes at a cost, as traditional knowledge loses some of its more radical implications in terms of indigenous rights or alternative cos-mologies. The political and strategic dimension of climatisation is also present in Edouard Morena's account of philanthropic foundations' involvement in the climate debate. In Chapter 5, he analyses how a small group of liberal founda-tions played a proactive but discrete role in orchestrating the final outcome of the conference and in generating the larger "momentum" that surrounded the conference. Foundations thus appear as key actors in the trend towards climatisa-tion. Finally, through their analysis of two mechanisms – the REDD+ scheme to avoid emissions from deforestation and forest degradation, and the instruments of climate adaptation finance – Aurore Viard-Crétat and Christophe Buffet show how climate change is used and mobilised to relabel existing practices and institu-tions of development aid. The climatisation of development thus appears, at least partially, as a strategic move to generate new legitimacy for this much-criticised and central feature of North-South relations.

A third group of chapters addresses the ambiguities of climatisation. In Chap-ter 3, Birgit Müller, Sarah Benabou and Nils Moussu analyse the private sectors' efforts to project a unified and "progressive" voice in Paris. This global political ambition was, however, overshadowed by differing – and at times conflicting – assessments of the climate crisis and its implications for the private sector, as well as by a voluntary vagueness concerning the concrete shape of regulatory solutions to the climate problem. The climatisation process's ambiguity is also illustrated in Joost de Moor, Edouard Morena and Jean-Baptiste Comby's analysis (Chapter 4) of the climate movement's involvement in and around the conference. The authors show that a central issue for social movements and NGOs was to situate oneself in relation to the negotiation process. Finding the "appropriate distance" between lobbying inside COP21 and bottom-up activism that participates in the broader climatisation process was a central element of activists' strategies in Paris.

It goes without saying that the chapters contained in this book do not cover all the objects, spaces and actors that have been or are in the process of being climatised. Other objects, such as agriculture – through climate-smart agriculture (CSA) – and religion – through Pope Francis's *Laudato Si* encyclical or the Islamic Declaration on Global Climate Change – among others, would also require fur-ther investigation.

## Interpreting climatisation: its origins, meanings and limitations

To fully grasp the multifaceted process of climatisation, we must understand its origins and meanings, examine its wider implications and analyse its limitations. A first step in this direction is to make sense of the climate regime's force of attrac-tion. The most obvious explanation of this attraction relates to the seriousness and scale of the climate problem. Climate change is the most emblematic feature of what scientists and historians call the Anthropocene,[5] the current geological epoch in which humanity acts as the driving force behind the transformations of the Earth's biosphere and lithosphere. Over the past twenty years, global warming has become more palpable, be it through the melting of ice caps, rising sea levels, the disruption of local climate patterns or the growing number of extreme weather events. Given its scale and scope, state and non-state actors as well as ordinary citizens are increasingly enticed to recognise the seriousness of the situation and the urgent need to take action. However, the scale of the climate problem does not by itself explain the climate regime's formidable force of attraction. Among the other factors that need to be examined are the climate regime's long-term dynamics and what can be termed an "institutional snowball effect": the more the climate regime grows, the greater its force of attraction.

As a consequence of its growing appeal, the international climate regime has become a place in which to be seen and heard in order to advance individual and collective agendas, expand networks and raise funds. Climate change is therefore no longer framed exclusively as a scientific and political problem of global proportions, but also and more significantly as a problem that has the power to break down the barriers that traditionally separate science, the environment, politics and the economy. By merging together intersecting and overlapping social, political and environmental issues, the climate plays a "totemic" function that brings together a variety of actors with different agendas and worldviews. It also turned into a global controversy that opposes competing understandings of the planet's socio-ecological system. In a similar vein to "atomic energy" in the 1980s and "globalisation" in the 1990s, it has become a "hypnotic focal point" and a metaphor for the world's most serious problems and predicaments, from North-South inequalities and questions of global equity to ideological struggles about industrial modernity and its impasses.

From a historical perspective, climatisation can be interpreted as the most recent and now dominant form of "environmentalisation" (Buttel 1992). The rise of climate change coincides with the surge of the "global environment" as a scientific and political category (Yearly 1996, Ingold 2000). As with environmentalism, climatisation can take on different ideological colourations, from more radical critiques against the growth paradigm and "fossil capitalism" (Altvater 2007) to more reformist calls for a "greening [of] modernity" (Beck 2010) by reflexively readjusting its core institutions to tackle the ecological crisis, and to policies focusing on incremental change through market- and technology-based solutions.

Climatisation also contributes to further marginalise or overshadow other important environmental concerns. By focusing almost exclusively on climate change, there is a risk of diverting the general public and policymakers' attention away from other important global environmental problems and planetary boundaries (Rockström et al. 2009). Climate mitigation efforts that minimise or omit other environmental challenges can have unintended and undesirable social and ecological consequences. Afforestation efforts or plantations for biomass production, for instance, can lead to a loss in biodiversity, the depletion of freshwater resources and the forced displacement of local populations. Climate change is without doubt a major and possibly the most important issue of our time, but it is by no means the only global problem requiring our urgent attention.

That being said, we should not exaggerate the scale of climatisation nor over-estimate its durability or robustness over time. It remains a very partial and frag-mented process. A number of issues – including vitally important ones like fossil fuel regulation – have resisted the climate regime's gravitational force. Further-more, when analysing the climatisation process in Paris, it is important to factor in the conference's historic and exceptional character. In the space of two weeks, the climate issue held centre stage, momentarily relegating other global concerns to the sidelines (war, terrorism, the global economic crisis). Thus, Paris projected an exaggerated sense of climatisation that does not reflect the actual situation. Just one year after COP21, Donald Trump's victory in the US presidential election offers a potent reminder of the climatisation process's incompleteness. His climate skeptic rhetoric, his threats to leave the Paris agreement and his nomination of cabinet members representing large polluter interests highlights the fact that climatisation can be reversed.

Finally, and perhaps most importantly, climatisation should not be confused with the actual measures put in place to address the climate problem. Clima-tisation is above all a symbolic and discursive process. Interpreting COP21 in terms of the climatisation of the world does not contradict analyses of the climate regime in terms of a growing "schism of reality" – seen as the rift that separates the climate regime from the geopolitical, economic and environmental realities of the world (Aykut and Dahan 2014, Dahan 2016). Following COP21, the cli-mate regime continues to be isolated from other international institutions and processes that regulate global trade, energy supply or finance. It also continues to move at a very slow pace when compared to a range of other global processes, especially economic and financial globalisation (Aykut 2016). The current focus on market-based solutions (Lohmann 2005) and technological fixes (Hamilton 2013) marginalises alternative approaches to global problems that highlight the need for more profound socioeconomic transformations. The idea that unbridled economic growth is compatible with climate mitigation continues to dominate the international agenda (Vogler 2016, 26–28).

These remarks serve to further qualify the historical meaning and origins of the climatisation process. Indeed, climatisation can be understood as an indirect consequence of the climate regime's failure to address some of the root causes of global warming, such as fossil fuel extraction and combustion or the intensification of economic and financial globalisation. In other words, climatisation can simultaneously be seen as a response to a worsening climate problem that increasingly affects other issues and domains, and as an effort to broaden the scope of climate action precisely because of our failure to tackle its root causes.

## Making sense of the "paradigm shift" in global governance

Beyond the climatisation process, the Paris conference signalled a much-discussed "paradigm shift" in global climate governance; a paradigm shift that translates into a bottom-up, voluntary approach to climate action where sending the right "signals" to economic actors and building "momentum" in society become just as important as the multilateral negotiations themselves. This is a remarkable evolution, as the climate regime has been frequently criticised for its "globalism" and its tendency to downgrade human experiences, erase territorial specificities and disempower local communities (Jasanoff 2001, 2010). While globalism continues to form a core element of international climate politics, there are signs of a trend towards a "de-globalisation" (in the territorial and political sense) of the climate regime. To begin with, COP21 marked a clear attempt at highlighting the role of bottom-up and local-level action, especially through its focus on indigenous and frontline communities (Chapter 8), corporate initiatives (Chapter 3) and the work of cities and local authorities (that were particularly present during the Paris COP).[6] This greater focus on and promotion of the local level went hand in hand with a reaffirmation of the role of states. Along with the traditional calls by Southern countries to abide by the principles of "common but differentiated responsibilities" and national sovereignty, the intended nationally determined contributions (INDC) mark both a major institutional innovation for the climate regime and a form of renationalisation of climate policies. While INDCs' bottom-up character has the potential to induce real change, their non-binding and voluntary character means that there is no way of ensuring that countries abide by their commitments.

If nation states continue to play a central role in the climate regime, COP21 also reaffirmed the principles of multi-stakeholder governance. In a post-Paris world, achieving the agreement's long-term targets – keeping global warming below 2°C (and aiming for 1.5°C) and reaching 100 billion dollars of annual climate finance for mitigation and adaptation in developing countries – no longer depends on states alone. Quite the contrary, attaining these objectives requires all sections of the "international community" to ramp up their climate actions, including non-state actors, in both the Global North and South. The consequence is a gradual shift in the global climate regime's centre of gravity away from the UNFCCC, and towards a more decentralised governance architecture. Climatisation subsequently appears as not just a historic process but also a political tool in support of this new, decentralised mode of governance whereby multiple state, interstate and non-state actors combine and align their efforts in order to reach a mutually agreed objective.

An additional feature of this new approach to climate governance is the promotion of less directive, "soft" methods of government. By referring to the Paris Agreement as a "self-fulfilling prophecy", Laurence Tubiana, head of the French delegation, points to the regime's shift away from the Kyoto approach – centred on legally binding emissions reductions commitments – towards a "soft law" approach to climate governance centred on voluntary and non-binding commitments.[7] By setting an ambitious long-term goal without legally binding reduction commitments, the Paris Agreement can be labelled as a "performative" agreement. For its architects and promoters, the agreement's primary function is to send the right signals and generate the momentum required for ambitious and decisive climate action by state and non-state actors alike – and in particular businesses and investors. The focus on "climate solutions" and showcasing of success stories of climate action at the different business spaces and events in Paris as well as through the UNFCCC's Non-state Actor Zone for Climate Action (NAZCA, formerly Lima-Paris Action Agenda) are illustrative of this shift away from a "command-and-control" approach to international law. In the name of pragmatism, the regulation-sanction combination, grounded on clear targets and time frames, has been replaced by voluntary pledges and regular review cycles. This approach is justified by its promoters by the belief that a non-binding agreement built on confidence and goodwill has a greater chance of rallying parties and thereby producing tangible results.

In sum, the US approach to climate governance has finally triumphed in Paris (Aykut and Dahan 2014). It should be noted, however, that this approach was also backed by a number of developing countries that preferred to voluntarily commit to mitigation actions rather than to have policies dictated to them by the COP. This trend towards a "softening" of international law is neither new nor specific to the climate debate. It already permeated the different multilateral environmental agreements signed in the 1990s (Maljean-Dubois 2005), as well as the instruments set up to govern techno-scientific objects (Pestre 2014) and market standards. Having said this, the Paris Agreement can nevertheless be seen as a high point for this approach to international law. The climate regime subsequently appears as a laboratory where new forms of global governance are tried and tested. This makes scholarly accounts of climate governance, especially those that go beyond an analysis of the negotiation process, all the more urgent and timely.

## A collaborative methodology

Our introduction to this volume would not be complete without a brief presentation of the project that gave rise to it. In particular our work has focused on collaborative research methods.

> The ethnographic delimiting of a mega-event is also problematic due to its complexity and fragmentary nature. When confronted with a conglomeration of over 30,000 people, from over 100 countries, that lasts for two weeks and is wired into a worldwide network of communications and transportation technologies, the illusion of capturing the "essence" of such a complex event is painstakingly revealed.
>
> (Little 1995, 281)

This is how Paul Little (1995) described the difficulty of conducting ethnographic fieldwork at the UN Conference on the Environment and Development, or "Earth Summit", in Rio de Janeiro in 1992. The same, of course, holds true for COP21, a conference of analogous proportions and political significance, with equally blurred spatial and temporal boundaries. The multiplication of such transnational mega-events since the Earth Summit – the Johannesburg (2002) and Rio+20 (2012) summits, annual climate conferences, biodiversity conferences and World

Social Forums, to name just a few – has given rise to an expanding social science literature on the ways of using and adapting fieldwork methodologies to adequately capture the "essence" of such events.[8] In the process, this research also contributes to wider discussions on the specific challenges that globalisation poses for social science research (Marcus 1995, Appadurai 1997, Markowitz 2001, Siméant 2015).

These reflections have contributed to direct scholarly attention towards collaborative research methodologies. Such collective inquiries have been conducted – and reflected upon – for example by a collective of French researchers from Sorbonne University at the World Social Forums in Nairobi 2007 and Dakar 2011 (Pommerolle and Siméant 2008, Siméant, Sommier and Pommerolle 2015) and by a North American group of political ecology scholars who studied the World Conservation Summit and a biodiversity COP (Brosius and Campbell 2010, Campbell et al. 2014). Both cases provide ample and compelling evidence that working in larger teams helps to better capture the diversity of actors, events and spaces of interaction, and the complexity and range of issues, as well as the countless temporal and spatial overflows that are so characteristic of global governance processes. However, as Campbell et al. (2014) explain in an article presenting their "collaborative event ethnography" framework, collaboration does more than just address the "limits of working" alone by providing "more eyes" to better cover a given event. If conducted properly, collaboration also provides "more ideas", as the practical benefits of working together are complemented by the intellectual benefits of crossing analyses and collectively elaborating hypotheses and a common research framework (Campbell et al. 2014, 10).

This last point was especially relevant to our research. Our conceptual framework was the product of earlier collaborations and the subsequent coming together of two research teams. The first team, a group of researchers working on biodiversity and agriculture governance, and the role and involvement of various actors, such as indigenous peoples, NGOs, trade unions and business groups, mobilised a collaborative methodology approach to observe and analyse the Rio+20 Summit on Sustainable Development in 2012 (Foyer 2015). The second team, a group of researchers from the Centre Alexandre Koyré (EHESS Paris), had conducted a series of sociological observations at climate conferences and developed a strong expertise on questions related to climate governance.[9] This led to two parallel analyses of the climate debates: while members of the first team specialising in areas not directly related to climate change observed the climate regime's growing influence on their objects of study, the second group witnessed how the climate regime increasingly took on new issues (Aykut and Dahan 2015). The idea that climate governance in general and the Paris conference in particular could be analysed as part of a broader trend towards the climatisation of the world and the globalisation of the climate subsequently arose out of earlier discussions between members of both groups who subsequently went on to form the ClimaCop project.

With COP21 approaching, the research team grew through the integration of PhD candidates and postdoctoral fellows interested in the COP21. The result is a fairly young research collective of approximately twenty researchers, representing a variety of different institutions, disciplines (political science, sociology, anthropology, history) and specialities and theoretical groundings (science and technology studies, political sociology, anthropology of international institutions, international relations, political economy, political ecology).[10] Such diversity logically required adopting an interdisciplinary approach that is structured by a common interest in global environmental governance. If shedding light on the same object through multiple perspectives constitutes an analytical advantage, it also represents a methodological challenge requiring constant discussions on theoretical and methodological issues.[11] To sum up, the object of study as much as the composition of our team encouraged us to adopt a collaborative methodology and to turn its development and improvement into a permanent preoccupation throughout the project's life cycle. This collaboration took different forms before, during and after COP21.

Monthly project meetings and regular research seminars at the Centre Alexandre Koyré played an important team-building role. They were an opportunity to discuss organisational and substantive research questions. This contributed to a shared project culture among project members and enhanced interactions with other members of the research community. Internal and external communication was enhanced through the use of web-based tools, such as a project mailing list; a file hosting system – or cloud – to share relevant information and primary data; and a website to showcase the project's work, events and output.[12] Collaborative fieldwork began before COP21 since members of our team observed different preparatory meetings, such as the Climate and Business Summit in Paris in May 2015, an intermediate negotiation session in Bonn in June 2015 and the scientific conference Our Common Future under Climate Change, organised in Paris in July 2015.

Logistical and organisational issues were a permanent concern, especially when it came to fieldwork access. Indeed, a specific challenge associated with research in UN settings relates to getting hold of accreditations to access the blue zone, where negotiations and most side events were taking place. This was complicated by the drastic access limitations imposed by the UNFCCC secretariat prior to COP21 and by the fact that most of our academic institutions were not officially recognised stakeholders. Despite our exchanges with various accredited institutions as well as the French COP presidency, a majority of researchers in the ClimaCop team still had no access to the conference on the eve of the conference. It was only at the start of the COP that most of the team was able to get hold of a badge through NGOs (including a youth and a Pygmy organisation!), trade unions or national delegations (France, Cameroun, Bangladesh). This indicates that collaboration through the activation and sharing of personal networks can help to overcome recurring challenges associated with the study of international events, such as the issue of access to fieldwork.

During the observation stage at COP21, an apartment was rented close to the Gare du Nord station. The apartment offered team members who didn't live in Paris quick and easy access to the various field sites outside and inside Paris. It also acted as a project hub to plan, organise and coordinate activities during the two-week conference. Regular team briefings were essential in order to get a clearer sense of who was observing what and what was happening. Team members could share observations and practical information about events, and discuss emerging research hypotheses. The apartment was also a useful venue to informally interact with other fellow researchers who were present in Paris. Another important collaborative tool was a standardised observation form for fieldwork notes, intended to offer general information about observed events (title, speakers, public, format, etc.), and details about their content. Over 150 forms were completed over the course of the COP.

Possibly the most important scientific benefit of collaboration during COP21 was what we called the "permanent-seminar effect". In addition to the planned briefings, discussions among team members continued at meal times, during journeys or breaks. Project members were thus constantly encouraged to share their observations, methods and perspectives. The efforts required to synthesise collected information and observations for other team members and to confront different points of view helped to strengthen work hypotheses and fostered the emergence of new research questions.

After the conference, the challenge was to preserve the collaborative dynamic in the output phase. We continued to organise monthly meetings and seminars, while focusing our efforts on writing. Two months after the COP, a writing workshop was organised to discuss the COP and possible hypotheses. Those discussions formed the basis for the present book. In July 2016, a second workshop was organised to present and discuss draft chapters. This collaborative reviewing process allowed authors to appropriate the general lines of the book and reinforced the structure and coherence of the main arguments.

Finally, as coordinators, we paid constant and very specific attention to an essential ingredient for successful collaboration: conviviality. This ingredient does not appear in methodological guides nor obey scientific rules. While one cannot decree conviviality, it does not suddenly appear either; it must be nurtured. Collaborative research projects are above all human endeavours and conviviality acts as an essential means of improving working relations and assuring overall intellectual coherence. We very much hope that this is reflected throughout the book.

## Notes

1 This notion has been coined by Pieke (1996) to describe the Chinese Tiananmen demonstration of 1989.
2 Exceptions are intermediate negotiations (or "intersessions") that take place mostly in Bonn, Germany, where the secretariat of the Climate Convention is located.
3 A similar argument has been made by academics working on "securitisation" (Wæver 1995, Buzan, Wæver and De Wilde 1998) of different issue areas. Following this line of work, Oels (2012) has analysed the securitisation of climate change and the climatisation of security. Our volume aims at developing and systematising this approach.
4 We use this notion in the sense of actor-network theory. See Callon (1986) and the contributions in Akrich, Callon and Latour (2006).

5 For the scientific debate, see Crutzen (2002) and Steffen, Broadgate, Deutsch, Gaffney and Ludwig (2015). A historical and political perspective is provided by Bonneuil and Fressoz (2016).

6 Consider, for instance, the Climate Summit for Local Leaders, organised on 4 December in Paris, which brought together some 700 representatives of local government and the mayors of the world's major cities.

7 Losson, Christian, "COP21: 'L'accord doit être une prophétie autoréalisatrice'", *Libération*, 17 December 2015.

8 See the special issues of *Global Environmental Politics* (2014, Vol.14, No.3) and *Critique Internationale* (Vol. 2012/1, No. 54), especially the respective introductions by Müller (2012) and Campbell et al. (2014).

9 See the different reports from the COP observation project led by Amy Dahan – for example Dahan, Armatte, Buffet and Viard-Crétat (2012).

10 A limit of our research project is that it is almost entirely composed of researchers from the Global North (despite the fact that some of the researchers have a long-standing engagement in research in the Global South).

11 An important moment in these discussions was a workshop on methodological questions relating to the study of transnational mega-events, organised in Paris in July 2015. See https://climacop.hypotheses.org/evenements/131–2.

12 https://climacop.hypotheses.org/.

## Bibliography

Akrich, Madeleine, Michel Callon, and Bruno Latour. *Sociologie de la traduction: textes fondateurs*. Paris: Presses des Mines, 2006.

Altvater, Elmar. "The social and natural environment of fossil capitalism." *Socialist Register* 43 (2007): 37.

Appadurai, A. "Fieldwork in the era of globalization." *Anthropology and Humanism* 22, no. 1 (1997): 115–118.

Augé, Marc. *Non-places: Introduction to an Anthropology of Supermodernity*. London: Verso, 1995.

Aykut, Stefan C. "Taking a wider view on climate governance: Moving beyond the 'iceberg', the 'elephant', and the 'forest'." *WIREs Climate Change* 7, no. 3 (2016): 318–328.

Aykut, Stefan C., and Amy Dahan. *Gouverner le Climat? 20 ans de négociations internationales*. Paris: Presses de Science Po, 2015.

Aykut, Stefan C., and Amy Dahan. "La gouvernance du changement climatique: Anatomie d'un schisme de réalité." In *Gouverner le progrès et ses dégats*, by Dominique Pestre, 97–132. Paris: La Découverte, 2014.

Beck, Ulrich. "Climate for change, or how to create a green modernity?" *Theory, Culture & Society* 27 (2010): 254–266.

Bendix, Regina. "Une salle, plusieurs sites: Les négociations internationales comme terrain de recherche anthropologique." *Critique Internationale* 54 (2012): 19–38.

Bonneuil, Christophe, and Jean-Baptiste Fressoz. *The Shock of the Anthropocene: The Earth, History and Us*. Brooklyn, NY: Verso Books, 2016.

Brosius, Peter J., and Lisa M. Campbell. "Collaborative event ethnography: Conservation and development trade-offs at the fourth world conservation congress." *Conservation and Society* 8, no. 4 (2010): 245–255.

Buttel, Frederick. "Environmentalization: Origins, processes, and implications for rural social change." *Rural Sociology* 57, no. 1 (1992): 1–27.

Buzan, Barry, Ole Wæver, and Jaap De Wilde. *Security: A New Framework for Analysis.* Boulder, CO: Lynne Rienner, 1998.

Callon, Michel. "Some elements of a sociology of translation: Domestication of the scallops and the fishermen of St Brieuc Bay." In *Power, Action and Belief: A New Sociology of Knowledge?*, by John Law, 196–223. London: Routledge, 1986.

Campbell, John L., Catherine Corson, Noella J. Gray, Kenneth I. MacDonald, and Peter J. Brosius. "Studying global environmental meetings to understand global environmental governance: Collaborative event ethnography at the tenth conference of the parties to the convention on biological diversity." *Global Environmental Politics* 14, no. 3 (2014): 1–20.

Crutzen, Paul J. "Geology of mankind." *Nature* 415 (2002): 23.

Dahan, Amy. "La gouvernance du climat: entre climatisation du monde et schisme de réalité." *L'Homme et la Société* 199 (2016): 79–90.

Dahan, Amy, Michel Armatte, Christophe Buffet, and Aurore Viard-Crétat. *Plateforme de Durban: Quelle crédibilité accorder encore au processus des négociations climatiques?* Rapport de Recherche, Koyré Climate Series, n° 4. Paris: Centre Alexandre Koyré, 2012.

Foyer, Jean. *Behind the Scenes at the COP21.* May 26, 2016. http://www.booksandideas.net/Behind-the-Scenes-at-the-COP21.html (accessed August 4, 2016).

Foyer, Jean. *Regards croisés sur Rio+20: La modernisation écologique à l'épreuve.* Paris: Editions du CNRS, 2015.

Hamilton, Clive. *Earthmasters: The Dawn of the Age of Climate Engineering.* New Haven: Yale University Press, 2013.

Ingold, Tim. "Globes and spheres: The topology of environmentalism." In *The Perception of the Environment: Essays on Livelihood, Dwelling and Skill*, by Tim Ingold, 209–218. London: Routledge, 2000.

Jasanoff, Sheila. "Image and imagination: The formation of global environmental consciousness." In *Changing the Atmosphere*, by Clark A. Miller and Paul N. Edwards, 309–337. Cambridge, MA: MIT Press, 2001.

Jasanoff, Sheila. "A new climate for society." *Theory, Culture & Society* 27 (2010): 233–253.

Little, Paul E. "Ritual, power and ethnography at the Rio Earth Summit." *Critique of Anthropology* 15, no. 3 (1995): 265–288.

Lohmann, Larry. "Marketing and making carbon dumps: Commodification, calculation and counterfactuals in climate change mitigation." *Science as Culture* 14 (2005): 203–235.

Maljean-Dubois, S. *La mise en oeuvre du droit international de l'environnement.* Paris: Iddri, 2005.

Marcus, George E. "Ethnography in/of the world system: The emergence of multi-sited ethnography." *Annual Review of Anthropology* 24 (1995): 95–117.

Markowitz, Lisa. "Finding the field: Notes on the ethnography of NGOs." *Human Organization* 60, no. 1 (2001): 40–46.

Mathieu, L. "L'espace des mouvements sociaux." *Politix* 77 (2007): 131–151.

Moncel, Rémi, and Harro van Asselt. "All hand on deck! Mobilizing climate change action beyond the UNFCCC." *Review of European Community & International Environmental Law* 21, no. 3 (2012): 163–176.

Müller, Birgit. "Comment rendre le monde gouvernable sans le gouverner: les organisations internationales analysées par les anthropologues." *Critique Internationale* 1, no. 54 (2012): 9–18.

Müller, Birgit. *The Gloss of Harmony: The Politics of Policy-Making in Multilateral Organisations.* London: Pluto Press, 2013.

Oels, Angela. "From 'securitization' of climate change to 'climatization' of the security field: Comparing three theoretical perspectives." In *Climate Change, Human Security and*

*Violent Conflict: Challenges for Societal Stability*, by Michael Brzoska, Hans Brauch, Günter Jürgen Scheffran, Peter Michael Link and Janpeter Schilling, 185–205. Berlin: Springer, 2012.

Okereke, Chukwumerije, Harriet Bulkeley, and Heike Schroeder. "Conceptualizing climate governance beyond the international regime." *Global Environmental Politics* 9, no. 1 (2009): 58–78.

Ostrom, Elinor. "Beyond markets and states: Polycentric governance of complex economic systems." *The American Economic Review* 100, no. 3 (2010): 641–672.

Pestre, Denis. *Le gouvernement des technosciences*. Paris: La Découverte, 2014.

Pieke, Frank N. *The Ordinary and the Extraordinary: An Anthropological Study of Chinese Reform and the 1989 People's Movement in Beijing*. London: Kegan Paul, 1996.

Pommerolle, Marie-Emmanuelle, and Johanna Siméant. *Un Autre Monde à Nairobi: Le Forum Social 2007 entre Extraversion et Causes Africaines*. Paris: Karthala, 2008.

Randeria, Shalini. "Glocalization of law: Environmental justice, World Bank, NGOs and the cunning state in India." *Current Sociology* 51, no. 3/4 (2003): 305–328.

Rockström, Johan, Will Steffen, Kevin Noone, Åsa Persson, F. Stuart III Chapin, Eric Lambin, Timothy M. Lenton, et al. "Planetary boundaries: Exploring the safe operating space for humanity." *Ecology & Society* 14, no. 2 (2009): 32.

Seyfang, Gill, and Andrew Jordan. "The Johannesburg Summit on sustainable development: How effective are environmental conferences?" In *Yearbook of International Cooperation on Environment and Development 2002–03*, by Olav Schram Stokke and Oystein B. Thommessen, 19–39. London: Earthscan, 2002.

Siméant, Johanna. *Guide de l'enquête en sciences sociales*. Paris: Presses du CNRS, 2015.

Siméant, Johanna, Isabelle Sommier, and Marie-Emanuelle Pommerolle. *Observing Protest from a Place: The World Social Forum in Dakar (2011)*. Amsterdam: Amsterdam University Press, 2015.

Sloterdijk, Peter, and Gesa Mueller von der Hagen. "Instant democracy: The pneumatic parliament®." In *Making Things Public*, by Bruno Latour and Peter Weibel, 952–955. Cambridge, MA: MIT Press, 2005.

Steffen, Will, Wendy Broadgate, Lisa Deutsch, Owen Gaffney, and Cornelia Ludwig. "The trajectory of the Anthropocene: The great acceleration." *The Anthropocene Review* 2, no. 1 (2015): 81–98.

Vogler, John. *Climate Change in World Politics*. Basingstoke: Palgrave Macmillan, 2016.

Wæver, Ole. "Securitization and desecuritization." In *On Security*, by Ronnie Lipschutz, 39–53. New York, NY: Columbia University Press, 1995.

Yearly, Steven. *Sociology, Environmentalism, Globalization: Reinventing the Globe*. London: SAGE, 1996.

# 1   Governing through verbs

## The practice of negotiating and the making of a new mode of governance

*Stefan C. Aykut*

> More than 150 world leaders have come to Paris and are here together in one room, with one purpose. A political moment like this may not come again. We have never faced such a test. But neither have we encountered such great opportunity. You have the power to secure the well-being of this and succeeding generations.
>
> (UN General Secretary Ban Ki-moon)[1]

> I recall that the objective is not to have discussions, but to produce a text.
>
> (Daniel Reifsneyder, co-chair of the ADP)[2]

## Introduction

Now that the dust has settled, and the euphoria of the immediate aftermath of COP21 has dissipated, the time has come for analysts and observers to examine and interpret the details of the Paris Agreement, weigh its strengths and ponder its weaknesses.[3] Most such analyses aim to answer the central question of whether the Paris deal has brought us anywhere closer to a resolution of the climate problem. In other words: is the Paris Agreement a better basis for "governing the climate" than was its much-criticised predecessor, the Kyoto Protocol? Will it contribute to curbing global emissions and will it kick-start a global clean energy transition? Or is it "cheap talk", in which the setting of long-term targets and complex governance mechanisms merely hide the fact that concrete action is – once more – postponed into the future?

In this chapter, I propose to take a detour before returning to these questions. Most scholarly accounts of COP21 seem to be primarily concerned with the meeting's outcome. In doing so, they take for granted that climate negotiations are indeed primarily and essentially about *solving* the climate problem. This is, however, far from obvious. Not only are multilateral negotiations far more complex than suggested by the simplified models of "negotiation games" between rational actors that are used frequently in academic discourse. A long-standing bulk of literature on the governance of social problems has also argued convincingly that policymaking is not so much about *solving* problems than about *dealing* with problems (Hoppe 2013), and showed how, in this process, new problems are framed according to dominant normative and cultural orders and inserted in existing institutional settings and organisational routines (Gusfield 1981, Lascoumes

1994). Instead of concentrating on the outcomes of policymaking, such as administrative decisions or laws, these accounts take a process-oriented perspective, insisting on the importance of administrative practices and cognitive dimensions, like the creation of common definitions of problems and possible solutions.

Process-oriented perspectives have recently become more visible in international relations research, as proponents of a "practice turn" (Bueger and Gadinger 2014) and ethnographers of international organisations[4] have turned to analysing negotiations as social practice that unfolds in time and space, functions according to specific logics and norms, produces meaning and creates artefacts that circulate and are taken up, but also reinterpreted and readapted, in local contexts. Following this line of reasoning, the chapter sets out to shift attention away from what climate negotiations are said to do (i.e. save the climate) to analysing what it means to make the climate problem "governable" in multilateral negotiations (Müller 2012). To do so, the chapter proposes an account of climate negotiations based on ethnographic observation at COP21 and at an intermediate negotiation session in Bonn in June 2015, interviews with participants and extensive analysis of negotiation documents, reports and grey literature that circulated at COP21.

The chapter is structured as follows: (1) Climate negotiations are analysed as a social practice that unfolds in a specific temporal and spatial setting, according to a set of rules. (2) The making of the Paris Agreement is examined as a sequence of text-related activities that separated "technical" practices of text editing from "political" bargaining. (3) Mechanisms are detailed through which different issues, problem framings and solutions found their way into the text while others were excluded. (4) The main outcome of this process, the Paris Agreement, is analysed with a view to understanding its significance in climate governance. (5) Finally, some reflections about the "social life" of the text are sketched, from its adoption at COP21 to its effects on national policymaking and social practice. The conclusion revisits the question of what "governing climate change" actually means, in the Paris conference and beyond.

## Process: the negotiated order of climate conferences

Paris was what observers of climate talks call a "high-stakes conference". It aimed to close a negotiation cycle begun in 2007 with the adoption of the "Bali Road Map", which called for a follow-up treaty to the Kyoto Protocol. The first attempt to produce such a document famously failed in Copenhagen two years later, before a new attempt was launched in Durban, South Africa, in 2011. Since then, the "Ad Hoc Group on the Durban Platform" (ADP) has been the main negotiation forum. Led by two co-chairs, the American Reifsnyder and the Algerian Djoghlaf, the ADP was tasked with elaborating a draft version of "a protocol, another legal instrument or an agreed outcome with legal force".[5] This drafting exercise was conducted in several intermediate negotiation sessions throughout 2015, which took place in Geneva, Switzerland (February) and Bonn, Germany (three sessions, held in June, August/September and October), as well as in December in Paris, before a draft text was submitted to the COP.

## Rules and procedures

As the ADP was established under the UNFCCC, the Climate Convention's rules structured the drafting process. Interestingly, though, rules of procedure were never formally adopted in climate negotiations, because parties were unable to agree on an article about voting rules.[6] The rules, except the controversial voting rule, have hence been tacitly "applied" ever since (Yamin and Depledge 2004, 433). Climate talks are thus a particularly striking illustration of what Anselm Strauss famously termed the "negotiated order" of social organisations: rules and norms not only are what structures human interaction; they also are subject to continuous renegotiation themselves (Strauss 1978). This situation exacerbates some of the more general characteristics of multilateral settings. Consensus decision-making for example is a common feature of environmental negotiations (Chasek 2001, 31–32) and it is generally assumed that the absence of formal disagreement indicates consensus (Zartman 1994, 5). However, in climate talks, varying interpretations have prevailed at different moments. The Copenhagen Accord is infamous in this respect: it was "adopted" despite vocal opposition by a minority of delegations, so its legal status remains unclear (Vogler 2016, 57). And while it is commonplace in multilateral settings that negotiations on substance are preceded by those on procedure (Bendix 2012, 30), climate talks have been characterised by a peculiar "politics of process", where endless discussions about rules often *replace* discussions on substance. This practice has favoured obstructionist tactics by some delegations[7] and transformed climate governance into a "fabric of slowness" (Aykut and Dahan 2015, 106) that stands in stark contrast to the accelerating pace of climate-induced environmental and social disruptions. On a more positive note, the de facto veto power of parties also had the effect of creating a relatively inclusive process, where small developing countries have a stronger voice than in other multilateral settings.

## Choreography and rhythm

As at other climate conferences, access to different spaces in the "blue zone" at COP21 and especially to the negotiation area was restricted and channelled through a complex system of badges distributed to participants based on their organisational affiliation – observers, negotiators, UN personnel, media and so forth. This organisational and spatial arrangement created a relatively protected zone where negotiators could mingle and engage in informal doorway chats, while also allowing for regular interactions among negotiators, and between them and other participants in neighbouring spaces. Such "interactional openness" is believed to be important because it facilitates learning and trust (Schüssler, Rüling and Wittnebe 2014). Another important characteristic of international conferences identified by Schüssler and colleagues is "temporal boundedness". Defining temporal boundaries, and especially setting a clear deadline, may, however, appear easier in theory than it is in practice, as climate conferences are very prone to last-minute drama, prolongations and even adjourning of controversial issues to follow-up meetings. At COP21, the ADP co-chairs and COP president Laurent

Fabius therefore tirelessly repeated that the conference would not be prolonged beyond Saturday night. This created a sense of urgency that was amplified because the crucial importance of COP21 had been almost ritually highlighted by the UNFCCC secretariat and French officials in the run-up to the conference. For example UNFCCC executive secretary Christina Figueres travelled the globe to remind world leaders and the general public that Paris was the "last chance"[8] to strike a deal, while media outlets stylised the Paris talks as "twelve days that will decide Earth's future".[9] Backed by results from modelling exercises that indicated a rapidly closing window for climate action,[10] alarmism also dominated opening statements, as exemplified in this quote from US president Obama's speech:

> For I believe, in the words of Dr. Martin Luther King, Jr., that there is such a thing as being too late. And when it comes to climate change, that hour is almost upon us. But if we act here, if we act now, if we place our own short-term interests behind the air that our young people will breathe, and the food that they will eat, and the water that they will drink, and the hopes and dreams that sustain their lives, then we won't be too late for them.[11]

There are, however, trade-offs between temporal boundedness and continuous interaction over time. While regular events create more interaction and exchange, punctual high-stakes events induce a stronger sense of urgency. This dilemma is addressed in climate negotiations through a specific temporal dramaturgy, which combines intersession meetings (see Figure 1.1) throughout the year

*Figure 1.1*  An ADP plenary meeting at the Bonn intersession meeting in June 2015. Country delegates sit in the central ring, while observers' seats are located at the back of the hall and on the balcony at the first floor.

Source: Caption Collective Climacop.

with high-stakes conferences like COP21. While intersessions receive less media attention, creating the possibility to engage in or maintain less formal interactions and explore areas for possible compromise,[12] COPs create a unity in time and space and impose a specific temporality and rhythm on negotiations.

### Socialisation

Negotiations not only are made up of rules, temporal boundaries and spatial arrangements but they are also social spaces. Repeated interactions among participants create personal ties that can be observed regularly during the early days of a COP, when members of different delegations greet each other vocally across the hallways of the blue zone, or hug frenetically like old friends meeting again after a long time. The importance of group dynamics and personal relationships in multilateral negotiations is recognised in the literature (Chasek 2001, 34), but mostly analysed with a view to understanding their impact on negotiation outcomes.[13] The emergence of social networks is, however, an interesting and significant phenomenon in itself. And the fact that climate negotiations are relatively old – the meetings of the intergovernmental negotiation committee (INC) began in the early 1990s – increases their importance, as one member of the French delegation confirms:

> One of the things that struck me immediately in these negotiations is at what point the climate negotiations milieu rests upon interpersonal relations. Your contacts even determine your importance in your negotiation team . . . of course, there is also the capacity to manage the technical complexity of your subject matter, the knowledge of details, etc. but I would say that 90% is the network, the people you know.[14]

Over time, people in such networks come to share a common experience, and common codes and understandings about the issues at stake. Bendix (2012) for example, who argues from an ethnographic point of view, considers this process of socialisation of participants from extremely diverse backgrounds to be one of the main outcomes of multilateralism. Independently of its formal output, climate governance can therefore be considered a process that creates shared language and shared problem framings among negotiators, who bring them "home" to their administrations and publics once negotiations are over. For Bendix, this convergence of negotiators' views and habits precedes and furthers a much larger movement: a slow but steady convergence between the distant sites that the negotiators are there to represent.

## The technical, the political and the progressive materialisation of a document

The spatial choreography and temporal dramaturgy of climate conferences – and of international conferences more generally (Müller and Cloiseau 2015) – are organised around the production of text. This was all the more important in Paris, as the expected outcome was not a simple COP decision like at most conferences, but a new treaty. COP21 and to a lesser extent the preparatory intersessions were therefore places of "high politics" under close public scrutiny. Given this particular setting, one could have expected a politicisation of negotiations, with controversial debates and open clashes. This was rarely the case. Instead, negotiations took the form of a technical exercise of text editing. Locating politics and identifying power struggles in this highly codified process is possible only through a close examination of its different steps, and through efforts to "decode" the polished language of UN talks.

### Technicising negotiations

A first-time observer of climate talks can only be puzzled by the form in which the politics of climate governance unfolds before his or her eyes. Coordinated by "chairs" or "facilitators", delegates engage in a strikingly banal exercise of text editing, organised around a central device: one or sometimes several monitors display a word document with the paragraphs currently under discussion (see Figure 1.2). Changes to the document are marked using "track changes" mode for modifications under discussion and highlighted through "colouring" to attract the attention of delegates to specific passages. "Brackets" are used to indicate

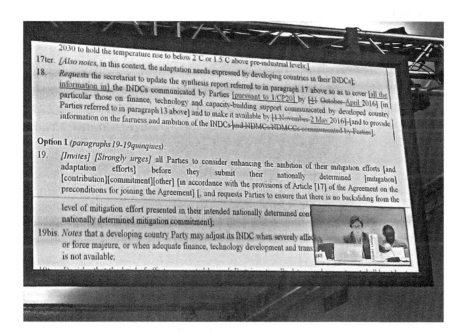

*Figure 1.2* A monitor at an ADP plenary meeting in Paris.

Source: Caption Collective Climacop.

a stabilised form of disagreement that can form the basis of further discussions. While this basic setting and the procedure remain stable, distinct text-editing practices are distributed in time and space.

The first intersession in Geneva dealt with simple "text compilation" by collecting contributions of all parties to a prospective treaty. As the option of a protocol was formally still on the table, and UNFCCC rules stipulate that the text of a protocol must be communicated at least six months before it is proposed for adoption,[15] this way of proceeding was presented as a mere procedural requirement. In practice, it also served two strategic purposes: first, the act of starting with a text entirely produced by parties was meant to create transparency and build trust. Second, the Geneva text contained only demands and options that parties had submitted "in time", in order to discredit attempts by parties to come up with "new text" in subsequent phases of the process. The subsequent Bonn intersessions introduced more complex forms of text editing, such as the "ordering" of text, "elimination of repetitions", "clarifying of options" and "streamlining", which were deemed purely technical (as opposed to political) by the ADP co-chairs. The stated purpose was to clarify options, to prepare for negotiations in Paris:

> The objective here is really to prepare the substantial work. So just to give an example: If you have two sentences: "It is not raining" and "I don't like cats," then you should not try to merge. These are two different concepts [laughs].
>
> (ADP co-facilitator F. Perrez)[16]

A new form of editing was introduced during the first week in Paris: parties were encouraged to propose "bridging proposals" that condensed different options into one, either because those options were similar or because a compromise had been reached. The "technical phase" ended at the start of the second week, when a draft text of forty pages was handed over to the newly created "Comité de Paris" that conducted the final, "political" phase of negotiations. The French COP presidency took things into its own hands, conducting extensive bilateral consultations and releasing successive drafts that were discussed in lengthy and sometimes heated plenary sessions. Text editing was replaced by more classical negotiation practices, such as bargaining over conflicting options, issue-linkage to facilitate the conclusion of deals, and coalition-building to support specific options.

## Incrementalism

To ensure that this process stayed inclusive and "party-driven" (a mantra since negotiations failed in Copenhagen), the ADP chairs produced successive documents whose legal status was voluntarily left unclear. These comprised several "non-papers", "co-chair's tools" and a "reflection note" released at the end of the first week, to take note of any disagreements by parties without reopening discussions on the main document. This resulted in multiple documents, which raised questions among delegates:

| | |
|---|---|
| *ADP co-facilitator (F. Perrez):* | "So, we hope that the outcome will be a shortening of the text, not a lengthening, which would be a surprising outcome, but you never know. Concerning the document that we put online: that is not an official document." |
| *Malaysia:* | "So there are three documents now: the Geneva text, the working document, and the non-text?" |
| *ADP co-facilitator:* | "No, this is not a document."[17] |

This incremental approach was designed to suggest that at each stage, anything was still possible, and to convince delegates that they maintained ownership of the process. At the same time, negotiations kept progressing towards a final document whose outline became more and more clear. "Nothing is decided until everything is decided": this leitmotiv was constantly repeated, but the more talks advanced, the more difficult it became to introduce new ideas or to revisit options that had been sidelined earlier. In this art of advancing without acknowledging it, the co-chairs counted on the "normative power of the factual" – that is on the weight of the document that was on the table.

The progressive materialisation of the document, always tacit, never explicit, was followed by media and civil society through a peculiar way of assessing progress based on two simple metrics: the size of each new draft text and the number of remaining brackets.[18] The publication of a new "co-chair's tool" of only twenty pages on October 5 – after there had been seventy-six pages in July and eighty-six pages in February – was for example hailed by observers as an important step towards a positive outcome. When developing countries insisted on reintroducing many of their initial formulations, and a new document of fifty-one pages was issued on October 23, it was interpreted as a sign that negotiations were backsliding and at risk of failing.

### Situating power and politics

Power struggles and political differences were generally hidden behind a depoliticised and technicised façade, but they were not absent. For example power asymmetries figured in a recurring complaint by small delegations about the proliferation of parallel processes, which grew stronger as negotiations advanced. Indeed, the ADP (and later the "Comité de Paris") regularly mandated "contact groups" on specific articles that in turn created "spinoff groups" on particular paragraphs, which were soon complemented by "informal informals" and "bilateral consultations" to address controversial issues. Parallel to this vertically organised architecture – in which each subsidiary body reported back to the next level – were meetings of country groups with sometimes overlapping membership. Such complexity is known to reinforce existing "capacity gaps" between delegations of highly unequal sizes; consequently, "negotiation by exhaustion" can be an effective strategy for large delegations (Schroeder, Boykoff and Spiers 2012, 835). A way for smaller countries to evade this trap has been to create alliances inside and outside of negotiations – for example with large environmental NGOs or resourceful developing states. An important downside is that countries like Saudi Arabia have frequently been able to instrumentalise smaller countries by trading logistical help for support of their preferred agenda items (Depledge 2008).

Throughout the process, "politics" appeared in highly coded forms, disguised as procedural issues and expressed in the polished language of UN multilateralism. Consider this extract of an ADP session:

| | |
|---|---|
| *Tuvalu:* | "We want to do an insertion." |
| *ADP co-chair (A. Djoghlaf):* | "This is not the time to make new proposals. Only bridging proposals." |
| *Tuvalu:* | "This is very important for us. We propose to insert, after 'agreement', 'in context of Article 17'." |
| *ADP co-chair:* | "Ok, I consider this to be not new." |
| *USA:* | "This is a new proposal, we would need to reflect on this and have consultation." |
| *Saudi Arabia:* | "We're not comfortable with this proposal here." |
| *Tuvalu:* | "I would then propose to put it into brackets in this text."[19] |

The background of this discussion is that Article 17 of the UNFCCC refers to the modalities for establishing a protocol to the Climate Convention. Referring to it would have transformed the legal status of the Paris text from an agreement to a protocol, meaning that all the dispositions of the Climate Convention (including for example the distinction between Annex I and Annex II countries) would have applied. This was unacceptable to the United States and Saudi Arabia. Instead of directly addressing this issue, however, discussions centred on questions of timing, rules and their interpretation:

| | |
|---|---|
| *ADP co-chair:* | "So we can have this discussion all morning. But I suggest really to move on. My suggestion would be to have it inserted with two brackets." |
| *Cuba:* | "We should discuss substance. But unless we have the rules clear, we cannot proceed. This touches on the right of Parties. Equal Parties. What Tuvalu was suggesting was in the Geneva text. So the proposal is not coming from the moon, it was there [. . .] I would suggest to have a note of the co-chair about what rules apply." |

The extract points to the ambiguity of editing rules (e.g. the difference between brackets and double brackets)[20] and also of concepts like "new text". As this example shows, the interpretation, renegotiation and "bending" of rules are themselves an important "political" negotiation strategy.

## Substance: the world in the text

Moving from process to substance, an essential question is understanding how, and under which form, issues get taken up in climate talks and find their way into negotiation documents, especially when they are as diverse as emissions reductions, adaptation strategies, energy markets, disaster risks, biodiversity protection and climate finance. Because climate change is, as some have noted, "the apotheosis of the idea that everything is related to everything else" (Skolnikoff 1993, 183), this immediately begs the opposite question of how and why, if climate change touches upon just about everything, certain issues or framings get excluded. The answers to both of these questions will help to characterise more precisely what it means to make climate change "governable".

### Globalising the climate: inscriptions

Bruno Latour's account of the role of inscriptions and "circulating reference" in scientific practice[21] constitutes a useful starting point for this discussion. As with Latour's scientists, much of the work of negotiators consists of producing "inscriptions" (i.e. fixed expressions or short sentences), introducing them in the negotiations, and defending their presence and exact location in the final document (in the agreement, the preamble and the COP decision). These inscriptions condense and represent wider assemblages of actors, "actants" and problem framings; they often result from yearlong struggles to find a convenient formulation that gathers sufficient support. The introduction of a specific formula in the text can constitute the main reason for the presence of certain actors at a COP, such as when the International Trade Union Confederation lobbied actively to include the phrase "a just transition of the workforce and the creation of decent work" in the document. Small island developing states backed by foundations and environmental NGOs conditioned their acceptance of an agreement on recognition of the goal of limiting temperature increase to 1.5 °C, and the concept of "loss and damage" that refers to climate change impacts to which adaptation is impossible. Youth activists defended "intergenerational equity", representatives of indigenous peoples defended the "rights" and "knowledge of indigenous peoples" (see Foyer and Dumoulin, this volume), and business representatives and the carbon trading industry championed "cooperative approaches" and "market-based instruments". While this list could be endless, the following paragraph of the agreement's preamble is an empirical example that clearly outlines this process of inscription:

> *Noting* the importance of ensuring the integrity of all ecosystems, including oceans, and the protection of biodiversity, recognised by some cultures as Mother Earth, and noting the importance for some of the concept of 'climate justice', when taking action to address climate change, . . .

The paragraph introduces several loosely related concepts, some of which (i.e. "Mother Earth", "climate justice" and "oceans") thus appear for the first time in a climate treaty. While the small word "some" that precedes the first two notions indicates that they are not recognised by all parties, the importance of "oceans" is acknowledged in the text without further qualification. This was the result of an unprecedented mobilisation of a diverse group of actors regrouped under the umbrella of the "Ocean and Climate Platform".[22] This "ocean community" comprised think tanks, scientific associations, NGOs and philanthropic foundations, like the Fondation Prince Albert II de Monaco, along with international organisations, like the Intergovernmental Oceanographic Commission of UNESCO. The platform organised side events during COP21, including an "ocean day" in the civil society space and events for the wider public in Paris; it formulated a list of nine recommendations for the conference, including a better articulation of the Climate Convention and ocean-related international treaties and dispositions. Their demands received support from the French COP presidency and several other country delegations. This (admittedly very specific) example shows the immense amount of work – that involved constituting legitimate spokespersons, building coalitions, attracting public attention and condensing and translating a larger agenda into specific requests for negotiators – required to introduce a small piece of text into the agreement. The lobbying work also led to the constitution of a new collective actor, the "ocean community", represented by the Ocean and Climate Platform. In other words, "inscriptions" and "spokespersons" can co-constitute each other.[23]

## Deglobalising the climate: discreet framings

Making climate change governable also entails a parallel movement that excludes issues, framings and actors. Political scientists have coined the notion of "discreet framing" to characterise processes that enable successful negotiation outcomes by preventively excluding issues that might block consensus (Gilbert and Henry 2012). Detecting such discreet framings is an analytical challenge: once established, they cease to provoke controversy or disagreement. Rather, they produce silence. To analyse them, we therefore must turn attention away from official negotiations at COP21, to retrace the historical evolution of dominant framings in the climate regime, and the discrepancies or dissonances between framings in the negotiations and the wider climate debate.

Historically, the basis for the Paris Agreement was laid at COP15 in Copenhagen (2009). Basic concepts that dominated discussion in Paris emerged and were codified there, such as the 2 °C target, the $100 billion promise for financial aid from developed to developing countries and the bottom-up process of national mitigation pledges. The conference in the Danish capital was also significant in that it laid bare a geopolitical shift in climate governance: the final agreement was crafted by the United States and China, associated with other major emerging economies but not the European Union. The uncrowned leader of climate talks was sidelined in the final hours of the conference, forcing it to accept an approach that ran fundamentally counter to its long-time orientations in the climate regime (Grubb 2010). It is important to understand that this result was not an accident. Rather, it reflected the basic positions of the world's two largest economies, which had clearly outlined their redlines before the conference: the United States rejected binding commitments and requested a common framework for developing and developed countries,[24] while China insisted on the priority of economic development, refused external monitoring and review that would interfere with its sovereignty, and called for official recognition of the 2 °C target.[25] The Copenhagen Accord combined those positions, which explains why it was much less criticised in the United States than in Europe, and even praised in official Chinese media.[26] These redlines have been internalised in climate talks since Copenhagen, and they formed part of the discreet framing that pre-structured the Paris talks. Thus, most of the actors that had vocally criticised the Copenhagen outcome, and denounced the US and Chinese positions in Copenhagen as inflexible, stayed silent in Paris, even though the same approach prevailed.

A second layer of this discreet framing concerns the exclusion of specific issue areas or sectors. As I have argued elsewhere (Aykut 2016), the current global governance architecture isolates the climate regime from other institutions that regulate issue areas that are relevant to climate policy, such as energy security and markets, international trade, finance and development. This fragmentation of the international scene is reflected in the dominant framing of climate change mitigation as a problem of emissions reduction, as opposed to, say, regulation of fossil fuel production and trade, reorientation of global financial flows or management of global trade volumes (see also Aykut and Castro, this volume). An interesting case in point is the climate-trade nexus. While several reports in the run-up to COP21 highlighted the necessity for reform of global economic governance to tackle climate change (Brandi, Bruhn and Lindenberg 2015), the potential trade-offs between efforts to intensify global trade and those to limit global emissions have never been problematised in climate talks. Quite the contrary, the dominant framing demands that the intensification of global trade would *advance* climate mitigation (Vogler 2016, 26–28, 33), and a so-called conformity clause in the Climate Convention and the Kyoto Protocol assures the priority of international commercial law over international climate law.[27] Scholars have argued that such dispositions exert a "chilling effect" (Eckersley 2004) on national regulators who are willing to take measures against environmental degradation that might contravene WTO rules. Such debates, however, never entered the Paris negotiations. The notion "trade" appears three times in the Geneva text: once to reaffirm the rejection of all forms of trade restrictions (Article 9 Option 1), once in reference to carbon markets (Article 69bis) and once in reference to a possible regulation of emissions from international aviation and shipping (Article 47.5 Option [a]). The final agreement makes no mention of international trade. Interestingly, the discreet framing can in this case be traced directly to at least one specific actor: according to internal EU documents leaked by Attac (an activist network in the anti-globalisation movement), EU negotiators were instructed explicitly to prevent trade issues from being put on the table in Paris.[28]

## The changing grammar of climate governance

Adopted on the evening of Saturday, December 12, 2015, the outcome of the yearlong drafting and editing process is a thirty-two-page document of two parts: a twenty-page COP decision with a preamble and 140 paragraphs, and an agreement of twelve pages, consisting of yet another preamble and twenty-nine articles. The two texts have a different legal status: the decision can be complemented, over-ridden or replaced by subsequent COP decisions, while the agreement undergoes a procedure of signature and ratification by parties, and is therefore seen as the central output of the conference. It contains procedural (Articles 1 and 16–29)[29] and substantial (Articles 2–15) dispositions. Among the latter, Article 2 defines three separate objectives, concerning mitigation, adaptation and finance. It con-tains the long-term goal of holding global temperature increase to "well below 2 °C" and introduces an even more stringent "aspirational" objective of 1.5 °C. Articles 4 to 6 translate the long-term temperature goal into a mitigation objec-tive, lay out modalities for the submission of national mitigation plans, contain provisions relating to the protection of forests, and establish voluntary market-based and non-market-based cooperation mechanisms for mitigation. Articles 7 and 8 relate to adaptation, and loss and damage. Article 9 treats financial support for developing countries' mitigation and adaptation efforts. It is acknowledged that financial resources can come from public and private sources, with their amount to grow from a bottom line of US$100 billion per year (Paragraph 54 of the decision). Developing countries are encouraged to contribute on a voluntary basis. Articles 10–12 treat matters like technology transfer, capacity building and education. This quick overview reveals little that is genuinely new: issues like mitigation, adaptation, finance, technology transfer and capacity building have been central since the 1990s.[30] The recognition of loss and damage and the 1.5 °C temperature goal are exceptions; their inclusion is generally considered a victory of the most vulnerable developing countries. The immediate consequences of this are, however, likely to be very limited: the 1.5 °C threshold is a goal that most scientists already consider unattainable in practice (Anderson 2015), and the inclusion of loss and damage in the agreement is weakened by Paragraph 52 of the decision, which excludes any claim to liability and compensation.

### Governing through verbs

Articles 3 and 13–15 help one to understand why Paris nonetheless constitutes a paradigm shift. Those articles establish a cyclical pledge and review system: par-ties are invited to regularly submit nationally determined contributions (NDCs) that are expected to become progressively more ambitious (the so-called ratchet mechanism). A "transparency framework" and a "facilitation mechanism" are created to assure comparability of the NDC objectives and to help parties attain them, and a "global stocktake" is organised every five years to assess progress.[31]

To further specify the Paris approach, it is instructive to look at the use of two seemingly inconspicuous *modal verbs*: "shall", which in legal language indicates binding dispositions, and "should", which introduces non-binding elements. The Paris Agreement contains fifteen mentions of the formulation "Party [or Parties] should", whereas "Party [or Parties] shall" appears twenty times. Two other non-binding formulations, "voluntary" and "encouraged", appear five times each. More specifically, half of the binding dispositions in the Paris Agreement (ten) deal with obligations to inform or communicate. Five others point, respectively, to domestic adaptation and mitigation policies, participation in the facilitation process, financial assistance and climate education. The remaining five are "false positives", meaning that they contain no specific obligations. In sum, the Paris Agreement appears as a mix of soft law and binding law, where binding provisions essentially concern reporting duties. This can be compared to the use of the same wordings in the Kyoto Protocol. In stark contrast, the non-binding formula "Party [or Parties] should" does not figure *at all* in the text and the words "should", "voluntary" and "encouraged" appear only once each. The binding formulation "Party [or Parties] shall", however, is used twenty-five times and the verb "shall" appears no less than 158 times. Also, virtually every paragraph of the mitigation section (Articles 2 and 3) is introduced by a specific obligation for parties.

While counting verbs might seem trivial, it helps to specify the characteristics of the Paris approach. The new agreement replaces a Kyoto governance based on legally binding reduction targets and sanctions for non-compliance (applying exclusively to developed countries) with a system based on national pledges that are regularly and collectively reviewed (applying equally to all parties). While the content of those pledges is non-binding and determined freely, reporting is mandatory. In other words, the core features of the Copenhagen framing prevailed in Paris. They were spelled out in greater detail and completed by supplementary elements, such as the cyclical review mechanism and the more ambitious long-term goal.

## The text and the world: black-boxing and circulation

Much like romantic movies, scholarly accounts of climate negotiations often end with the moment that "seals the deal" – for example when parties reach agreement on an important treaty.[32] But this is not where the story ends. What happens with the text once it is stabilised? How does it circulate? Through which mechanisms does it affect policymaking and social practice "on the ground"? While a detailed account of the agreement's "social life" is beyond the scope of this chapter, it is possible to make a rough sketch of the first steps of its journey.

Formal adoption of the treaty took place at the closing plenary of COP21, which was convened in "La Seine", the biggest and most impressive meeting hall of the conference centre (see Figure 1.3). Access was restricted to ministers, heads of delegation and selected media representatives, with live transmission provided to several "overflow" rooms and screens in the hallways of the conference centre. Presided over by French foreign minister Laurent Fabius, it started with some confusion and an unscheduled interruption. The reason for this soon became clear: the US delegation unofficially blocked adoption of the final draft, claiming that a

*Figure 1.3* COP21 meeting hall "La Seine".

Source: Caption Collective Climacop.

"shall" in Article 4.4 (mitigation pledges by developed countries) would change the legal status of the document and force ratification by the US Senate. In a rare diplomatic masterstroke, the "shall" was replaced by a "should" in what was termed a purely "technical" revision, after which M. Fabius announced the closure of the Comité de Paris and the opening of a session of the COP, the supreme body of the Climate Convention. After a short look at the floor, he declared to see no objections and, in a swift movement, used a gavel to mark adoption of the Paris Agreement. In reaction, the hall erupted in applause. The floor was then given to country delegates, who made a series of statements that underlined the "historic" significance of the moment and the importance of the agreement, and thanked the French COP presidency for its work.[33]

    This short description reveals different techniques used to ritually[34] mark the conclusion of the agreement, including the convening of high-level delegations (ministers) into a specific setting (the most significant conference hall), the raising of stakes through media presence and live transmission, the execution of a formal routine that indicates closure (swinging the gavel) and the performing of a ceremonial speech act where participants express their adherence (closing statements). To this, we may add the signature ceremony convened four months later at the UN Headquarters in New York, which marked the beginning of the next phase – signature, ratification and entry into force[35] – in the life of the agreement. Even if this sequence is purely "symbolic", its significance should not be underestimated; each step in the chain of ritualised practice increases the symbolic and reputational costs of individual countries questioning the process or opting out. It also ensures that the text is "black-boxed" (Latour 1986, Akrich 1992), so that it can circulate globally without being reopened.

The adoption of the agreement fixes its content. That is followed by a phase where every sentence of the text is publicly scrutinised, commented on and interpreted, both in subsequent negotiation sessions and in various media outlets, where public representatives, legal scholars, stakeholders and activists express their views and try to impose their interpretations. That process is enabled by the voluntarily vague language that is often used in international agreements to facilitate consensus. Despite this "constructive ambiguity" (Biniaz 2016), there are limits to interpretation: the text *de facto* excludes certain readings, while facilitating others. Within this space of "interpretability", a new round of political struggles unfolds (Geden 2015). Again, structural power asymmetries are an important aspect of the process. As low-stakes COPs and intersessions attract much fewer delegates, especially from developing countries with limited resources, experienced negotiators and influential delegations can more easily impose their readings.

Finally, the text serves different purposes among national contexts. Treaties or elements of treaties are transposed in national law; they serve as a reference point for public debates, form the basis of court decisions or rulings and become a lever for lobbying activities. Thus, actors that managed to inscribe their formulations into the document can now count on a new powerful ally to advance their agenda "on the ground". As one trade union delegate explained to me, the main motivation of the decade-long struggle for including a phrase on "just transition" in the agreement was to change the discursive context under which national and local energy transitions play out.[36] This *performative* dimension is particularly important in the case of documents which, like the Paris Agreement, are based mainly on soft law. Of course, the discreet framings that shape the drafting exercise also constrain and orient its use: issues and framings that are excluded from negotiations will also be less legitimate in public debate, and problematic framings in the text may cause problematic real-world effects.

## Conclusion: climatising the world?

In what sense, then, is climate change "governed" in climate negotiations? Based on this analysis of the negotiations for the Paris Agreement, we can distinguish three distinct responses to the question. First, transnational mega-events like COP21 function as political ritual that creates or enacts a specific political cosmology. This has been most eloquently depicted by Paul Little in his ethnographic study of the 1992 UN Conference on the Environment and Development in Rio de Janeiro (Little 1995). Examining the marathon of statements by heads of state at the closing ceremony, he argued that it is not so much the *content* of such declarations that is important. Instead, this "illocutionary performance" by world leaders can be deciphered "as something like: 'I am concerned about the environment and development and I am actively involved in finding solutions to these problems'" (ibid., 276). It is important in this respect that, just like the

Rio Earth Summit, COP21 was a conference of superlatives: the presence of an unprecedented number of world leaders and massive coverage by international media created a global event of singular symbolic importance that in itself performs "climate governance", because it suggests that there is something like an "international community" in charge of the world's problems. Put negatively, this symbolic aspect of the global circus of climate conferences corresponds to what Blühdorn (2007) calls "politics of simulation": empty talk and agitation in the face of political stalemate and accelerating climate disruptions.

Second, climate conferences constitute the central node of a transnational political space or network that connects distant sites through the circulation of skilled individuals (delegates, experts, activists and stakeholders), discourses and material artefacts (e.g. reports and treaties). A main feature of such conferences is that they bring together and *socialise* actors with very different cultural backgrounds, problem framings and interests, and make problems "governable" by diffusing common cultural norms and producing shared understandings (Bendix 2012, Müller 2012). This means that the *process* of elaborating a text – and not the outcome as such – is central, and that the slow pace of climate talks has to be interpreted in the light of the laborious process of acculturation of delegates and the even more time-consuming dynamic of convergence among the sites that constitute the network. From this point of view, the Paris Agreement can be conceived of as a patchwork of "inscriptions", which link actor coalitions that successfully "climatised" beforehand to the UNFCCC arena. In other words, the "globalisation of the climate", through the inscription in negotiation documents of a growing number of issues, corresponds *in fine* to an extension of the network of climate governance. That is true not so much because these issues will indeed be "resolved" (they may or may not be), but because legitimate spokespersons have come to represent them in the climate regime.

Third, international treaties and decisions contain concrete instructions for signatory states. However, the way such instructions "work" – that is how they are supposed to produce real-world effects – is changing with the Paris approach: if scholars of international relations were able to affirm in the 1990s that "the main goal" of international regimes "is to harmonise national legislation or to establish rules that can be applied by and to states" (Zartman 1994, 6), this is no longer valid for Paris-type agreements. From a system that aimed at governing through "rule-making", organised around the production of a document with more or less immediate legal consequences, climate governance has evolved into a system that governs through the setting of global goals (e.g. the 2 °C and 1.5 °C temperature thresholds, and the $100 billion objective for climate finance), to be attained by a mix of voluntary pledges and obligatory information and review cycles. The status of the text changes: rather than a body of legislative rules to be transposed into national law, or a document that contains detailed information about what to do, it is part of a strategy that aims at changing the expectations of a variety of public and private actors. The backdrop of this "governance by signals" is that the global "momentum" that assures the performativity of the text must be continually re-actualised, to prevent more urgent matters from supplanting the focus on climate politics. This means that climate governance "après Paris" fundamentally depends on the capacity of actors to sustain the process of climatisation and extend its scope.

## Notes

1 Speech at the opening plenary of COP21. http://www.ibtimes.co.uk/cop21-ban-ki-moon-full-speech-start-paris-climate-change-talks-1531133 (all links were last accessed on July 31, 2016).
2 ADP contact group, morning session, 1.12.2015, 10–13h, Paris. All negotiation transcripts were made by the author. Difficulty of transcribing in real-time may have resulted in minor imprecisions or omissions.
3 See the recent special issues of *Climate Law* (2016, Vol. 6, No. 1–2) and *Review of European, Comparative & International Environmental Law* (2016, Vol. 25, No. 2).
4 For an overview, see the special issues of *Global Environmental Politics* (2014, Vol. 14, No. 3) and *Critique Internationale* (Vol. 2012/1, No. 54), as well as the edited volume by Müller (2013).
5 UNFCCC. 2011. "Establishment of an Ad Hoc Working Group on the Durban Platform for Enhanced Action". FCCC/CP/2011/9/Add.1.
6 Rule 42 of the Draft Rules of Procedure would have allowed for majority decisions. See UNFCCC. 1996. "Organizational Matters: Adoption of the Rules of Procedure". FCCC/CP/1996/2.
7 The extensive use of such techniques by Saudi Arabia is documented by Depledge (2008).
8 http://www.foxbusiness.com/markets/2015/07/22/ap-interview-un-climate-chief-says-paris-last-chance-tells-doubters-to-think.html.
9 http://mashable.com/2015/11/25/paris-climate-conference-cop21/#IQgjbde2Ekq4.
10 As one observer puts it, such modelling results consistently depicted a situation where "Time is running out, but we can still make it if we start to act now" (Geden 2015).
11 https://www.whitehouse.gov/the-press-office/2015/11/30/remarks-president-obama-first-session-cop21.
12 Consultations also take place outside official negotiations. For example the French presidency engaged in extensive high-level meetings, issuing joint climate statements with the United States (12.11.2014), India (11.4.2015), Mexico (16.7.2015) and China (2.11.2015). This strategy has been described as "multiple bilateralism" (Belis, Joffe, Kerremans and Qi 2015).
13 For example Benedick (1991, 49) and Depledge (2008, 19).
14 Interview with a member of the French delegation, 25.11.2015.
15 See Article 37 of the Climate Convention.
16 ADP group on section D, 4.6.2015, Bonn, Germany.
17 ADP group on section D, 4.6.2015.
18 Of course, substantive analyses of the draft texts by observers did also exist. Both of these metrics were, however, widely used both in mainstream media and detailed analyses.
19 ADP contact group, 1.12.2015, 10–13h, Paris.
20 See Biniaz (2016) for an excellent compilation of negotiation techniques that exploit such ambiguities.
21 See the chapter "Circulating Reference: Sampling the Soil in the Amazon Forest", in Latour (1999).

22  http://www.ocean-climate.org/?cat=121.
23  A similar argument is made by Bellier (2007) in her ethnographic study of the struggle for recognition of the term "indigenous peoples" (as opposed to "indigenous people"), where she shows how the activism of indigenous leaders in the UN arena led to the constitution of a political actor in charge of the governance of "indigenous matters".
24  See the report on *International Climate Agreements* by Joseph E. Aldy and Robert N. Stavins (2008), two Harvard professors close to Democratic circles, which reflects a long-term orientation of US climate politics that was reaffirmed in the US submission to the Paris talks (USA, U.S. Submission – September 2014, UNFCCC, Bonn, 17.9.2014).
25  As outlined in a document crafted before the conference by China in association with India, Brazil, South Africa and G77 chair Sudan, which was published in the journal *Le Monde*, in its edition of December 11, 2009.
26  A summary of the international reception of the accord is given in the report of the House of Lords (2010, 11).
27  Article 3.5, UNFCCC and Article 2.3, Kyoto Protocol.
28  See Hilary (2015).
29  Article 1 fixes definitions and Articles 16–29 treat organisational matters, such as the creation of subsidiary bodies, signature and ratification and entry into force.
30  The respective importance of these issues has changed over time, with the latter three – dear to developing countries – having gained in prominence since the 2000s (Aykut and Dahan 2015).
31  The first "global stocktake" is scheduled for 2023. A light version of the stocktake – called "facilitative dialogue" – will be convened in 2018.
32  Among many others: "The Inside Story of the Climate Convention" (Mintzer and Leonard 1994); "Prologue to the Climate Convention" (Bodansky 1994); "Framework Convention on Climate Change: A Scientific and Political History" (Hecht and Tirpak 1995); "Tracing the Origins of the Kyoto Protocol" (Depledge 2000).
33  The intervention of the Nicaraguan delegate who expressed dissatisfaction with the outcome and the procedure was an exception. As Nicaragua's objection had not been raised "in time", this dissonance had no effect on the outcome.
34  For an analysis of transnational mega-events as ritual, see Little (1995).
35  The Paris Agreement enters into force after the ratification by at least fifty-five countries that account for 55% of greenhouse gas emissions.
36  Interview with a trade-union delegate, December 3, 2015.

## Bibliography

Akrich, Madeleine. "The de-scription of technical objects." In *Shaping Technology / Building Society: Studies in Sociotechnical Change*, by Wiebe E. Bijker and John Law, 205–224. Cambridge, MA: MIT Press, 1992.

Aldy, Joseph E., and Robert N. Stavins. *Designing the Post-Kyoto Climate Regime: Lessons from the Harvard Project on International Climate Agreements*. Belfer Center for Science and International Affairs, Harvard Kennedy School, Belfer Center for Science and International Affairs, 2008.

Anderson, Kevin. "Duality in climate science." *Nature Geoscience* 8 (2015): 898–900.

Aykut, Stefan. "Taking a wider view on climate governance: Moving beyond the 'iceberg', the 'elephant', and the 'forest'." *WIREs Climate Change* 7, no. 3 (2016): 318–328.

Aykut, Stefan, and Amy Dahan. *Gouverner le Climat? 20 ans de négociations internationales*. Paris: Presses de Science Po, 2015.

Belis, David, Paul Joffe, Bart Kerremans, and Ye Qi. "China, the United States and the European Union: Multiple bilateralism and prospects for a new climate change diplomacy." *Carbon & Climate Law Review* 9, no. 3 (2015): 203–218.

Bellier, Irène. "Partenariat et participation des peuples autochtones aux Nations unies: intérêts et limites d'une présence institutionnelle." In *Démocratie participative, cultures et pratiques*, by Catherine Neveu, 175–192. Paris: L'Harmattan, 2007.

Bendix, Regina. "Une salle, plusieurs sites: les négociations internationales comme terrain de recherche anthropologique." *Critique Internationale* 54 (2012): 19–38.

Benedick, Richard Elliot. *Ozone Diplomacy: New Directions in Safeguarding the Planet*. Cambridge, MA: Harvard University Press, 1991.

Biniaz, Susan. *Comma but Differentiated Responsibilities: Punctuation and 30 Other Ways Negotiators Have Resolved Issues in the International Climate Change Regime*. Sabin Center for Climate Change Law. 2016. http://www.ColumbiaClimateLaw.com (accessed 2016).

Blühdorn, Ingolfur. "Sustaining the unsustainable: Symbolic politics and the politics of simulation." *Environmental Politics* 16, no. 2 (2007): 251–275.

Bodansky, Daniel. "Prologue to the climate change convention." In *Negotiating Climate Change: The Inside Story of the Rio Convention*, by M. Mintzer and J. Leonard Amber, 45–74. Cambridge, MA: Cambridge University Press, 1994.

Brandi, Clara, Dominique Bruhn, and Nanette Lindenberg. *The Global Regulatory Framework for Decarbonisation – 3x3 Starting Points for the Reform of Global Economic Governance*. Briefing Paper 19, Bonn: German Development Institute, 2015.

Bueger, Christian, and Frank Gadinger. *International Practice Theory: New Perspectives*. Basingstoke: Palgrave Macmillan, 2014.

Chasek, Pamela S. *Earth Negotiations: Analyzing Thirty Years of Environmental Diplomacy*. Tokyo: United Nations University Press, 2001.

Depledge, Joanna. "Striving for no: Saudi Arabia in the climate change regime." *Global Environmental Politics* 4, no. 2 (2008): 24–50.

Depledge, Joanna. *Tracing the Origins of the Kyoto Protocol: An Article-by-Article Textual History*. 2000. http://unfccc.int/resource/docs/tp/tp0200.pdf (accessed February 2, 2011).

Eckersley, Robyn. "The big chill: The WTO and multilateral environmental agreements." *Global Environmental Politics* 4, no. 2 (2004): 24–50.

Geden, Oliver. "Paris climate deal: The trouble with targetism." *The Guardian*, 14 December 2015.

Gilbert, Claude, and Claude Henry. "La définition des problèmes publics: entre publicité et discrétion." *Revue française de sociologie* 53, no. 1 (2012): 35–59.

Grubb, Michael. "Copenhagen: Back to the future." *Climate Policy* 10, no. 2 (2010): 127–130.

Gusfield, Joseph R. *The Culture of Public Problems: Drinking-Driving and the Symbolic Order*. Chicago: Chicago University Press, 1981.

Hecht, Alan D., and Dennis Tirpak. "Framework convention on climate change: A scientific and policy history." *Climatic Change* 29 (1995): 371–402.

Hilary, John. "There Is No EU Solution to Climate Change as Long as TTIP Exists." *Independent*, 7 December 2015.

Hoppe, Robert. *The Governance of Problems: Puzzling, Powering and Participation*. Bristol: Policy Press, 2013.

House of Lords. *Debate on 14th January: The Copenhagen Conference on Climate Change*. London: House of Lords Library, 2010.

Lascoumes, Pierre. *L'éco-pouvoir: Environnements et politiques*. Paris: La Découverte, 1994.

Latour, Bruno. *Pandora's Hope: Essays on the Reality of Science Studies*. Cambridge, MA: Harvard University Press, 1999.

Latour, Bruno. "Visualization and cognition: Thinking with eyes and hands." *Knowledge and Society: Studies in the Sociology of Culture Past and Prese* 6 (1986): 1–40.

Little, Paul E. "Ritual, power and ethnography at the Rio Earth Summit." *Critique of Anthropology* 15, no. 3 (1995): 265–288.

Mintzer, Irving M., and J. Amber Leonard. *Negotiating Climate Change: The Inside Story of the Rio Convention.* Cambridge: Cambridge University Press, 1994.

Müller, Birgit. "Comment rendre le monde gouvernable sans le gouverner: les organisations internationales analysée par les anthropologues." *Critique Internationale* 54 (2012): 9–18.

Müller, Birgit. *The Gloss of Harmony: The Politics of Policy-Making in Multilateral Organisations.* London: Pluto Press, 2013.

Müller, Birgit, and Gilles Cloiseau. "The real dirt on responsible agricultural investments at Rio+20: Multilateralism versus corporate self-regulation." *Law & Society Review* 49, no. 1 (2015): 39–67.

Schroeder, Heike, Maxwell T. Boykoff, and Laura Spiers. "Equity and state representation in climate negotiations." *Nature Climate Change* 2 (December 2012): 834–836.

Schüssler, Elke, Charles-Clemens Rüling, and Bettina B. F. Wittnebe. "Climate summits: The limitations of field-configuring events as catalysts of change in transnational climate policy." *Academy of Management Journal* 57, no. 1 (2014): 140–171.

Skolnikoff, Eugene B. *The Elusive Transformation: Science, Technology and the Evolution of International Politics.* Princeton, NJ: Princeton University Press, 1993.

Strauss, Anselm. *Negotiations: Varieties, Processes, Contexts, and Social Order.* San Francisco: Jossey-Bass, 1978.

Vogler, John. *Climate Change in World Politics.* Basingstoke: Palgrave Macmillan, 2016.

Yamin, Farhana, and Joanna Depledge. *The International Climate Change Regime: A Guide to Rules, Institutions and Procedures.* Cambridge: Cambridge University Press, 2004.

Zartman, I. William. *International Multilateral Negotiation: Approaches to the Management of Complexity.* San Francisco: Jossey-Bass, 1994.

## 2 The necessary and inaccessible 1.5°C objective

### A turning point in the relations between climate science and politics?

*Hélène Guillemot*

### Introduction

For many, it was the great surprise of COP21: whereas the commitment to avoid global warming of more than 2° above pre-industrial levels adopted at COP15 in Copenhagen had been constantly repeated for six years, the Paris COP21 saw the emergence of an even more ambitious temperature objective of 1.5°. With the support of an increasingly broad coalition, this goal was ultimately adopted in the Paris Agreement, whose first article sets out the plan to

> [hold] the increase in the global average temperature to well below 2 °C above pre-industrial levels and to pursue efforts to limit the temperature increase to 1.5°C above pre-industrial levels, recognizing that this would significantly reduce the risks and impacts of climate change.

While this mention of a 1.5° target in the agreement was almost unanimously welcomed by state delegations and NGOs, initially it surprised, and even shocked, many climate scientists. According to model-based scenarios, limiting warming to 2° would require immediate and drastic cuts in global greenhouse gas emissions (chiefly $CO_2$), and even that would not be enough. The socioeconomic scenarios also include the removal of $CO_2$ from the atmosphere in the second half of the twenty-first century through "negative emissions technologies" (NETs) – technologies that currently do not exist on the required scale, and that may create negative side effects. Since the official adoption of the 2° target in 2009, greenhouse gas emissions have risen further, making the goal increasingly inaccessible – and yet in Paris an even more stringent target was being proposed.

In this chapter, we use the story of the 1.5° target to discuss the relationship between science and politics at the COP. Climate change has been science-based since its beginnings, but COPs are political negotiating spaces where few scientists are present. Spaces include a handful of scientific side events, a few climate science institutions have display stands, and influential scientists, sometimes members of national delegations, are present for a few days; but generally researchers consider that they have little place at the COPs, seeing them as political rather than scientific events. Yet, the sciences played a particularly important role at the Paris COP: because of the exceptional scope of the event, but also because relations between climate science and climate politics are undergoing profound changes, linked to shifts in the framing of the climate problem. The 1.5° target is one of the principal questions blending together science and politics that emerged during the conference.

How should we understand the paradoxical success of an arguably unattainable target? The first level of explanation is political: from this perspective, the reference to the 1.5° target in the Paris Agreement is not surprising, since it results from years of obstinate efforts by highly determined actors. But this explanation is partial: while 1.5° is a political target, it is based on scientific research and is criticised by other scientific publications. This was a new situation: the 1.5° target revealed disagreement in a domain where previously, scientific consensus was publicly expressed.

Here we will attempt to analyse the debate on the 1.5° target among scientists, surveying its history (as in fact there was already disagreement on the 2° target) and detailing the arguments and dynamics between the actors involved. The disagreements bear on long-term temperature goals, and in particular on their "safety" and feasibility. These debates are neither scientific controversies nor political disputes, but sit at the boundary between these domains. Long-term temperature goals inherently involve science-politics relations within the climate regime, and disagreements on the 1.5° target can be seen as reflecting a transformation in those relations. The Copenhagen turning point, by upsetting the framing of the problem, modified the role of science in the regime. The emergence of the 1.5° target and the resulting disagreements among scientists may be seen as a politicisation of this domain that led to a weakening of the sciences' role. However, the heated debate set off by the 1.5° target may not expand; following the Paris conference, we could instead see attempts by the climate science community to retake control over research agendas, as well as a recomposition of science-politics relations.

To address the questions raised by the 1.5° target, the debates it has stimulated, and the associated transformations in science-politics relations, this chapter combines two approaches. The first, from science and technology studies, relates to the co-production of climate science and politics and to the circulation between science and politics in translating and aligning issues (Latour 1999, Jasanoff 2004, Miller 2004). The second, based on the sociology of public problems, deals with the specific ways in which groups of actors frame the climate problem, orienting perceptions and representations of what is at stake as well as proposed solutions.

Analysing what took place around COP21 is not enough: the 1.5° issue can only be understood by situating it in the history of temperature goals and of relations between climate science and climate politics more generally. To clarify this history, this text is structured in a partly chronological fashion. The first section of this chapter presents the dominant framing of the climate problem and science's role in that framing, and examines the Copenhagen COP, the shift in climate governance and the history of the 2° long-term goal. The second section analyses the period from the aftermath of Copenhagen up to the Paris COP, reviewing the debate on the 2° target and the rise of the 1.5° target until its inclusion in the agreement. It also documents the resulting turmoil in the scientific community, analysing different groups' respective the positions. The third section looks at the preparation of the IPCC's upcoming special report on the 1.5° target and the evolution in science-politics relations, during and after COP21.[1]

## From the "science-first" framing to the Copenhagen turning point (1988–2009)

### A consensual, hegemonic model of science-politics relations

Science has played a crucial role in defining the climate problem since the beginning of the regime in the late 1980s and early 1990s (with the creation of the IPCC in 1988 and the UNFCCC in 1992). In this domain, science-politics relations have often been presented in terms of a "linear" model, whereby scientists provide knowledge to political actors, who draw on these diagnoses to make decisions, with science and politics acting independently. In this framing of the climate problem, science is the principal authority that justifies political action, leading some to speak of a "science-driven" or "science-first" problem. The IPCC adopts this model when it describes itself as "policy-relevant but not policy-prescriptive" and every five to seven years publishes its scientific assessment reports, including its "Summary for Policymakers" for use in UN negotiations (Dahan and Guillemot 2015).[2]

The linear model has long been shown to be inaccurate: the links between science and politics are more complex, and the boundaries between them more mobile and negotiated. The IPCC does not merely summarise the results of peer-reviewed research, but produces special reports ordered by governments, orchestrates consensus and more or less directly influences research programmes. The IPCC is in fact a hybrid scientific and political institution; indeed, it is precisely to its dual legitimacy, scientific and political, that the IPCC owes its remarkable authority. The place of the sciences in the climate issue thus cannot be reduced to diagnoses and assessments: in defining the problem, they also contribute to defining the proposed solutions. Climate science provides the indicators and metrics used in negotiations (mean temperature, carbon budget, $CO_2$ equivalent, estimates of climate change impacts, etc.).

More generally, as STS scholars have shown, climate change exemplifies the co-production of a global knowledge order and a (nascent) global political order (Miller 2004). Certain social scientists have criticised the framing of the climate regime and the claim of a policy founded on scientific authority. This model, they write, leads less to a "scienticised" politics than to a politicised science. It serves to disguise political disagreements as scientific ones (Pielke 2002), and to polarise debates around science rather than around political responses (Sarewitz 2004, Hulme 2011). This strong polarisation around the scientific reality of climate change long made it difficult to express any critique of the climate regime (Guillemot 2014). Furthermore, this hegemonic, consensual framing was backed by a broad coalition of actors – scientists, media, NGOs, UN agencies and so forth (Aykut, Comby and Guillemot 2012).

### The Copenhagen shift and the adoption of a long-term temperature goal

The Copenhagen COP deeply challenged this framing. With the failure of negotiations, it became clear that scientific consensus was not sufficient to trigger political action.[3] While the scientific evidence on climate change was by then widely accepted,[4] this widespread acceptance also highlighted the failure of the framing, since universal recognition did not produce the required political effects. This inability to reach an agreement on the reduction of greenhouse gas emissions reflected an underestimation of geopolitical and economic factors. Far from leading antagonisms to disappear into a "common future," climate change instead revealed these contradictory interests (Aykut and Dahan 2015). Following the failure of twenty years of "top-down" strategy, with burden sharing and legally binding reduction targets, Copenhagen saw the adoption of a "bottom-up" approach: the "pledge and review" system, whereby countries set their own emissions reductions commitments. Yet Copenhagen also delivered a major "top-down" innovation: the goal of limiting global temperature increase to 2°.

The 2° global limit has a long and complex history (Randalls 2010, Aykut and Dahan 2011, Cointe, Ravon and Guérin 2011). Since the 1970s, the 2° figure has appeared in climate change talks in various contexts: as the mean estimate of climate sensitivity,[5] the reference value for the first cost-benefit studies and the proposed threshold for dangerous climate change in first international conferences. In 1990, Article 2 of the Climate Convention specified an "ultimate objective": "to achieve (. . .) stabilization of greenhouse gas concentrations in the atmosphere at a level that would prevent dangerous anthropogenic interference with the climate system" – without specifying the level in question. However, until the late 1990s, the issue of the long-term goal remained at the margins of climate debate, despite the adoption of 2° as a long-term objective by the European Union. It was in the 2000s that the long-term goal – first formulated in terms of concentrations of greenhouse gases – took on its central role in the IPCC reports and in climate negotiations. In 2005, Europe launched the proposal of a 2° target for a global agreement, at first unsuccessfully. But in 2007, the Bali COP proposed the adoption of a "shared vision" including a long-term goal. The 2° target crystallised through the continuous interaction between scientific experts and policymakers, initially associated to an atmospheric concentration of 450 parts per-million (ppm) of $CO_2$. The 2° target came to dominate in the months leading up to Copenhagen due to its ability to connect emissions and impacts and the ease with which it can be communicated, but also because this figure is sufficiently vague to allow several interpretations and is "less accurate and less clearly measurable than concentrations, which affords it an ambiguity that is very useful in the negotiation process" (Cointe et al. 2011, 28).

The result of a political and scientific co-construction, the 2° threshold benefited from a clear legitimacy. And yet the consensus around it was more fragile than it seemed. While politicians repeated that the 2° target was determined by "the science," scientists recalled that it was a subjective, political choice, and were divided on the subject, as we will see. Moreover, even before the Copenhagen conference certain groups were pushing for a more "ambitious" target: the Alliance of Small Island States (AOSIS) argued that 2° of warming would mean that their islands would be wiped off the map by rising sea levels. Along with the group of least developed countries (LDC) and the Africa group, and with the support of leaders such as Bangladeshi Saleemul Huq, an IPCC specialist on adaptation to climate change, these countries supported the targets of 350 ppm $CO_2$ and 1.5° of warming. When the 2° target was adopted, these countries, grouped together in the Climate Vulnerable Forum, succeeded in pushing for the Copenhagen Declaration to call additionally for "strengthening the global long-term goal during a review by 2015, including in relation to a proposed 1.5°C target." Thus, the debate on the 2° and 1.5° targets was already in the making at the Copenhagen conference.

## From a hushed debate on 2° to the public emergence of disagreement on 1.5° (2009–2015)

Between the COPs in Copenhagen in 2009 and in Paris in 2015, the 2° target was constantly reaffirmed in climate arenas, but a much wider range of views on long-term goals was expressed in scientific journals. Some articles emphasised the extreme difficulty of attaining the 2° target; others were more optimistic on its feasibility; still others affirmed the need for a 1.5° target due to the gravity of the impacts of 2° of warming; only very few, however, claimed that it is also possible to limit warming to 1.5°. These disagreements, initially confined to a narrow scientific milieu, emerged publicly at the time of the Paris COP.

### Warning on the feasibility of the 2° target

In 2009, a survey by the British newspaper *The Guardian* showed that 85% of climate scientists did not believe it would be possible to limit warming to 2°.[6] This level of warming by 2100, considered likely in 1995, seemed extremely difficult to attain fifteen years later, due both to growth in greenhouse gas emissions over this period (+30% between 1995 and 2010) and to progress in the climate sciences.

Since 2010, the global mean temperature has been often associated with a new dominant metric, the "carbon budget" (Allen et al. 2009). Due to the long life of $CO_2$ in the atmosphere, global mean surface warming by 2100 will be determined by cumulative $CO_2$ emissions. Thus, a carbon budget is associated to each temperature target, with a probability distribution reflecting the associated uncertainties.

A two-thirds chance of remaining under 2° of warming translates into a carbon budget of 1,000 GtC (gigatonnes of carbon). Since we have consumed around 520 GtC since the start of the Industrial Revolution, this leaves another 480 GtC. If we content ourselves with a 50% chance of remaining under 2°, the total budget is 1,300 GtC, and the remaining budget is 820 GtC. If the aim is a 66% chance of limiting warming to 1.5°, the remaining carbon budget decreases to 400 GtC (Rogelj et al. 2011).[7] At the emissions rate of recent years we will have used up the budget for the 2° target (at 66% probability) in two decades – and in three to ten years for the 1.5°C target.

Between 2010 and 2015, various scientific articles and reports warned of the challenge of reversing the trend of emissions for attaining the 2° target (Peters et al. 2013, Friedlingstein et al. 2014). The review of the 2° target launched by the Climate Convention to respond to the demand in the Copenhagen agreement spurred a debate on the long-term temperature target. To give but one example, in a *Nature* article entitled "Ditch the 2° Warming Goal," the political scientist David Victor and the physicist Charles Kennel criticised not only the 2° target but also the very principle of a long-term mean temperature target, which they argued is both politically counterproductive and of little scientific relevance, and called for it to be replaced with "an array of planetary vital signs" (Victor and Kennel 2014, 30). The article spurred dozens of responses from scientists and environmentalists defending mean temperature as the best scientific indicator (because of its direct link to both emissions and impacts) and the 2° figure as accessible and politically effective.

### Optimistic scenarios and negative emissions

Alongside articles criticising the 2° goal or highlighting the difficulties of meeting it, other scientific publications concluded, to the contrary, that it was attainable. Paradoxically, between 2010 and 2015, as greenhouse gas emissions continued to grow, a series of increasingly optimistic decarbonisation scenarios were published (van Vuuren et al. 2011, Rogelj, Luderer et al. 2015). This paradox is easily explained: the 2° scenarios rely overwhelmingly on "negative emissions technologies" (NETs) that remove carbon from the atmosphere on a large scale. These scenarios are produced by integrated assessment models,[8] which set out pathways for socioeconomic evolution according to a given global temperature target and time horizon. On the basis of a portfolio of technologies with associated costs, these models choose the most cost-effective technology for the assigned target. Remaining below 2° of warming in this century (or not exceeding the carbon budget of 1,000 GtC) requires a very rapid drop in global $CO_2$ emissions to "zero emissions" within a few decades. Given that this is highly unlikely, the alternative is a temporary overshoot of atmospheric $CO_2$ concentrations followed by a "sucking up" of carbon from the atmosphere in the second half of the twentieth century through NETs.

Among these technologies, the most commonly referred to in 2° scenarios is "bioenergy with carbon capture and storage" (BECCS). It consists of growing plants for bioenergy, burning them, capturing the carbon dioxide released in the process, liquefying it under pressure and storing it underground. The (theoretical) net result is that atmospheric $CO_2$ is absorbed through photosynthesis and then stocked under the Earth's surface while producing energy. These technologies have only been tested experimentally, and they pose various problems: they may be very costly, they require safe geological storage on a large scale, leakage rates could be high and, above all, they would require an enormous proportion of the Earth's total arable land (the surface area of India according to some estimates). In the fifth IPCC report (published in 2013), out of the 400 scenarios with a 50% probability of warming below 2° in 2100, 344 assumed large-scale use of BECCS (the others assumed that emissions would peak in 2010, and are thus already obsolete).

NETs' central place in the IPCC scenarios is due to the adoption of the 2°C target, which pushed scientists to develop simulations capable of reaching it (Guivarch and Hallegatte 2013). "A few years ago, these exotic Dr. Strangelove options were discussed only as last-ditch contingencies. Now they are Plan A," writes Kevin Anderson (2015a, 437), deputy director of the Tyndall Centre for Climate Science Research. The incentives to provide 2° scenarios are not only political but also moral (abandoning the 2° target is defeatist) and even financial (funding agencies reward technological optimism). The political imperative can also bias the scientific diagnosis, as "when a stringent target is revealed as infeasible with a given model, it simply does not appear in the literature" (Guivarch and Hallegatte 2013, 185).

### The rise of the 1.5°C target

During the same period, between the Copenhagen and Paris conferences, the 1.5° target progressively gained momentum, both politically and scientifically. Following demands to "[strengthen] the global long-term goal" in Copenhagen, the Climate Convention tasked the SBSTA[9] with creating a "Structured Expert Dialogue" that brought together scientists and state representatives (between 2013 and 2015). In May 2015, the Dialogue produced a 200-page report arguing that the 2° target, although beneficial, would fail to save some countries, populations and ecosystems, and that "limiting global warming to below 2°C is still feasible and will bring about many co-benefits, but poses substantial technological, economic and institutional challenges."[10] The same diagnosis was offered in 2010 in a report by the Grantham Institute on Climate Change and the Environment,[11] and in 2014 in a Climate Analytics report for the World Bank.[12]

In the months leading up to the Paris COP, the Climate Vulnerable Forum effectively lobbied politicians, civil society and the media, promoting the 1.5° target with the help of scientific advisors from the powerful European Climate Foundation, a major philanthropic initiative (see Morena, this volume, and Morena 2016). They recalled that a global increase of 2° would have severe impacts, which would affect ecosystems, sea levels and extreme events, and that the impacts would be greatest in vulnerable countries. They affirmed, on the other hand, that the 1.5°

objective was accessible, citing the low-emission scenarios in the last IPCC report. The 2° target was set by Europe and the developed countries, they argued, but for poor countries the danger threshold is 1.5°: not accepting this target is tantamount to telling vulnerable countries that we do not care to protect them. Shortly before the Paris conference, the government of the Marshall Islands (assisted by a non-profit advisory group) launched a "High Ambition Coalition," which demanded a reference to the 1.5° threshold as a prerequisite to any agreement. Rallying the support of NGOs as well as more than 100 countries before and during the COP, the coalition succeeded in its goal, almost unanimously hailed as a victory.

Politically, this target pleased nearly everyone. For vulnerable countries, it represents a bargaining chip for future negotiations: if it is officially recognised that more than 1.5° of warming is dangerous, they can subsequently seek reparations for resulting losses and damages. For developed countries, backing the 1.5° limit meant obtaining the signatures of these states without explicitly committing to financial compensation. And institutions and think tanks backing the 1.5° target were all concerned with avoiding a repetition of the failure in Copenhagen, creating favourable "momentum" and obtaining an "ambitious" agreement. The success of the 1.5°C target thus resulted from long-term political aspirations – although it also played out in the final days and hours of the conference.

### Surprise at the COP

Many climate scientists first expressed surprise – and in some cases, even indignation – at the inclusion of the 1.5°C target in the agreement,[13] before resigning themselves to it, viewing it above all as a political compromise.[14] One event that reflected these questionings was an improvised press conference organised in the Bourget convention centre on Friday, December 11 – the eve of the adoption of the agreement – by the communications officers of the International Council for Science (ICSU) and several major research centres present at the COP. Although it was assembled at the last minute, the press conference brought together 200 journalists and other observers to hear the comments of five prominent scientists on the draft agreement, in particular the long term goals and the 1.5° target.[15] In principle, these scientists represented divergent positions, with leaders from institutions producing both 2° and 1.5° scenarios among them, as well as a famous critic of these scenarios, the Tyndall Centre's Kevin Anderson. But the message they delivered was coherent, constructive and relatively critical. They welcomed the inclusion of the 1.5°C target in the draft, affirming that it was consistent with the science, but criticised the rest of the text as insufficiently ambitious to achieve this goal. The panellists emphasised that to limit warming to 1.5°, emissions would need to begin decreasing by 2020, reaching zero by 2050; Anderson also pointed out the text's failure to mention emissions from shipping and aviation.

Until the Paris conference, debate on the 2° long-term goal had been confined to the relevant scientific circles, and its implications had not been publicly discussed (although the 2° scenarios and NETs were mentioned in the Summary for Policymakers of the latest IPCC report). Since 2015 and the COP21, however, this debate has exploded in scientific journals (particularly from the Nature Publishing Group), as well as the press and the Internet. It is not the goal in itself that stirred these various actors to speak out, as both goals require massive transformations of the economy and a very high degree of political will (although the 1.5° target imposes more stringent requirements).[16] The difference between the 2° and 1.5° goals doubtless lies less in their implications than in how they were adopted. As mentioned earlier, the 2° threshold was co-constructed in a long process that took place between science and politics. It was considered legitimate and there was an official consensus around it, although internal debate existed. The 1.5° target, in contrast, obviously responded to a political demand. The tensions and difficulties surrounding a long-term goal that will be very difficult to meet, which remained latent at 2°, came to be expressed openly both within and beyond the scientific community. The 1.5° target shattered the previous consensus.

### The blurry region of long-term goals

While the success of the 1.5° target is political, it is based on scientific reports and articles. The disagreement on the 1.5°C target does not oppose scientists and politicians; nor is it a scientific controversy. The debate is on long-term temperature objectives, and more particularly on their "safety" (or dangerousness) and "feasibility," notions that simultaneously involve scientific elements and value judgments. Neither purely scientific nor exclusively political, the debate on the 1.5° target, and on long-term goals more generally, takes place in a blurry region between these two domains, and brings their relations into play.

In reality, safety (or dangerousness) is no longer at stake in the debate: first, because recent research has demonstrated the severity of the impacts associated to 2° of global warming; but also because scientists are reluctant to identify a danger threshold, seeing this as "a compromise between what is deemed possible and desirable, rather than a 'planetary boundary' that clearly separates a 'safe' from a 'dangerous' world" (Knutti, Rogelj, Sedlacek and Fischer 2016, 14). The debate around the Paris COP has focused instead on the "feasibility" of the 1.5° (or 2°) target.

The researchers involved in these debates on long-term goals belong to a number of communities, including climatologists working on long-term projections of climate change (authors from IPCC Working Group I), specialists on the impacts of global warming on different ecosystems and societies (Working Group II) and economists from Working Group III on mitigation. The debate also includes social scientists and experts working on climate policies, and representatives of think tanks and institutes defending the 1.5° target. But the central actors here are scientists developing and using integrated assessment models to produce scenarios known as "deep decarbonisation pathways". A handful of research centres in the world develop integrated models, including three particularly influential European institutes: the International Institute for Applied Systems Analysis (IIASA), based in Vienna and founded in 1972, played a major role in global pollution assessment in the 1980s; the PBL (Netherlands Environmental Assessment

Agency), which has been developing integrated models since the late 1980s; and the Potsdam Institute for Climate Impact Research (PIK) in Germany, which has had a central role in this field in recent years. There are other centres producing such models in the United States, Japan and France. Among these centres, some are academic institutions, while others are more oriented towards a political advisory role.

### Divergences at the boundary between science and politics

There are in reality very few scenarios based on the 1.5° target (Rogelj, Luderer et al. 2015), although those that have been produced are widely cited by think tanks and NGOs promoting this target. The scientists who produced these scenarios all belong to one of the influential institutes mentioned earlier: IIASA, PBL or PIK. They do not speak out in favour of this goal and do not hide the extremely stringent conditions that it would impose. At first glance, different scientists seem to hold very similar views on the 1.5° target (as we saw with regard to the press conference): all consider that 1.5° of warming would be preferable, recognise the extreme difficulty of achieving this target and criticise the inadequacy of mitigation goals. Nonetheless, these scientists express diverse perspectives on feasibility, which they themselves sometimes label as "optimistic" and "pessimistic." The "optimists," most associated with the institutes producing 2° and 1.5° scenarios, mainly emphasise the severity of the impacts of 2° of warming, rather than the impacts of NETs. They do not consider the social or political feasibility of the goal: Ottmar Edenhofer, director of PIK and ex-co-chair of IPCC Working Group 3, says that his work is to set down a "cartography of pathways," which it is up to politicians to navigate (Edenhoffer and Kowarsch 2015). These scientists focus above all on the "signal" that this ambitious target represents for politicians and industrialists, its potential to leverage action, more than on its means of attainment.

"Pessimistic" scientists – that is those who are critical of the 2° and 1.5° targets – give greater weight to the implications of these long-term goals. According to some political scientists, a goal that is very difficult to attain, rather than leveraging action, acts as a "substitute for appropriate action" (Geden 2015), and its lack of credibility can undermine the negotiation process. Critical scientists view the long-term target as involving physical, economic, political and social constraints; they often criticise the simplistic character of the integrated models and their implicit hypotheses, which neglect uncertainties and inertia – the constraints of geology and agriculture as well as of labour markets and finance. Kevin Anderson (2015b) presents a political critique of the 2° scenarios: this target, he argues, supposes a virtual elimination of $CO_2$ from the energy system by 2050 and demands profound and immediate changes to the consumption and production of energy. But paradoxically, he adds, experts continue to claim that these drastic transformations will have little effect on economic growth. Moreover, to critical authors, the 1.5° (or 2°) scenarios involving massive recourse to NETs suggest a future more dystopian than utopian, a "brave new world" requiring the management and exploitation of land on a planetary scale. An official from the Natural Environment Research Council (UK) for instance claims that large-scale $CO_2$-removal could "cause a loss of terrestrial species at the end of the century perhaps worse than the losses resulting from a temperature increase of about 2.8°C above pre-industrial levels" (Williamson 2016, 154). According to a number of accounts, pessimistic scientists were pressed not to openly cast doubt on the 1.5° goal during the Paris negotiations.

These groups of scientists differ not in terms of their discipline or their political orientations but rather in terms their divergent conceptions of the political role of the target and the prerogatives of scientists. Critical scientists see these scenarios as akin to "magical thinking" or "science fiction"; others argue that they can have a political effect, spurring change. These different conceptions seem to be linked to scientists' institutional affiliations and to their institutions' links with politics and expertise. This connection has already been studied in the case of climate modelling: there are a number of distinct ways to practise modelling, which are tied to the culture of particular research centres and their relationship to politics (Shackley 2001). Depending on what institution they work within, scientists are more or less inclined to "adjust to policy expectations" (Shackley, Risbey, Stone and Wynne 1999, 413). We may hypothesise (noting that further evidence is needed) that the same is true for scientists studying decarbonisation pathways, which are more directly linked to politics. These scientists maintain connections to policymakers and NGOs, are involved in the IPCC or in the definition of research programmes and have responsibilities at multiple levels (national, European, international). The co-production of global types of knowledge and politics that shape the role of decarbonisation scenarios takes place concretely and locally through these multiple connections (Hulme 2010).

## A new role for science

### From the narrative of consensus to the narrative of the gap

The debate surrounding the 1.5° target can be interpreted as signaling a shift in the relationship between climate science and climate politics. One manifestation of this change is the emergence of a central theme in the climate change narrative: the topos of the gap. The gap has become a major subject of scientific climate expertise since the adoption of a long-term temperature goal: the coexistence of "bottom-up" commitments and a long-term goal calls for the measurement of the gap between them, which is done notably in the "Emissions Gap Report" published annually by UNEP since 2010, as well as other research comparing the INDCs and the 2° target. But beyond these scientific measurements, the theme of the gap has also become ubiquitous in how the climate problem is represented, via various wordings – for example inconsistency and schism (Aykut and Dahan 2015). What is novel here is not the reality of a gap between what "the science" recommends and what politicians accomplish but the gap's place in the climate change narrative. Before the Copenhagen COP, what was important was to come together behind a single scientific diagnosis that was expected to lead to a global agreement (without specifying the means). Since Copenhagen, the climate regime is no longer characterised by continuity between science and politics, but by the gap that separates them. The consensus on the science having proven to be unable to spur political action, it is now seen as less essential; critics – of climate governance, the UN and the framing of the climate problem – now express themselves more freely. Copenhagen confirmed that scientific consensus does not automatically translate into public policies. Politics must choose between conflicting priorities, and is generally not coherent with scientific knowledge: inconsistency is inherent to policymaking (Geden 2015).

If we admit that there exists a gap between science and politics, does this mean that science's authority in the climate regime is being undermined? The problem of the 1.5° target suggests that this is the case. An IPCC researcher involved in the 2013–2015 Structured Expert Dialogue on the long-term goal admitted that the 1.5°/2° target "is about our respective willingness to understand and buffer against risk and to pay for abatement and compensation, not merely about reaching or not reaching a single-index number goal" (Tschakert 2015, para. 31). This politicisation of the climate problem may seem like a natural evolution: following a phase of alarm grounded in a consensual scientific diagnosis, the phase of economic and technological choices is necessarily more conflict-laden and political. Have we moved, then, from a "science-first" to a "policy-first" framing? From a scientific consensus that was supposed to unify politics to political division that has spread into the scientific arena?

## The challenges of the 1.5° special report: crisis and reframing

It is not clear that disagreements surrounding the 1.5° target will continue and lead to durable rifts inside the scientific community. The situation has been evolving rapidly since the Paris COP, as time is short for climate scientists: in December 2015, the COP requested that the IPCC "provide a Special Report in 2018 on the impacts of global warming of 1.5°C above pre-industrial levels and related global greenhouse gas emission pathways."[17] The IPCC, at a plenary meeting in April 2016, responded positively, explaining that this special report will look at global warming of 1.5°C "in the context of strengthening the global response to the threat of climate change, sustainable development and efforts to eradicate poverty."[18] However, this report presents a challenge for the climate science community: first, there are few studies on the 1.5° target, and the deadline is very tight to produce more; second, the 1.5° target has major diplomatic implications, so the report will be subjected to scrupulous political examination by all parties; and thirdly and above all, many researchers find working on the 1.5° target problematic.

Responding to governments' requests forms part of the IPCC's mandate; the report can be justified insofar as the target is recognised as legitimate and the related domain little explored. But while the request is consistent with the relationship between the IPCC and the political process, it is more controversial in the context of relations between the IPCC and the research community (Hulme 2016). Climate research has indeed long been structured around the problem of climate change, but many researchers are uncomfortable working on a 1.5°C target that they consider "a lost battle." They see this research as a waste of time and resources, which "may distract the community from focusing research efforts on the risks and impacts of warming scenarios between 2°C and 4°C," which are "more likely to happen" – and even as "a form of hypocrisy, sustaining false hope from the public and most vulnerable countries" (Boucher et al. 2016, 7287). Some argue, as a French agricultural economist said bluntly, that "science should not respond to issues of partisan politics." Others feel that they are caught in a double bind, forced to live with the contradiction inherent in a target that is both necessary and inaccessible: "Personally, I'm in a fix," one CIRED researcher said. "If we don't make these scenarios, we're absent; if we say it's not possible [to meet the 1.5°C target] we're the bad guys; if we do it, people will say our scenarios are useless." Moreover, researchers have in mind many other research topics that they see as more interesting, both scientifically and politically.

Scientists working on climate change are thus caught between a rock and a hard place: most of them do not believe in the possibility of reaching the 1.5° target, or even the 2° target for that matter, yet they also want to respond to environmental concerns and the demands of developing countries. Their challenge is thus to reframe the 1.5° report by transforming the obligation to issue the report into an opportunity to perform interesting and novel research. As they prepare the report's outline, the co-chairs of the three working groups are at work on this reframing.[19] Climatologists and economists are making proposals aimed at launching "new directions for climate change research" (Boucher et al. 2016, 7287). By doing so, these researchers are working to align the interests of scientists and policymakers (Latour 1999), re-appropriating a political demand to make it of interest to researchers.

The special report may change the dynamic around long-term goals, creating convergence of interests rather than deepening rifts. All scientists in the domain, regardless of whether they are critics of the 1.5° target, recognise that the hypotheses underlying 2° and 1.5° scenarios must be made more explicit (Edenhoffer and Kowarsch 2015). Whereas advocates of the 1.5° target were defending it "at all costs" to save small island countries, since its success at the Paris COP, civil society actors have been taking a greater interest in its implications.[20] Research has begun to specify the conditions and limitations of negative emissions technologies (Smith et al. 2015). The 1.5° special report will be an opportunity to study the impacts, not only of 1.5° of warming but also of the economic and technological measures suggested to meet this target.

In the climate sciences, the 1.5° special report may also provide an opportunity to bridge research gaps. Most articles on the 1.5° target have been published in the "opinion" pages of scientific journals. Opinions must now be grounded in specific research – for example (as suggested by a climatologist from the LSCE) by renewing the study of methane and aerosol emissions, which will play a greater role if $CO_2$ emissions are lower. The 1.5° report can offer the community a chance to study the limitations of existing tools, clarify uncertainties and connect the perspectives of different disciplines. It should also allow climate economists to advance with what has been missing from Working Group III: studies on how to trigger the transition, connecting short-term efforts to long-term objectives and national economic scenarios to global ones (Boucher et al. 2016). Reformulating the problem of the 1.5° target may also mean, in the words of a CIRED economist, asking not whether the target is attainable but why it is not (conditions of implementation, land use). In short, this reframing could clarify not only technical but also social sources of inertia.

## Conclusion: in search of a new form of co-production between science and politics

Inevitably, the paradigm shift in climate governance at the Copenhagen COP affected the relationship between science and politics that is at the heart of the framing of the climate problem. The case of the 1.5° temperature goal is symptomatic of this change. Although the demands and difficulties created by the 1.5° goal already existed with the 2° goal – and in that sense the shift is not a dramatic break – the success of the stricter target on political grounds, which caught the scientific community off guard, attests to a shift in the balance of power between science and politics. The climate sciences have never been independent of politics, and the model of co-production continues to account for their interrelations. Nevertheless the 1.5° target reflects a form of co-production distinct from that which led to the 2° target: this shift could be described as one from "science-driven co-production" to a "policy-driven co-production."

The climate science community faces the unprecedented task of having to produce a report on a long-term target that it knows is unattainable so as to satisfy a political agenda. The IPCC accepted this request, and many researchers do not want to be left out of the process, cutting themselves off from the political process and from developing countries. They must thus make sense of this target. Although some researchers consider that more work must be done on the issue of feasibility, many want to move beyond this problem and reformulate the demand in terms that are both more scientifically relevant and engaging. The 1.5° special report will probably include a much broader investigation of the target's implications, exploring the connections between the short and the long term, and between climate change and other environmental, social and economic problems. The aim is also to produce "policy-relevant" knowledge, a requirement for the sciences to preserve their central role, and thus to contribute to "solutions" to the climate problem, another pressing demand facing scientists today.

To conclude, let us return to the question posed throughout this book: How are science-politics relations changing in an increasingly "climatised" world? What is the "climatisation of the world" doing to climate science? Following the Copenhagen turning point, and even more after the Paris COP, the phase of a global, consensual alarm is now behind us. The priority is no longer to inform negotiators and the wider public on the scope of the problem but to respond to a more diverse and fragmented set of scientific and political questions. While the sciences have largely contributed not only to defining the climate problem but also to extending it into numerous domains (agriculture, economics, etc.), today these climatised domains are presenting the sciences with numerous questions: regionalising climate change, solutions to climate problems and insights into trade-offs with other problems (environmental or otherwise). In this extension of the domain of expertise, the climate question is no longer isolated. Scientific research must take into account other factors, including political factors, which constitutes a profound change in the role of the sciences in the climate regime. The 1.5° target, which responds to a demand from small island states, can also be seen through this prism.

## Notes

1  This text is based on fieldwork conducted at and around the Paris COP, on the analysis of numerous scientific publications in various journals and websites, and on interviews with scientists. I want to thank for their help and availability: Olivier Boucher (Laboratoire de Météorologie Dynamique, LMD), Philippe Ciais (Laboratoire des Sciences du Climat et de l'Environnement, LSCE), Pierre Friedlingstein (University of Exeter), Céline Guivarch (Centre International de Recherche sur l'Environnement et le Développement, CIRED), Franck Lecoq (CIRED), Corinne Le Quéré (Tyndall Centre), Valérie Masson Delmotte (LSCE, co-chair IPCC Working Group 1) and Denise Young (International Council of Scientific Unions, ICSU). Most interviews were conducted in collaboration with Amy Dahan, whom I thank for stimulating exchanges.
2  The climate problem involves many areas in the natural sciences as well as the social sciences and economics, which have different relationships to politics. However, in public discourse, the use of the term "sciences" is usually reserved for the natural sciences.
3  The "consensus" in question is that on the scientific reality of global warming and its anthropic origins. Beyond this consensus, there are scientific debates in all domains: on the intensity of climate change, its effects, its manifestations in different regions, its impacts, the risks associated to a given level of warming, the corresponding costs and so forth.
4  Although climate scepticism persists in certain political circles, notably in the United States and Australia.
5  "Climate sensitivity" is the change in mean temperature at the Earth's surface that results from a doubling of the atmospheric concentration of $CO_2$
6  For the poll, the *Guardian* contacted all registered participants in the scientific conference organised in Copenhagen in March 2009, in the lead-up to the December COP. Out of 1,756 participants, 261 responded, including 200 climate scientists. https://www.theguardian.com/environment/2009/apr/14/global-warming-target-2c.
7  These figures are subject to large uncertainties, and vary depending on whether emissions linked to land use, non-$CO_2$ greenhouse gases and aerosol emissions are taken into account.
8  Integrated assessment models (IAMs) differ from global climate models (GCMs). GCMs are physical models (very similar to those used for weather forecasting), whose algorithms are drawn from physical laws and that describe atmospheric movements and their evolution with increasing greenhouse gas concentrations. IAMs are

socio-economic models consisting of several modules (climate, land use, energy use, etc.) that describe how different parameters change over time under different constraints (e.g. a temperature target).

9   The SBSTA (Subsidiary Body for Scientific and Technical Advice) is a body of scientific experts whose role is to advise the Climate Convention on matters of science, technology and methodology. It is open to the participation of all parties, and has a key role in science-politics relations in the climate regime.

10   Report on the structured expert dialogue on the 2013–2015 review, UNFCCC, Message 6, p. 21, http://unfccc.int/resource/docs/2015/sb/eng/inf01.pdf.

11   http://www.lse.ac.uk/GranthamInstitute/wp-content/uploads/2014/02/PB-global-warming-mitigating.pdf.

12   One of the authors of the World Bank report, Bill Hare, is also one of the most influential experts promoting the 1.5°C target. A regular at COPs for more than two decades, Hare, previously the climate policy director for Greenpeace International, is founder and CEO of Climate Analytics, a German think tank whose mission is "to help provide scientific and technical advice about climate change to the poorest and most vulnerable developing countries." See also the chapter by Edouard Morena in the present volume.

13   "To me 1.5° is delusional," a French climatologist said. "It's the stupidest thing they could do," a World Bank economist exclaimed. "When I hear 1.5° I want to cry," admitted a Tyndall Centre researcher.

14   "It's a diplomatic compromise that has little basis in the sciences. But you can understand vulnerable countries playing this card," declared a climatologist from the LMD. "Poor countries and small islands have been focused on this target for ten years, their delegates can't go home without getting it," according to one expert on the negotiations. "I wasn't surprised: it's how they got poor countries into the agreement," said a climate economist from the CIRED. "There's been a lot of research, the vision on the impacts has changed, it's getting more and more alarmist."

15   The panel of scientists at the December 11 press conference consisted of Hans Joachim Schellnhuber, Director of the PIK; Johan Rockstrom, Director of the Stockholm Resilience Centre; Steffen Kallbekken, Research Director at CICERO; Kevin Anderson, Deputy Director of the Tyndall Centre; and Joeri Rogelj, IIASA.

16   "The technologies required for the 1.5°C scenarios are the same as for the 2°C pathway, but need to be deployed faster, and energy demand needs to be reduced earlier, implying a higher cost than in the 2°C scenarios." Report on the Structured Expert Dialogue on the 2013–2015 review, UNFCCC.

17   UNFCCC COP Decision Report, article 21, p. 4, https://unfccc.int/resource/docs/2015/cop21/eng/l09.pdf.

18   Sixth Assessment Report (AR6) Products, UNFCCC: "Outline of the Special Report on the Impacts of Global Warming of 1.5°C above Pre-industrial Levels and Related Global Greenhouse Gas Emission Pathways, in the Context of Strengthening the Global Response to the Threat of Climate Change, Sustainable Development, and Efforts to Eradicate Poverty," http://www.ipcc.ch/apps/eventmanager/documents/40/210920161043-INF.6-Outline1.5.pdf.

19   As of this writing, in May and June 2016, the content of the 1.5° special report is unknown.

20   The first session of the Climate Convention after the Paris Agreement, held in Bonn in May 2016, saw a heated debate on BECCS technologies. Several African networks issued a joint statement entitled "Sacrificing the Global South in the

Name of the Global South: Why the 1.5°C Goal Must Not Be Met with Land Grabs."

## Bibliography

Allen, Myles, David J. Frame, Chris Huntingford, Chris D. Jones, Jason A. Lowe, Malte Meinshausen, and Nikolai Meinshausen. "Warming caused by cumulative carbon emissions toward the trillionth tonne." *Nature* 458 (2009): 1163–1166.

Anderson, Kevin. "Duality in climate science." *Nature Geoscience* 8 (2015b): 898–900.

Anderson, Kevin. "Talks in the city of light generate more heat." *Nature* 528, no. 7583 (2015a): 437.

Aykut, Stefan, Jean-Baptiste Comby, and Hélène Guillemot. "Climate change controversies in French mass media 1990–2010." *Journalism Studies* 13, no. 2 (2012): 157–174.

Aykut, Stefan, and Amy Dahan. *Gouverner le climat? Vingt ans de négociations internationales*. Paris: Presses de Sciences Po, 2015.

Aykut, Stefan, and Amy Dahan. "Le régime climatique avant et après Copenhague: Sciences, politiques et l'objectif des deux degrés." *Nature, Sciences, Sociétés* 19, no. 2 (2011): 144–157.

Boucher, Olivier, Valentin Bellassen, Hélène Benveniste, Philippe Ciais, Patrick Criqui, Céline Guivarch, Hervé Le Treut, Sandrine Mathy, and Roland Séférian. "In the wake of Paris agreement, scientists must embrace new directions for climate change research." *PNAS* 113, no. 27 (2016): 7287–7290.

Cointe, Béatrice, Paul-Alain Ravon, and Emmanuel Guérin. *2°: The History of a Policy-Science Nexus*. Working Paper, IDDRI, 2011: 28.

Dahan, Amy, and Hélène Guillemot. "Les relations entre science et politique dans le régime climatique: À la recherche d'un nouveau modèle d'expertise?" *Natures, Sciences, Sociétés* 23 (2015): 6–18.

Edenhoffer, Otmar, and Martin Kowarsch. "Cartography of pathways: A new model for environmental policy assessment." *Environmental Science and Policy* 51 (2015): 56–64.

Friedlingstein, Pierre, Robbie M. Andrew, Joeri Rogelj, Glen Peters, Josp G. Canadell, Reto Knutti, Gunnar Luderer, Michael R. Raupach, Michiel Schaeffer, Detlef P. van Vuuren, and Corinne Le Quéré. "Persistent growth of $CO_2$ emissions and implications for reaching climate targets." *Nature Geoscience* 7 (2014): 709–715.

Geden, Oliver. "The trouble with targetism." *The Guardian*, 15 December 2015.

Guillemot, Hélène. "Les désaccords sur le changement climatique: au-delà d'un climat bipolaire." *Natures, Sciences, Sociétés* 22 (2014): 340–350.

Guivarch, Céline, and Stéphane Hallegatte. "2°C or not 2°C?" *Global Environmental Change* 23 (2013): 179–192.

Hulme, Mike. "1.5° and climate research after the Paris agreement." *Nature Climate Change* 6 (2016): 222–224.

Hulme, Mike. "Problems with making and governing global kinds of knowledge." *Global Environmental Change* 20 (2010): 558–564.

Hulme, Mike. "Reducing the future to climate: A story of climate determinism and reductionism." *Osiris* 26, no. 1 (2011): 245–266.

Jasanoff, Sheila. *States of Knowledge: The Co-production of Science and Social Order*. London: Routledge, 2004.

Knutti, Reto, Joeri Rogelj, Jan Sedlacek, and Erich Fischer. "A scientific critique of the two-degree climate change target." *Nature Geoscience* 9 (2016): 13–18.

Latour, Bruno. *Pandora's Hope: Essays on the Reality of Science Studies*. Cambridge: Harvard University Press, 1999.

Miller, Clarke. "Climate science and the making of a global political order." In *States of Knowledge: The Co-production of Science and Social Order*, by Sheila Jasanoff, 46–66. London: Routledge, 2004.

Morena, Edouard. *The Price of Climate Action: Philanthropic Foundations in the International Climate Debate*. Basingstoke: Palgrave, 2016.

Peters, Glen, Robbie M. Andrew, Tom Boden, Josp G. Canadell, Philippe Ciais, Corinne Le Quéré, Gregg Marland, Michael R. Raupach, and Charlie Wilson. "The challenge to keep global warming below 2°." *Nature Climate Change* 3 (2013): 4–6.

Pielke, Jr, Roger. "Policy, politics and perspective." *Nature* 416 (2002): 368.

Randalls, Samuel. "History of the 2°C climate target." *Wiley Interdiscip Review: Climate Change* 1 (2010): 598–605.

Rogelj, Joeri, William Hare, Jason Lowe, Detlef P. van Vuuren, Keywan Riahi, Ben Matthews, Tatsuya Hanaoka, Kejun Jiang, and Malte Meinshausen. "Emission pathways consistent with a 2° global temperature limit." *Nature Climate Change* 1 (2011): 413–418.

Rogelj, Joeri, Gunnar Luderer, Robert C. Pietzcker, Elmar Kriegler, Michiel Schaeffer, Volker Krey, and Keymar Riahi. "Energy system transformations for limiting end-of-century warming to below 1.5°." *Nature Climate Change* 5 (2015): 519–527.

Sarewitz, Daniel. "How science makes environmental controversies worse." *Environmental Science and Policy* 7 (2004): 385–403.

Shackley, Simon. "Epistemic lifestyles in climate change modeling." In *Changing the Atmosphere: Expert Knowledge and Environmental Governance*, by Clarke Miller and Paul Edwards, 107–133. Cambridge: MIT Press, 2001.

Shackley, Simon, James Risbey, Peter Stone, and Brian Wynne. "Adjusting to policy expectation in climate change modeling." *Climatic Change* 43, no. 2 (1999): 413–454.

Smith, Pete, Steven Davis, Felix Creutzig, Sabine Fuss, Jan Minz, and Benoit Gabrielle. "Biophysical and economic limits to negative $CO_2$ emissions." *Nature Climate Change* 6 (2015): 42–50.

Tschakert, Petra. "1.5°C or 2°C: A conduit's view from the science-policy interface at COP 20 in Lima, Peru." *Climate Change Responses* 2, no. 3 (2015).

van Vuuren, Detlef, Elke Stehfest, Michel G. J. den Elzen, Tom Kram, Jasper van Vliet, Sebastiaan Deetman, Morna Isaac, et al. "RCP 2.6: Exploring the possibility to keep global mean temperature increase below 2°." *Climatic Change* 109 (2011): 95–116.

Victor, David, and Charles Kennel. "Climate policy. Ditch the 2° warming goal." *Nature* 514 (2014): 30–31.

Williamson, Phil. "Emissions reduction: Scrutinize $CO_2$ removal methods." *Nature* 530 (2016): 153–155.

# 3 The business voice at COP21

## The quandaries of a global political ambition

*Sarah Benabou, Nils Moussu
and Birgit Müller*

## Introduction

One of the salient features of COP21 was the pervasive presence of corporate representatives and their business associations. This presence has been interpreted in various ways: from a radical critique of the "corporate capture" of climate negotiations, to a more pragmatic acknowledgement of business roles in climate governance, to a praise of business leadership in the fight against global warming. In any case, this involvement points to the need to take into account business's ambition not only as lobbyists but also as climate governors to get a full picture of the current transnational climate change governance.

Interestingly, business's overall positioning at COP21 seemed to conclude a cycle of three phases begun during the run-up to the UN Framework Convention on Climate Change (UNFCCC) more than twenty years ago. At that time, business's first reaction to any attempt to regulate greenhouse gas (GHG) emissions, led by oil and gas corporations, was almost unanimously defensive and obstructive, challenging climate science and emphasising the economic costs linked to such regulations . By the end of the 1990s, this "united front" began to crack, due to diverging strategies and conflicts inside the oil and gas sector and the emergence of a more plural set of interest groups involved in the climate change negotiation process. This development was fostered by the progressive implementation of the Kyoto Protocol flexibility mechanisms, in which at least some corporations and business groups were enthusiastically involved (Meckling 2011, Matt and Okereke 2015). More recently, the prospect of COP21 finally initiated what could be seen as a new moment in business's positioning towards climate negotiation.

This third phase saw an impressive amount of work by key business leaders and associations in order to restore the lost unity of the private sector. Expressed forcefully and repeatedly during COP21, the new "business voice" proved to be the exact opposite of the initial obstructive and defensive one, and keen to demonstrate that "business has changed," in line with the changing climate. Fuelled by the IPCC's latest conclusions, and shared by the vast majority of the private sector beyond sectoral and geographical divides, business's main proposals were the following:

1   A universal and ambitious agreement that includes a long-term goal – such as the 2°C limit and/or the need for net zero $CO_2$/GHG emissions, well before the end of the century – to provide a predictable framework and send clear policy signals to corporations (BFC 2015, B-Team 2015, Business & Climate Summit 2015, OGCI 2015, Wei, Carmeron, Prattico, Scheerder and Zhou 2015);
2   A price on $CO_2$ emissions as one of those policy signals, and, as carbon pricing had been mentioned in many "intended nationally determined contributions" (INDCs), provisions for international market linkage (IETA 2015a,b);
3   A deepening of the dialogue between the private sector and public authorities inside the UNFCCC process, following both the establishment at COP20 of the Lima-Paris Action Agenda that allows and promotes the engagement of non-state actors, as well as the so-called business dialogues leading up to COP21 (BFC 2015, Business & Climate Summit 2015, TBD 2015).

This unified "business voice" could be understood as the signal of a fully "climatised" business, aligned unanimously around progressive climate objectives. Although impressive and significant, we argue that this "climatisation" was still ambiguous and fraught with contradictions, despite the "gloss of harmony" (Müller 2013) it strived to present at COP21. The cost of building such a consensual and widely shared positioning was indeed its high level of generality, far from the detailed, technical, and complex negotiations among country delegations. Moreover, this positioning often struggled to hide divergent political views about the respective tasks of states and the private sector during the transition towards a low-carbon economy, and deep sectoral disagreements about how to implement concrete mechanisms that could steer this transition.

To get a sense of that Janus-faced business position, this chapter draws on the interrelated movements of climatisation of the world and "globalisation of the climate" developed by the editors of this book (see introduction). Focusing on business actors, this dialogic movement acknowledges the effects of the climate change issue and negotiations on the private sector, along with the way corporations and their associations try to simultaneously shape the current transnational climate governance. In the first part of this chapter, the climatisation of business during COP21 is discussed using a panorama of its mobilisation, and a short account of its attempts to build a common, proactive position in order to preserve its legitimacy and social licence to operate. Drawing on an analysis of two important business reports, the second part of the chapter focuses on the ideas of governance that underlie the constant vagueness that business discourses have maintained regarding the respective roles of states and business in climate governance, and how they relate to distinct views on democratic decision-making.

Finally, the contradictions and tensions of the globalisation of the climate are then illustrated with the business demand for global carbon pricing in the context of the bottom-up Paris Agreement made of INDCs. Particular attention is paid to conflicting views on how this price on carbon should be implemented in this context.

## The business sector at COP21

One striking feature of the private sector mobilisation during COP21 was the plethora of business spaces, forums, and events inside and around the official negotiations. Inside the so-called UNFCCC blue zone, the main business focal point was the "business hub" set up by the World Business Council for Sustainable Development (WBCSD) and the International Emissions Trading Association (IETA). Roughly 100 side events were held inside this hub, gathering representatives from corporations, business associations, international organisations, and policy makers. Alongside this forum, business also had the opportunity to express its voice through traditional UNFCCC side events, press conferences, and, more importantly, the new Lima-Paris Action Agenda (LPAA). This last platform, established by the COP20 and COP21 presidencies, gathered cities, regions, businesses, investors, and civil society organisations around various commitments that were showcased on the Non-State Actor Zone for Climate Action website.[1] The LPAA gave rise to a series of events about specific issues (transport, forests, building, private finance, etc.) during COP21.[2] But business mobilisation was not restricted to the blue zone, as many events took place during the negotiations in various locations. Two spaces, *La Galerie* in Le Bourget and *Solutions COP21* in Paris, were available for individual corporations to showcase their climate change "solutions" and demonstrate their commitment to action. In addition, many business forums were taking place, such as the *Sustainable Innovation Forum 2015* organised by Climate Action and UNEP, the *World Climate Summit 2015* by World Climate LTD, and the *Energy for Tomorrow* summit by the *New York Times*, among others.

These diverse business events reflected the variety of business corporations, sectors, and associations represented at COP21, with more than 110 associations officially registered (UNFCCC 2015b). These associations aggregate business corporations at the levels of sub-national (e.g. Quebec Business Council on the Environment), national (e.g. Australian Industry Group), supranational (e.g. Wind Europe), and global (e.g. World Steel Association) levels. Most importantly, many economic sectors were represented, although unevenly, particularly including the following sectors: extraction (e.g. World Coal Association), manufacturing (e.g. European Chemical Industry Council), electricity and gas (e.g. Eurelectric), transportation (e.g. International Air Transport Association), and finance and insurance (e.g. Institutional Investors Group on Climate Change). The largest private sector delegations at COP21 were, however, those of multi-sectoral business associations, such as WBCSD and IETA, with over 100 delegates each. Altogether, more than 1,000 business representatives were present, with the vast majority from business associations and a few from national delegations.

Despite this variety of business events, forums, and associations, the private sector seemed to have attained an unprecedented level of coordination at COP21, undoubtedly due to the early work of key multi-sectoral business associations. These associations can be seen as scaled versions of the wider business landscape: as multi-sectoral platforms, they first have to internally accommodate diverse corporatist interests in order to build a common position. After stabilising the main building blocks of this position, they can undertake the task of building broader coalitions with other business associations. The case of the WBCSD is particularly illustrative here: it started to build its positioning for COP21 in 2014 after wide consultation with its member corporations (WBCSD 2014). This process was part of a broader effort initiated with the Vision 2050 report that led to intermediate objectives for 2020 within the so-called Action 2020 programme,[3] around which all WBCSD activities were reorganised (WBCSD 2010). Action 2020 has nine priority areas, stemming partly from the Stockholm Resilience Centre planetary boundaries framework, with related objectives entitled "societal must-haves" and "business solutions" (Rockström et al. 2009). Regarding climate change, the goal of Action 2020 is to maintain global warming under 2°C, corresponding to a carbon budget of one trillion tonnes, while meeting societal and development needs. The WBCSD COP21 position paper further operationalised this goal, by asking for "an international commitment to achieving global net zero emissions within the 21st century" (WBCSD 2014, 4). This process of shared objective-building is quite remarkable, especially considering that the WBCSD unites corporations from sectors as diverse as mining and quarrying, manufacturing, electricity and gas, and finance and assurance. Eventually, related "business solutions" were coupled to climate change objectives and collected into the Low-Carbon Technology Partnerships initiative, one of the preeminent business initiatives at COP21 that allowed corporations (regardless of whether members of the WBCSD) to be involved in selected domains of action (cement, carbon capture and storage, forests, climate-smart agriculture, renewables, etc.).

This kind of early groundwork allowed for the establishment of strong connexions among the main business associations, well before COP21. This was achieved around a series of business events, such as the annual NYC Climate Week, most notably in September 2014 and 2015, and the Business & Climate Summit held in Paris in May 2015. These events enabled business associations and their members to progressively build a common positioning, or what is commonly referred to as a unified "business voice." Particularly critical in this process was the launch of the We Mean Business coalition during NYC Climate Week 2014. We Mean Business unites numerous partners, including the WBCSD, Business for Social Responsibility, CDP Worldwide, The B-Team, The Climate Group, The Prince of Wales' Corporate Leaders Group, and the Coalition for Environmentally Responsible Economies. Claiming to gather more than six million corporations worldwide, the coalition's actions included: releasing a widely reviewed report on the economic opportunities from corporate "low-carbon actions"; helping to gather individual corporations' commitments that later fuelled the Non-State Actor Zone for Climate Action; and making eight "key asks for the Paris Agreement" in a "business brief" (WMB 2014, 2015). These requests had a strong impact during COP21, according to We Mean Business: "Governments heard our call loud and clear. The Paris outcome included all 8 of our asks, in many cases using the language that we had proposed" (Wei et al. 2015, 1). Furthermore, the coalition and its member associations were among the partners of the Business & Climate Summit, which brought together an even wider range of business groups, such as the International Chamber of Commerce, the UN Global Compact, the Consumer Goods Forum, and the Institutional Investors Group on Climate Change. To our knowledge, it was the first time that such an extensive collaboration among associations succeeded in the climate change domain; it produced a communiqué endorsed by all participants (Business & Climate 2015), very much in line with the WBCSD and We Mean Business positioning. Hence, this summit was a critical step in developing this unified business voice. Indeed, it brought together business associations that were historically more or less strongly committed to climate change actions, and that were also all struggling to maintain their advocacy niche and engaging in a competition to attract new corporate members.

Of course, this process was not limited to a progressive linkage among business associations. Key corporations and their senior managements were heavily involved before and during COP21. Such was the case for influential businessman Paul Polman, CEO of Unilever, chairman of the WBCSD, "leader" of We Mean Business and the B-Team, and board member of the UN Global Compact, the International Chamber of Commerce, and the Consumer Goods Forum, as well as member of the World Economic Forum International Business Council and The Global Commission on the Economy and Climate. As part of the Netherlands' delegation at COP21, he was a preeminent speaker at many events, and Unilever was one of the most committed corporations in the LPAA. Similar examples include Gérard Mestrallet (CEO of Engie), Jean-Pascal Tricoire (CEO of Schneider Electric), and Jean-Pierre Clamadieu (CEO of Solvay). While detailed discussion of these CEOs is beyond the focus of this chapter, it is nonetheless interesting to note that these "business leaders" hold important places in business associations, and that their corporations are members of a significant number of the associations registered at COP21. As bridge-makers among associations, these key individuals were instrumental in building the unified business voice.

The unprecedented preparation and coordination of the private sector before and during COP21 are fascinating examples of the strategic work required of business associations and key business leaders in order to create consensus concerning the parameters of what is feasible in climate change politics. The increasing involvement/encroachment of the private sector in climate policy is clear: not only via financial assistance, technological innovations, and investments but also in actually shaping the policy agenda. A main outcome of COP21 was indeed the official acknowledgement of the private sector's role as "advisor of the Prince" in future climate policy. Whether this is merely empty rhetoric, and how business views and fills its newly endorsed political role, remains to be seen.

## Business as a political actor

Global companies and their associations claimed an active political role for business during the numerous business forums and side events of the climate summit. Whereas nation states could only imagine non-global climate pledges through INDCs as a key instrument of COP21, business claimed to have solutions to drive collective action towards a common low-carbon future. Comfortable with manoeuvring in a world economy that is governed by international trade agreements and investment treaties, private firms claimed to have global visions and strategies for educating consumers and restructuring the supply chain, to achieve change in spite of the new borders traced by the heterogeneous policymaking proposed in the national commitments. This vision of the business role was encouraged by leading politicians, such as US secretary of state John Kerry, who stated in addressing a group of eighty business leaders after the climate talks,

> I do not believe that governments are going to end up making the fundamental decisions that effect changes to get the world on a low-carbon economy. [. . .] We are going to set a stage . . . but in the end it is business and the choices that you make, the kind of buildings you build and the investments you make [that will make the difference].[4]

At COP21, however, the role that business associations attempted to assume was more than purely economic. The French chair of the climate negotiations reminded business enterprises

> to encourage governments to increase their commitment and make ambitious decisions in Paris, it is essential that businesses actively lobby the governments of the countries in which they are operating to develop public policies which encourage emissions reductions, in particular by introducing carbon pricing.
>
> (TBD 2015, 61)

At the global level, what active political role was assigned to international business associations while governments focused on national commitments?

In order to avoid an over-idealised presentation of the business sector's environmental strategies, it is useful to recall that many of the most vocal climate advocates at COP21 were among the companies that have contributed most to historical GHG emissions and/or now possess fossil fuel reserves that, if burned, would irreparably undermine any attempt to limit global warming (Heede 2014).[5] Over recent decades, these corporations have intervened in environmental policy mostly in negative ways: legally, by blocking stringent environmental regulations through lobbying and lawsuits, and illegally, through bribes and the creation of revolving doors that offer policy makers the prospect of lucrative positions on company boards if they defend corporate interests. Their interventions have favoured lowering standards and making extractive and polluting industrial activities more profitable. For instance, US oil and coal companies have aggressively attempted to block any serious climate legislation in their country for decades (Schapiro 2014).

At COP21, however, and on their corporate websites, leading oil and gas companies ExxonMobil, Shell, and BP, among others, positioned themselves as strong climate defenders. They officially acknowledged the risks and consequences of their key products by stating,

> Public officials charged with addressing this challenge can learn valuable lessons from what has worked in the private sector. Our experience – harnessing efficiency measures and developing beneficial technologies – is illustrative: ExxonMobil has long taken action by reducing greenhouse gas emissions in our operations, providing products that help consumers reduce their emissions and supporting research into technology breakthroughs.[6]

ExxonMobil and four other oil corporations indicated that they were integrating a cost from $40 (BP and Shell) to $60 (ExxonMobil) per tonne of $CO_2$ emitted into their in-house accounting (Schapiro 2014).[7] In contrast to these commitments, however, at a recent Exxon shareholder meeting on the 22nd June 2016, a large coalition of "climate-activist investors" did not obtain satisfaction when they demanded more transparency from the Company Board on Exxon's hydraulic fracking activities, on lobbying, on the diversity and composition of the board, and on plans to adapt to a renewable energy economy.[8] In seemingly Orwellian doublespeak, Exxon CEO and chair Rex Tillerson replied, "For many years now, ExxonMobil has held the view that the risks of climate change are serious, and do warrant thoughtful action," yet when asked to cut the company's ties with groups denying climate change, such as the American Legislative Exchange Council,[9] Tillerson declined.

This example – among many others – strongly suggests that corporate intervention at COP21 was merely a public-relations enterprise. Reputation was indeed a strong driver of climate statements by multinational corporations, as a table produced by We Mean Business shows (WMB 2014, 12). However, protecting and enhancing their reputations cannot fully explain business's intervention at COP21. Climate reports and policy briefings, such as those of the two most important business initiatives, WBCSD and We Mean Business, are programmatic texts in their own right. This begs the questions, what ideas of climate governance circulated and were promoted among global business associations, and how do they relate to ideas of democratic decision-making?

Produced in 2010, WBCSD Vision 2050 is probably the most comprehensive programmatic text on climate change coming from business associations to position themselves as global political actors (WBCSD 2010). The report was endorsed by the almost 200 member companies of WBCSD, with input from hundreds of representatives from business, government, experts, and civil society. The content of the report is not detailed here, as what interests us are the visions on political governance that the report reflects. Vision 2050 aimed to provide "a basis for interaction with other enterprises, civil society and governments" about how to address three questions: "What does a sustainable world look like? How can we realize it? What are the roles business can play in ensuring more rapid progress toward that world?" (WBCSD 2010, 64). The report was intended to become "the guiding star" that helps "leaders across governments, businesses and civil society avoid repeating mistakes of the past – making decisions in isolation that result in unintended consequences for people, the environment and planet Earth." It did not aim to offer a prescriptive plan or blueprint, but rather to provide a platform for dialogue and for asking questions.

The fresco of the pathway towards 2050, a giant mural that accompanies the report and is destined for decorating the hallways of corporate headquarters, shows a smooth evolution towards a carbon-free future. Technological progress and efficient technocratic problem solving compensate easily for conflicts presented not as structural but as occasional mishaps in a harmonious world. Politics, and for that matter representative democracy which acknowledges the dimension of antagonism that the pluralism of values and interests entails, disappear from this vision of the future (Mouffe 2005). Parliamentary democracy and national elected governments that make decisions about the future are superseded by "governance systems that make decisions" (WBCSD 2010, 6).

What form do these "governance systems" take? The national level where political decisions are typically taken vanishes, in favour of an international level where "nations pool sovereignty," and a local focus where "much governance happens at community, city and regional levels" (WBCSD 2010, 6). It is no longer the democratic polity that defines objectives; rather, the system itself "defines targets and creates a level playing field and eliminates barriers" (WBCSD 2010, 6).

Who is part of that "system"? The report states,

> Government, academia, business and a range of stakeholders, including society, work together closely on trade and economic development, the design of systems and metrics to measure progress, climate change solutions, technology deployment, improving forest and farm yields, urban renewal, health and education, and shifting values and behaviours toward sustainability.
>
> (WBCSD 2010, 10)

An idea of society based on cooperation and conflict of social actors stratified by statuses and classes disappears in this definition and is subsumed under the category of "stakeholders." Central to this fiction of close collaboration is the assumption of the equality of stakeholders. It ignores the asymmetries of power in the arena of climate governance and the alignments and conflictual relationships between stakeholders. Government, academia, business, and "stakeholders" become typified categories that "design systems and metrics," "improve," and shift values and behaviours. The citizens and their elected representatives are not identified as actors. Instead, the only actors that the report identifies are consumers who "can choose" (WBCSD 2010, 6), and business leaders who "want and need to lead" (WBCSD 2010, 64).

The report describes the "system" in a way that resembles Foucault's concept of a *dispositif* (i.e. assemblage or apparatus) that constantly attracts new players, involving them as interlocutors, consultants, and experts and formatting them through forms of calculation, technical reasoning, and capacity building (Foucault 1994, Müller 2013). The system blends "the best of each sector's knowledge, assets and capabilities in *seamless partnerships* to tackle many of the challenges we face" (WBCSD 2010, 66). Opposing worldviews and interests do not exist in this vision of the future; instead "the partners" provide multiple perspectives and areas of expertise that make "issues" easier to spot (WBCSD 2010, 61). "Critics are engaged as customers rather than adversaries" (WBCSD 2010, 62); their critique is integrated in the system and used to the business's advantage. "As business evolves, these contrarians and their skills will become more valuable" (WBCSD 2010, 62). Independent, publicly funded fundamental research is placed at the service of business: "As it develops new technologies and ideas, academia will collaborate more with business at earlier stages to integrate and mainstream these ideas" (WBCSD 2010, 61). Non-governmental organisations are allowed to retain their role as critics and challengers and are used as a vehicle for diffusing the practices that business wants to promote: "NGOs will continue to serve as the challengers of regulators and business, and as a conduit to collect and spread best practices, capacity and attention to those traditionally underserved parts of the world" (WBCSD 2010, 61).

As elected legislators have disappeared from this vision of the future, the conclusion of the eighty-page report is at a loss to explain answers to these questions: "How will success be defined? Who defines the incentives and mechanisms?" As taxes are mentioned in the visionary report mainly in the form of incentives, where will the money come from? "Who finances the transition processes (especially research and development, and enhanced technology deployment)?" (WBCSD 2010, 64). "Who will (or should) be the first mover – people, governments or business? Or [. . .] do all need to move at once?" Whatever the answers to these questions, business has intended to grasp the climate crisis primarily as an opportunity: "Crisis. Opportunity. It is a business cliché, but there is truth in it. The perfect storm we face, of environment, population, resources and economy, will bring with it many opportunities" (WBCSD 2010, 64).

Five years after this report was published, however, "the perfect storm" has moved closer, and business spokespersons show less confidence that they will weather the social and physical consequences of climate change without strong political intervention. In the WBCSD Vision 2050 business presented itself as capable of self-governing through stakeholder forums, while the We Mean Business statement prior to COP21 now called for strong and decisive political measures. Governments were strikingly absent in the Vision 2050 report, yet they returned in force in the We Mean Business coalition's report. It was not only business that approached governments and called for intervention; government representatives also solicited business directly. French environment minister Ségolène Royal and foreign minister Laurent Fabius invited members of the business community to discuss commitments expected during COP21:

> Partnerships between States and the private sector should be strengthened to accelerate the development of key technologies for a low-carbon economy. This exercise ensures representation from all key sectors and all continents. It should build on the CEOs most committed to the fight against climate change.
>
> (TBD 2015, 36)

In an unprecedented move, the French presidency attempted to count on business support to adopt a framework and a common narrative that the chair had prepared for companies participating in COP21 (TBD 2015, 61). UNFCCC executive secretary Christiana Figueres declared on the final day of the LPAA, "We emerge from a historical period where everything that was good for business was bad for the environment. One feels a substantive motion: the cost of inaction becomes more expensive than the action" (fieldnotes, 8th December 2015).

With its cheeky title "The Climate Has Changed," the We Mean Business report (WMB 2014) largely broke with the enthusiastic, unified Vision 2050 of the WBCSD. More realistic and based on concrete data, it demonstrated the limits of a win-win approach to climate-related investments. While certain investments (e.g. in advanced low-carbon technologies, such as LED lighting and energy-efficient information technology equipment) are immediately profitable for most enterprises, due in part to their declining costs, other investments are profitable only in the long run. Enterprises that adopt the latter can keep up with their more polluting competitors only if overall regulations change. As the report points out,

> in Europe, some of the most cost-effective measures to improve building efficiency may have already been seized. However, the findings in this study indicate that companies are still moving ahead and investing in more aggressive opportunities for cutting their energy bills. Motivations for this include increasingly stringent building regulations and increasing demand for energy efficient buildings, to combat rising energy costs.
>
> (WMB 2014, 10)

The report shows persuasively the limits of voluntary engagements, by comparing carbon reduction targets set by the studied companies versus reduction levels required under a low-carbon pathway, in order to evaluate whether corporate actions and ambition are on track (WMB 2014, 13). It concludes that the large majority of company engagements would be grossly insufficient to achieve the required emission reductions by 2050 (WMB 2014, 16). Once "the low hanging fruit that delivers quick financial returns" has been harvested, to continue making cuts in carbon emissions, policy measures, such as financial incentives, carbon pricing, and reduction in subsidies that incentivise high-carbon energy, will be needed to make low-carbon investments more financially attractive. The report demands not only incentives – carrots – from governments but also sticks, such as regulations, standards, limits and taxes. "Finding a balance between the 'carrot' that incentivises investment and the regulation 'stick' by encouraging close collaboration between a positively engaged business lobby and pragmatic policymakers is at the heart of the We Mean Business agenda" (WMB 2014, 16).

The report considers regional differences in technological development that require differentiated responses from governments. While quite profitable investments in low-carbon technology remain to be made in regions that have not done so previously, such as India and South Africa, it becomes more and more difficult to make a profit with low-carbon investment in regions that are already fairly advanced in this respect, such as Europe. Here the carrot is no longer as effective, so the regulation stick is needed. Making the investments that hurt financially will depend on a clear and ambitious roadmap to 2050 – because it will persuade businesses to make these necessary, transformational investments sooner rather than later: eliminating subsidies that incentivise high-carbon energy, enacting meaningful pricing of carbon, putting in place robust energy efficiency standards, supporting the scale-up of low-carbon energy and ensuring that all policy regimes dealing with fiscal, energy, industry and trade-related issues provide actionable incentives for an early transition to a low-carbon future.

In another paper prepared specifically for the COP21 negotiations, We Mean Business went so far as to prepare actual alternative text for negotiations of the Paris Agreement, on purpose, targets, regulations, carbon pricing, monitoring and tracking commitments of the individual nation state. The language they demanded went clearly beyond that to which governments were ultimately ready to agree. In particular, they wanted constraining language that contributed to shaping a new agreement that goes beyond "a diplomatic settlement" amongst nations and becomes "a catalytic instrument" for climate ambition (WMB 2015, 1).

After decades of participating in increasing numbers in multiple international policymaking forums, the business sector had become savvy enough about negotiations to understand the power of verbs in internationally agreed-upon text. They paid attention to where the text they wanted to introduce was placed – "for example whether it appears in the preamble of the agreement, which does not create enforceable obligations, in the operative language of the agreement, which is intended to be universal and durable, or in COP Decisions, which implement the agreement" (WMB 2015, 7). They paid attention to "the power of the text, including the use of modal verbs such as 'shall,' 'should,' and 'may,' the active and passive voice, and the specificity or ambiguity of text" (WMB 2015, 11). To give an example, We Mean Business saw the need for "aggressive emissions reductions" during the period 2015 to 2030 as critical to holding global warming below 2°C. "Leaving scope to raise ambition progressively over this period is therefore vital. In contrast, capping government ambition for 15 years will make it difficult, if not impossible, to meet the below 2°C goal" (WMB 2015, 11). They therefore asked to strengthen the article on mitigation in the following way: "Each Party *shall progressively strengthen* the ambition of their successive nationally determined commitment every 5 years from 2020 onwards, informed by the *global stocktake* set out in Article 10 and by *the best available science*" (WMB 2015, 11). The agreed text of the Paris Agreement in Article 4.11 (UNFCCC 2015a) did not meet their expectations. It states, "A Party *may* at any time adjust its existing nationally determined contribution *with a view to* enhancing its level of ambition." Instead of an obligation expressed by the verb "shall" the agreed text compromises, using the verb "may." It expresses only the vague possibility that a negotiating party "may [. . .] adjust its existing NDC" and not "shall progressively strengthen" it, as the business sector had asked for.

This call for constraining language by the private sector stands in stark contrast to the recent contributions of the private sector to other international negotiations. For the Principles for Responsible Agricultural Investment at the UN Committee for Food Security, for instance, private sector representatives sat for two years from 2012 to 2014 with civil society and governments around the same negotiating table. Civil society and private sector were clearly in opposite camps. The reluctance of private sector representatives to accept any mention in the text of regulations, taxes or obligations destined to regulate land grabbing was such that even the neutral word "governance" became suspicious to them (McMichael and Müller 2014).

In the reports from the We Mean Business coalition, civil society is not expressly mentioned but rather subsumed under the term "stakeholder," which most of the time includes mention of the private sector: "stakeholders including the private sector." As in the WBCSD report, a division/separation/contrast between civil society and business points of view disappears; however, the We Mean Business reports emphasise a division of tasks between governments and business. Governments and stakeholders should all be in the same boat to fight climate change, but it is governments who should set clear regulatory frameworks that enable effective action.

In recent issues of *Environmental Politics*, several authors criticised the reliance on emissions trading and a market-determined carbon price as abdication of the political, abandonment of rational, political decision-making through democratic process, and reliance on the blind forces of the market (Kenis and Lievens 2014, Felli 2015). Instead of relying on price to determine the choices of profit-maximising individuals who seek to satisfy their wants and needs, a political discussion should take place to determine which use values should be given preference in a polity conscious of climate change. The We Mean Business reports express a similar point of view, calling to move beyond a market-determined outlook on climate politics, and asking for political intervention.

Was the voice of We Mean Business actually representative of the business sector at COP21? In the next section, we address the contradictions and ambiguities we observed in the statements of representatives from various business representatives, particularly in their call for a carbon price.

## The contested meaning of carbon pricing

For an external observer, following business events during COP21 was a laborious and somewhat Sisyphean task, but nevertheless crucial to get a grip on the actual "business climate" that was shaped beyond official communication campaigns. Conversations in business meetings were rife with discussions on (seemingly) consensual topics, from putting a price on carbon to removing fossil fuel subsidies, to changing investment thinking from short-term profit to longer-term goals. Closer engagement, however, revealed latent and antagonist structural constraints that went against the grain of the private sector's claim to hold parts of the solution to climate change.

Carbon pricing was clearly the most popular topic in business meetings. "We know who the enemy is – this is carbon," the secretary general of the OECD said forcefully during the Business & Climate Summit a few months before the COP. "We should hit it on the head with a blunt instrument as hard as possible . . . a big fat price" (Doyle and de Clercq, 2015). One can easily understand why the idea of carbon pricing has gained such momentum among business leaders and governments. As explained by the World Bank, "Instead of dictating who should reduce emissions where and how, a carbon price gives an economic signal and polluters decide for themselves whether to discontinue their polluting activity, reduce emissions, or continue polluting and pay for it."[10] Carbon pricing is a product of our time, where the global economy is driven by the pursuit of flexibility and cost-effective measures, and where the radical critique of the alleged inefficiency of direct regulation by legislation (the so-called command-and-control approach) formulated by proponents of the *law and economics* movement and the *property rights school* is now grounded firmly in environmental policy (Aykut 2014). In September 2014, the idea of a Carbon Pricing Leadership Coalition initiated by the World Bank Group – and launched officially at COP21 – gathered support at UN Climate Week from seventy-four countries and more than 1,000 companies. For those who are still reluctant, it is commonly argued that clear economic signals are needed, and a strong and steadily rising price on carbon emissions that survives political cycles will provide the proper incentive for long-term investments.

If the principle of putting a price on carbon was thus widely shared at business events, the way it was going to be implemented, mainly through an emissions trading scheme (ETS) or a carbon tax, and its most efficient and fair amount, remained largely open to debate. The World Bank special envoy for climate change kept all options on the table, favouring a "bottom-up" approach, country by country, region by region, city by city, with each entity choosing the mechanism (ETS, tax or a mix) and price deemed appropriate. Coordination among these various initiatives, but also procedures of validation and verification, was put off to a later time. Among corporations who operate at the global level and advocate a "level playing field," there was no place for such granularity/heterogeneity. Debates were raging about whether ETS or taxes were the most appropriate tool, and how to scale up and harmonise existing mechanisms. Arguably, cap-and-trade systems seemed more popular among the business community, strongly backed by IETA, which was omnipresent during business events. A key advantage enjoyed by ETS enthusiasts was that, potentially, they could be linked into carbon "clubs," to create larger and more "liquid" carbon markets – in other words, to keep trading volumes and the number of market players as high as possible. The issue under discussion was achieving fungibility, or comparability across jurisdictions – that is to treat carbon like a currency rather than a commodity. The fragmented landscape of the carbon market, with various national and regional initiatives, was thus attracting much interest; most notable was the development of a national carbon market in China that would become the largest by far in the world, as well as the joint carbon market of California, Quebec, and Ontario. The European Union ETS was of course a centre of attention, but opinions diverged strongly about whether it was a success or a failure. For many participants of the Business & Climate Summit, the EU ETS, in a Churchillian fashion, was the worst form of government, except for all the others. Despite its poor functioning, it was seen as a central policy instrument for the fight against climate change in Europe, the most efficient and cost-effective to date, as underlined by a representative of Dow Chemical. For others, such as the business association Swiss Clean Tech, from the point of view of simplicity, taxes would be much better, as nobody understands how the EU ETS works nor where it is going. For the mining company Glencore, the EU ETS has indeed a plethora of flaws, starting with a dysfunctional energy market and a misallocation of resources.

Unanimity behind a carbon price, in whatever form it might take, was sometimes sharply broken. During the Business & Climate Summit, a few hours after the OECD secretary general's rallying cry, coal and solar executives clashed on the issue of broad-scale industrialisation in countries like India or China. The chairman of mining company Glencore strongly emphasised that renewable energy cannot replace coal in countries such as India, being too intermittent to supply the steady power needed for the metallurgical industry. Before talking about setting a tax or price on $CO_2$ emissions, he said, it would be sensible to end fossil fuel subsidies. What is at stake, he continued, is for rich countries to help industrialising nations to build coal power stations with newer and cleaner systems. India, where some 300 million people have no access to electricity, is indeed about to build 200 gigawatts of coal-fired power plants, all using conventional technology instead of the less polluting but more expensive supercritical coal-fired plants. The issue of how developing countries should lift their populations from poverty, and whether this will require the use of fossil fuels or will be able to use cleaner alternatives, was a key argument of companies in the fossil fuel industry. Poorer nations, it was argued, should be allowed to use high-carbon fuels to build their economies, as industrialised nations have done. Glencore, needless to say, has major interests in fossil fuels and other commodities that would be hit by a carbon tax or other form of carbon pricing.

It is thus quite striking to notice that although business representatives claim that carbon pricing is key for the world to achieve the required reductions in emissions, confusion actually prevails when it comes to the concrete shape this "solution" should take – when it is not simply discarded. "Business" is indeed a highly heterogeneous community that shares common ground, but also has conflicting interests, as demonstrated regularly by these international conferences (Benabou and Müller 2015). By trying to speak with one voice, the private sector somehow reproduces the model of multilateralism, where consensus is obtained at the cost of a reformulation in extremely general terms. Carbon pricing is, in that sense, the equivalent for business of the UN's "sustainable development": an empty signifier that means different things to different people and is subject to radically different interpretations (Brown 2016). What is implied by qualifying carbon pricing as an empty signifier is not just that its content is vague. Following Laclau (1996), an empty signifier is the hegemonic representative of a collection of various demands. At the same time, it retroactively groups together these diverse sources of concern, thus opening a new field that invites criticism. If business organisations campaigned hard to (re)launch carbon pricing as a universal tool able to solve the world's most pressing problem, the COP was a moment of struggle to fill its indeterminate content.

## Conclusion

COP21 saw an unprecedented level of coordination among antagonistic business interests, and *prima facie* succeeded in building a common, proactive, and *fully climatised* position. This (self-designated) business voice, however, came at a price. The analysis of the WBCSD report Vision 2050 written in 2010 and the We Mean Business report of 2015 indicates a shift over the last five years from corporate self-governance to a call for government regulation. However, observations at business-sponsored meetings at COP21 showed dissenting opinions regarding the respective tasks of business and governments in the transition to a low-carbon economy. We found great confusion as to the shape that solutions should take. The debates on carbon pricing were a case in point, as underlying tensions and contradictions within the private sector came out into the open when the specifics of this tool were actually concretely discussed. The pervasive narrative of extractive industries that there is at present no obvious (i.e. low-cost and low-carbon) alternative source of energy for the tens of millions of Indians struggling to emerge from poverty was also a request to maintain permanence in change. It was a way to evacuate radical approaches, such as divestment campaigns that urge to leave 80% of the world's known remaining fossil fuel reserves in the ground, as "unrealistic" (see Aykut and Castro, this volume). Much effort was made to reassure investors that the risks of "stranded assets" and the bursting of a "carbon bubble" would be kept at bay. Emphasising national differences was also a way to evacuate agonistic politics and confrontation, by iterating that business, including extractive industries, was not the convenient enemy that the civil society was trying to portray.

Extractive industries were, however, not the only component of the business voice at the COP, and calls for "change" were clearly audible, even if they remained within the usual and coexisting business strategies of dealing with the climate imperative: (1) hiding inaction behind a rhetoric of compliance or green washing, (2) believing in the self-healing capacities of the market and/or

(3) calling for the establishment of "smart" regulatory frameworks, with the right incentives and policy signals, in order to provide a global level playing field. What was remarkable was the capacity of business to think internationally where states had national interests in mind and were ready to maintain a climate-unfriendly business environment to attract investments. In spite of their discrepancies, the business voice that emerged from COP21 showed actual awareness for the disruptive power of climate change as an investment handicap, an unwanted uncertainty compromising strategic planning.

What is more, at several occasions the private sector followed its own (business) agenda, far from what was at stake in the official negotiations. While the aviation sector (along with international shipping) was not bound by the COP21 deal, this sector was very active in the business hub, coordinating many sessions. Conversely, while the issue of vulnerability and adaptation to climate change had taken on considerable importance in the negotiations, it was quasi-absent in business meeting discussions. In other words, if the COP21 was to mark a turning point in the private sector's role in the climate regime, it wouldn't be because of its (poor) influence on the negotiation outcome, but rather because of what could be named a *tour de force* – that is how the private sector somehow succeeded in shedding its old polluter's skin and appearing as one of the legitimate partners, along with governments and civil society, of the fight against climate change – and not anymore as an object of regulation.

## Notes

1 http://climateaction.unfccc.int/ (accessed June 14, 2016).
2 See http://newsroom.unfccc.int/lpaa/cop-21/ (accessed June 14, 2016), and the related Caring for Climate Business Forum, organised jointly by the United Nations, the United Nations Environmental Program (UNEP), the UN Global Compact and various business partners, at https://www.unglobalcompact.org/take-action/events/71-caring-for-climate-business-forum /accessed June 14, 2015). Note that a platform similar to the LPAA will be maintained in the next COP, according to COP21 Decision 117 and following (UNFCCC 2015b).
3 See the dedicated WBCSD web site for Action 2020: http://action2020.org/ (accessed June 14, 2016).
4 Michael Stothard and Kiran Stacey, "COP21: Big Polluters See No Short-Term Change", in *Financial Times*, 13 December 2015, https://next.ft.com/content/441249f2-a19e-11e5-8d70-42b68cfae6e4 (accessed June 14, 2016).
5 On fossil fuel reserves, see http://fossilfreeindexes.com/research/the-carbon-under ground/ (accessed June 14, 2016).
6 http://corporate.exxonmobil.com/en/current-issues/climate-policy/climate-perspectives/statement-on-cop-21 (accessed June 14, 2016).
7 http://www.climatechangenews.com/2013/12/06/exxon-shell-and-bp-operating-internal-carbon-prices/ (accessed June 14, 2016).
8 http://www.wired.com/2016/05/exxonmobil-climate-change-real-%c2%af_%e3%83%84_%c2%af/ (accessed June 14, 2016).
9 https://www.alec.org/person/cynthia-bergman/ (accessed June 14, 2016).
10 http://www.worldbank.org/en/programs/pricing-carbon (accessed June 14, 2016).

# Bibliography

Aykut, Stefan C. "Gouverner le climat, construire l'Europe: l'histoire de la création d'un marché du carbone (ETS)." *Critique Internationale* 62, no. 1 (2014): 39–55.

Benabou, Sarah, and Birgit Müller. "De l'autojustification du capitalisme. Les ambitions du secteur privé à Rio+20." In *Regards croisés sur Rio+20*, by Jean Foyer, 137–157. Paris: Editions CNRS, 2015.

BFC. *Business Proposals in View of a 2015 International Climate Change Agreement at COP21 in Paris*. 2015. http://www.businessforcop21.org/ (accessed June 14, 2016).

Brown, Trent. "Sustainability as empty signifier: Its rise, fall, and radical potential." *Antipode* 48, no. 1 (2016): 115–133.

B-Team. *A Long-Term Goal at COP21 Is Critical: Open Letter to World Leaders*. December 11, 2015. http://bteam.org/announcements/global-leaders-call-for-long-term-goal/ (accessed June 14, 2016).

Bulkeley, Harriet, Liliana B. Andonova, Michele M. Betsill, Daniel Compagnon, Thomas Hale, Matthew J. Hoffmann, Peter Newell, Matthew Paterson, Charles Roger, and Stacy D. VanDeveer. *Transnational Climate Change Governance*. Cambridge: Cambridge University Press, 2014.

Business & Climate Summit. *Conclusive Messages*. 2015. http://www.businessclimatesummit.com/conclusive-messages/ (accessed June 14, 2016).

Doyle, A., and G. de Clercq. "France's Hollande Concerned about Slow Progress in Climate Talks." *Reuters*. May 20, 2015. http://www.reuters.com/article/us-climatechange-business-hollande-idUSKBN0O51ZQ20150520 (accessed November 16, 2016).

Falkner, Robert. *Business Power and Conflict in International Environmental Politics*. Basingstoke: Palgrave Macmillan, 2008.

Felli, Romain. "Environment, not planning: The neoliberal depoliticisation of environmental policy by means of emissions trading." *Environmental Politics* 24, no. 5 (2015): 641–660.

Foucault, Michel. "Le jeu de Michel Foucault." In *Dits et écrits III. 1976–1979*, by Michel Foucault, 298–329. Paris: Gallimard, 1994.

Hanegraaff, Marcel. "Transnational advocacy over time: Business and NGO mobilization at UN climate summits." *Global Environmental Politics* 15, no. 1 (2015): 83–104.

Heede, Richard. "Tracing anthropogenic carbon dioxide and methane emissions to fossil fuel and cement producers, 1854–2010." *Climatic Change* 122, no. 1–2 (2014): 229–241.

IETA. *The 2015 Paris Agreement, Carbon Pricing and Markets: Connecting the Dots*. November 2015a. http://www.ieta.org/International-Position-Papers/3878513 (accessed June 14, 2016).

IETA. *What Business Wants: Carbon Pricing in Paris. Business Association Statements on the Importance of Carbon Markets in the Paris 2015 Climate Agreement*. 2015b. http://www.ieta.org/page-18192/3766347 (accessed June 14, 2016).

Kenis, Anneleen, and Matthias Lievens. "Searching for 'the political' in environmental politics." *Environmental Politics* 23, no. 4 (2014): 531–548.

Laclau, Ernesto. *Emancipation(s)*. London: Verso, 1996.

Levy, David L., and Daniel Egan. "A neo-Gramscian approach to corporate political strategy: Conflict and accommodation in the climate change negotiations." *Journal of Management Studies* 40, no. 4 (2003): 803–829.

Matt, Elah, and Chukwumerije Okereke. "A neo-Gramscian account of carbon markets – The case of the European Union emissions trading scheme and the clean development mechanism." In *The Politics of Carbon Markets*, by Benjamin Stephan and Richard Lane, 113–132. London: Routledge, 2015.

McMichael, Philip, and Birgit Müller. *The Land-Grab Trap: Is There a Will to Govern Global Land Grabbing?* September 19, 2014. http://www.focaalblog.com/2014/09/19/philip-mcmichael-birgit-muller-the-land-grab-trap-is-there-a-will-to-govern-global-land-grabbing/ (accessed June 14, 2016).

Meckling, Jonas. *Carbon Coalitions – Business, Climate Politics, and the Rise of Emission Trading.* London: MIT Press, 2011.

Mouffe, Chantal. *On the Political.* Abingdon: Routledge, 2005.

Müller, Birgit. *The Gloss of Harmony: The Politics of Policy-Making in Multilateral Organisations.* London: Pluto Press, 2013.

Newell, Peter, and Matthew Paterson. *Climate Capitalism: Global Warming and the Transformation of the Global Economy.* Cambridge: Cambridge University Press, 2010.

OGCI. *Oil and Gas CEOs Jointly Declare Action on Climate Change.* 2015. http://www.oilandgasclimateinitiative.com/news/oil-and-gas-ceos-jointly-declare-action-on-climate-change/ (accessed June 14, 2016).

Oreskes, Naromi, and Erik M. Conway. *Merchants of Doubts: How a Handful of Scientists Obscured the Truth on Issues from Tobacco Smoke to Global Warming.* New York: Bloomsbury, 2010.

Rockström, Johan, Will Steffen, Kevin Noone, Asa Persson, F. Stuart Chapin, III, Eric Lambin, Timothy M. Lenton, et al. "Planetary boundaries: Exploring the safe operating space for humanity." *Ecology & Society* 14, no. 2 (2009): 32.

Schapiro, Mark. *Carbon Shock: A Tale of Risk and Calculus on the Front Lines of the Disrupted Global Economy.* Vermont: Chelsea Green, 2014.

TBD. *The Business Dialogue. A High Level Dialogue on Climate Change Negotiations Issues between Negotiators and CEOs from All Business Sectors and Countries.* 2015. https://www.engie.com/wp-content/uploads/2016/02/global_business_sector_report_hd_def1.pdf (accessed June 16, 2015).

UNFCCC. *Conference of the Parties, Twenty-First Session: Adoption of the Paris Agreement.* 2015a. http://unfccc.int/documentation/documents/advanced_search/items/6911.php?priref=600008831 (accessed June 16, 2016).

UNFCCC. *Conference of the Parties, Twenty-First Session: List of Participants.* 2015b. http://unfccc.int/documentation/documents/advanced_search/items/6911.php?priref=600008825 (accessed June 16, 2016).

WBCSD. *Net Zero. 2015 Climate Change Agreement: An Accelerator for Business Actions.* 2014. http://www.wbcsd.org/Pages/eNews/eNewsDetails.aspx?ID=16324&NoSearchContextKey=true (accessed June 16, 2016).

WBCSD. *Vision 2050 – The New Agenda for Business.* 2010. http://www.wbcsd.org/vision2050.aspx (accessed June 14, 2016).

Wei, David, Edward Carmeron, Emilie Prattico, Gareth Scheerder, and Joanna Zhou. *The Paris Agreement: What It Means for Business.* 2015. http://www.bsr.org/en/our-insights/report-view/the-paris-agreement-on-climate-what-it-means-for-business (accessed June 16, 2016).

WMB. *The Business Brief: Shaping a Catalytic Paris Agreement.* 2015. http://www.wemeanbusinesscoalition.org/businessbrief (accessed June 14, 2016).

WMB. *The Climate Has Changed: Why Bold, Low-Carbon Action Makes Good Business Sense.* 2014. http://www.wemeanbusinesscoalition.org/sites/default/files/The Climate Has Changed_2.pdf (accessed June 16, 2016).

# 4 The ins and outs of climate movement activism at COP21

*Joost de Moor, Edouard Morena and Jean-Baptiste Comby*

## Introduction

In an article entitled "High Pressure for Low Emissions: How Civil Society Created the Paris Climate Agreement" (published in March 2016), Michael Jacobs of the Grantham Institute writes that although it will go down in history as a diplomatic success, the Paris Agreement is a "display of the political power of civil society". According to Jacobs, a "broad coalition of forces from global civil society" – including NGOs, businesses, the scientific community, think tanks – "effectively identified the landing ground for the agreement, then encircled and squeezed the world's governments until, by the end of the Paris conference, they were standing on it." When describing NGOs' impact, Jacobs is not only referring to their successful lobbying tactics inside the negotiations space but also stresses the important role of grassroots campaigns and mobilisations at its periphery. In particular, he highlights the role of "newer NGOs", such as Avaaz and 350.org, in focusing the world's attention on dirty oil and coal, and "building a global supporter base". As he writes, these and other groups played a vital role in "orchestrating the narratives of science and economics to demand strong climate action". NGOs' roles in raising awareness and shaping public opinion are, according to Jacobs, just as influential as their lobbying activities. By highlighting the collaborations between NGOs – both inside and outside the negotiations space – and between NGOs and other non-state actors – think tanks, businesses and scientists – Jacobs suggests an important shift in terms of the climate movement's involvement in the international climate debate.

Given his pro-market and pro-business credentials and active role and support for the Paris Agreement, Jacobs's analysis is inevitably biased. In particular, he tends to overstate NGOs' support for the final text. Concomitantly, he also tends to present "global civil society" as a unified and coherent whole, minimising the ideological and tactical differences that cut across it. While groups like Greenpeace International, Avaaz and CARE International were generally satisfied with the Paris outcome, a number of other groups – including Friends of the Earth International, LDC Watch, Third World Network, the Asian Peoples Movement on Debt and Development or Attac, to name a few – were far more critical. Asad Rehman from Friends of the Earth International, for instance, described a "Titanic scenario" where the "ship is sinking and the band plays on to the warm applause of our political leaders [. . .] and the poor are being denied a place in the lifeboats" (Friends of the Earth International 2015).

It is interesting to note that the vast majority of NGO reactions, including groups mentioned by Jacobs, were very ambivalent, combining elements of praise and criticism. While praising the deal's global character and ambitious long-term goal, many members of the climate movement pointed to its vagueness when it comes to securing the means of implementing and reaching its stated targets. For Bill McKibben from the campaign group 350.org, "every government seems now to recognize that the fossil fuel era must end and soon. But the power of the fossil fuel industry is reflected in the text, which drags out the transition so far that endless climate damage will be done."[1] Development groups welcomed the ambitious target while simultaneously highlighting the fact that through the Paris Agreement, developed countries were not committing to doing their fair share of the required efforts. For Harjeet Singh, global lead on climate change with ActionAid,

> what we needed out of Paris was a deal which put the world's poorest people first [. . .] Yet what we have been presented with doesn't go far enough to improve the fragile existence of millions around the world. Despite disappointment, the Paris agreement provides an important hook on which people can hang their demands.
>
> (Voorhaar 2015)

Furthermore, Jacobs largely overlooks – which is logical given the angle of the piece – those groups that are active in the climate movement but for whom the Paris outcome was of little importance in terms of their agendas and strategies. These include in particular – but not exclusively – smaller, more radical grassroots action groups, such as Reclaim the Power or GroenFront!,[2] for whom the Paris conference was first and foremost an opportunity to mobilise and build up a global climate justice movement. This reflects a growing scepticism – in particular following the Copenhagen conference of 2009 – on behalf of certain members of the climate movement over the UNFCCC's relevance when it comes to dealing with the climate problem (Dietz 2014, Hadden 2015).

Despite its limitations, Jacobs' analysis does raise important questions about the influence and functions of NGOs and other climate movement actors (trade unions, grassroots action groups involved in the international climate regime), and by extension the continued relevance of the traditional distinction between "insider" and "outsider" groups. In the social movement literature, insiders are typically defined as advancing moderate, reformist political views through lobby-oriented strategies, whereas outsiders are presented as having more radical transformative views, and leaning towards more or less radical protest tactics (Keck and Sikkink 1998, Bennett 2005). A similar distinction is operated in the literature on the climate movement (Fisher 2010). By grouping together political agendas and mobilising tactics, the insider/outsider distinction fails to account for the diversity of positions within both categories. In response to this, Peter Newell came up with a more elaborate account of how climate movement groups engage in the international climate debate. He distinguishes between "inside-insiders", who "employ more traditional patterns of lobbying and interest representation", "inside-outsiders", who are "involved in the formal policy process but adopt more confrontational strategies to influence it" and "outside-outsiders", who are "not involved in the formal policy negotiations on climate change, but rather seek to draw on the impacts of the problem on existing patterns of inequality and social injustice through a variety of campaigning tools and technologies of protest" (Newell 2006, 100). While he breaks up the insider category, Newell's framework still presents groups active outside of the negotiation space as a relatively homogenous entity, which he associates with a more transformational discourse and confrontational approach.

Our rapid overview of the reactions to the Paris Agreement signals a need to reevaluate the continued applicability of prevailing categorisations of climate movement actors. In particular, they point to the existence of a "two-level split" within the climate movement, a split that challenges somewhat the existing tendency to systematically tie together a group's favoured area of action – inside or outside the negotiation space – with its framing of the climate problem and attitude towards the official negotiations – reformist or more systemic/transformational. As we will see, both spaces of action combine reformist and systemic/transformational approaches. Specifically, our observations at the Paris climate conference point towards the existence of two outsider subcategories: "outside-insiders" and "outside-outsiders". Broadly speaking, outside-insiders can be defined as movement actors who actively support and promote the formal negotiation process without directly engaging in it. Through their actions, they raise awareness on the climate issue and negotiations in a way that is supportive of the official process. Outside-outsiders do not align their strategies to the official negotiations process, but capitalise on its global reach to pursue alternative strategies to tackle the climate crisis.

Keeping with the broad outsider/insider distinction, our chapter presents and analyses three discernible climate movement dynamics in the run-up to and during COP21. In a first instance, we focus on climate movement actors inside the Le Bourget conference centre. In a subsequent section, we look at social movement mobilisations outside of the official negotiation space. Thirdly and finally, we explore an original form of narrative- and cultural-based mobilisation: "Place to B". Each of these spaces offers an original vantage point from which to uncover the climate movement, explore ongoing insider and outsider dynamics within it, and examine the relevance and merits of a further distinction between outside-outsiders and outside-insiders.

## The changing face of climate insiders

Ever since the UNFCCC's beginnings in the early 1990s, non-state actors have been active within the climate negotiations space. Initially dominated by a handful of large, predominantly Northern environmental groups – especially through the Climate Action Network (CAN) – the space has progressively opened up to an increasingly wide array of non-state "observers" from the Global North and South – trade unions, indigenous groups, women's organisations, development NGOs and youth organisations. In addition to representing their specific constituency interests, observers of the Climate Convention act in accordance with shared worldviews, ideologies and theories of change. This leads to the formation of alliances and networks that cut across thematic constituencies. Examples include the launch of Climate Justice Now! (CJN) in 2007 in response to CAN's perceived lack of interest in social justice and equity concerns. Another noteworthy example is the Global Call for Climate Action (GCCA), a global coalition of over 270 organisations launched in 2008 to ramp up ambition and generate momentum on the eve of the Copenhagen climate conference (COP15) (GCCA 2010, 7, Cox 2011, 27).

Given the relatively small size of its membership, the UNFCCC space has also fostered the emergence of a series of loose, "below-the-radar" networks where participants can informally share information and intelligence, and align individual and organisational strategies to more effectively weigh in on the negotiations process. These networks and alliances cut across the official constituencies, linking together observers, negotiators and members of the UNFCCC secretariat. Recent examples include the so-called Climate Seven, an ad hoc platform of policy experts representing some of the largest development (Oxfam, ActionAid, ChristianAid), environmental (Friends of the Earth International, Greenpeace International, WWF) and labour organisations (International Trade Union Confederation) involved in the UNFCCC process.[3] They are widely credited with having orchestrated a walk-out of observers from COP19 in Warsaw (2013) in protest against parties' lack of ambition and slow progress in the talks. Loose networks such as these can be likened to organisational fields where various actors come "into routine contact with one another under a common frame of reference, in pursuit of an at least partially shared project" (Bartley 2007, 233). While keeping with their organisational specificities, participants devise ways of working towards a predetermined and collectively agreed outcome.

### The International Policies and Politics Initiative (IPPI)

One such network was especially active and influential in the lead-up to the Paris COP. Bringing together a variety of groups – working inside and outside of the negotiations space – its main contributors were associated with a foundation-backed initiative: the International Policies and Politics Initiative (IPPI) (see Morena, this volume, and Morena 2016). Launched in 2013, the IPPI acted as a platform for various groups and individuals to collectively secure a "positive" outcome in Paris. Climate movement actors associated with the IPPI include networks such as CAN International and GCCA, campaigning groups like Avaaz.org and 350.org, NGOs such as Greenpeace and Christian Aid and influential think tanks such as the World Resources Institute (WRI), Potsdam Institute for Climate

Impact Research (PIK) and E3G. Their distinctive worldviews and underlying framings of the climate problem notwithstanding, groups affiliated with the IPPI were united by (1) a common benchmark for success in the Paris climate conference, and (2) a common "roadmap" to reaching this successful outcome.

Cutting across a variety of organisations and interests, this loose group of activists, consultants, policy analysts, public figures, climate experts, communications and media specialists and data analysts was bound by a common yardstick for measuring success in Paris. They all believed that meaningful progress could be made through a loose international framework that sets an ambitious emissions reduction target and incentivises bottom-up climate action by a variety of stakeholders. This required an agreement that sets a long-term goal, a mechanism to regularly review and ratchet up national mitigation and financial commitments and finally, a global framework to ensure transparency (Morgan 2015).

The IPPI marks a significant departure from 2009 and the climate movement's calls for a "Fair, Ambitious and Binding" agreement. Groups associated with the IPPI strategy adopted a more bottom-up approach centred on voluntary national commitments – an approach that mirrors the overall trend in international climate negotiations since Copenhagen (COP15). In this respect, they generally played a supportive – rather than oppositional – role in the negotiations. In addition to maintaining close links with the UNFCCC secretariat and incumbent French COP presidency, they also backed initiatives such as the Cartagena Dialogue for Progressive Action, a loose and informal platform set up in 2010 for "forward-looking" countries and coalitions representing the North and South and determined to reach a global agreement in Paris. This approach towards the negotiation process sets them apart from other groups within the negotiation space that continued to push for a more top-down, legally binding and equitable agreement, and from groups that monitored the process, but without actively seeking to influence its outcome. The IPPI approach builds on the belief that an agreement that simultaneously stresses the urgency of the situation while sending an optimistic and galvanising message will catalyse ambitious action on behalf of state and non-state actors alike. Hence the need for Paris to send "unambiguous signals that the world will shift its economic and social activity toward more climate-friendly and sustainable pathways" (Oberthür, La Vina and Morgan 2015, 1).

Beyond their shared understanding of what constitutes a positive outcome at the Paris COP, groups associated with the IPPI also adopted a common roadmap to success. In other words, they actively set out – in partnership with key stakeholders in the negotiations – to create the conditions for a "successful" Paris outcome (grounded in the aforementioned principles). Rather than simply focusing on the big polluters and UNFCCC – as was the case in Copenhagen – they adopted a holistic approach to climate diplomacy through the simultaneous orchestration of actions at multiple levels (international, national, subnational) and locations (G8, G20, IPCC, UNFCCC), targeting a wide range of stakeholders: business leaders, the media and general public, religious leaders and representatives from the Global South. Through their actions, groups associated with the IPPI sought to shape stakeholders' understandings of the climate problem and generate momentum in the lead-up to what was commonly referred to as the "Paris moment". Shaping interpretations of the Paris process was just as important as the agreement itself. As Laurence Tubiana, lead negotiator for France explains in a post-COP press interview, "we had to anticipate the interpretation of the agreement. Words contribute as much to change as the agreement itself: it is what I call the convergence of rational anticipations." As she adds, "the agreement has to be a self-realizing prophecy" (Losson 2015).

Followers of the IPPI strategy adopted an "unbranded flotilla approach" to communications whereby groups would coordinate their actions but without explicitly displaying their affiliation to a shared strategy (Figure 4.1). Actions were in large part organised through the Climate Briefing Service (CBS), a discreet platform whose purpose was to provide real-time and ready-to-use information to selected members of the climate community and "[coordinate] voices at national and international levels to help shape the national offers as they are being drafted and the thinking around the international agreement."[4] While initially cautious about public mobilisations, climate movement actors involved in the IPPI strategy soon realised that, if properly managed and oriented, they could act as a powerful "booster" in the run-up to Paris. Whereas, for sections of the climate justice movement, the Paris conference marked an opportunity to build up an autonomous global climate movement, irrespective of the climate negotiations. The IPPI viewed popular mobilisations as a means of mobilising the public, generating media attention and subsequently pressuring world leaders to seal the

*Figure 4.1* Climate movement action inside the Le Bourget conference centre.

Source: Climacop Collective.

deal. This goes to explain their support for an international day of action at the start of the Paris conference (on November 29) rather than at its conclusion (see following section).

The IPPI undeniably signals a new stage in the climate movement's short-lived history. It points to the emergence of a new brand of collective engagement in the climate arena, a brand whose defining attribute is neither a favoured space of action – the negotiations space or its periphery – nor a shared framing of the climate problem, but rather a common yardstick for success in Paris – an agreement that sets an ambitious target, creates an enabling environment for action but ultimately delegates the real action to stakeholders on the ground – and attendant multilevel strategy. With IPPI, a group's outsider or insider status has therefore less to do with its preferred space of engagement (inside or outside the negotiations), action repertoire (confrontational or more reformist) or underlying worldview, for that matter, than with its level of alignment with a given approach to change – an approach that mirrors the broader evolution of climate diplomacy since COP15. Through this prism and referring back to our earlier discussion, groups associated with the IPPI and active on the periphery of the negotiations space can therefore be regarded as insiders, or more specifically outside-insiders.

## The climate movement in the streets of Paris

In appearance, the popular mobilisation around Paris distinguished itself from the one around Copenhagen in terms of its relative unification across the political and strategic spectrum (Hadden 2015). In view of the fact that internal dividedness along the climate justice line had contributed to the movement's inability to use COP15 to its advantage, many climate movement actors felt it necessary to adopt a more collaborative approach to mobilising around COP21. This collaborative spirit gave rise to the Coalition Climat 21 (CC21), the largest coalition of French and international social movement organisations involved in COP21. Moreover, CC21 engaged in close collaboration with the radical grassroots network called Climate Justice Action (CJA).[5] A priority was therefore to construct a unified space for groups to negotiate and coordinate actions.

On the face of it, the broad collaboration within CC21 and between CC21 and CJA supports the idea of a fairly unified and homogeneous outsider group. On closer scrutiny, however, the dynamics and tensions between the various groups that made up these coalitions point to the existence of two distinct outsider approaches – approaches that contribute to the relegation of the previously divisive climate justice issue to a secondary position. In particular, while both approaches share a common appreciation of the benefits of grassroots action, they differ in terms of the appreciation of, and attitudes towards, the formal negotiations process. To illustrate this, we will begin by briefly presenting the CC21 and CJA planning process in the run-up to the Paris conference, and then focus on events as they actually played out in Paris – especially given the fact that the COP took place shortly after the terrorist attacks in Paris on November 13, 2015 (Wahlström and de Moor 2017).

## Towards a joint call for action

Organised by CAN France, Attac France and the Centre de Recherche et d'Information pour le Développement (CRID),[6] CC21 held its first meeting in January 2014. The meeting brought together a large number of French organisations to begin exploring possibilities for mobilising around COP21. It is interesting to highlight that the hosts (CAN France, Attac France and CRID) and participants (e.g. Friends of the Earth France, Alternatiba and WWF France) were representative of the breadth of approaches and worldviews contained in the French chapter of the climate movement (including groups from both sides of the climate justice cleavage). At its first international meeting in August 2014, CC21 was joined by 170 organisations from thirty-seven countries, including various national and international chapters of groups like Friends of the Earth, Greenpeace, CAN and Attac, representing a similarly diverse array of approaches and worldviews. Over the next fifteen months, the coalition grew in size and capacity through the establishment of a permanent secretariat and thematic commissions. Six more international meetings were organised,[7] as well as countless coordinating meetings and conference calls.

In parallel and in close cooperation with CC21, CJA began meeting from October 2014 onwards. While dominated by small and more grassroots groups, larger groups linked to CC21 – 350.org and Greenpeace for instance – were also involved in CJA planning activities. While very different in terms of its core constituency, CJA collaborated closely with CC21 in a variety of different ways, and played an important role when it came to organising and staging the more radical actions.

While climate justice rapidly emerged as a shared mobilisation framework within the CC21/CJA network, disagreements surfaced when it came to devising the movement's approach towards the official negotiations space and process. In particular, this was reflected in discussions over the timing of the large climate march that was planned for the Paris conference. The choice was between the first or the last weekend of the COP. Traditionally the climate movement organised its main demonstration on the middle weekend. This was justified by a desire to push for greater ambition and commitment on behalf of parties within the negotiation processes. Interestingly, among those pushing hardest for a march on the first weekend was Avaaz, which, as we have seen, was involved in IPPI. Yet, given the growing level of scepticism as to the UNFCCC's capacity to actually deliver a strong agreement, many within CC21 felt that collective efforts should be set on "having the last word". In practice this required staging the actions on the last weekend, as the conference was ending. Given the divergent views within the movement, and in an attempt to preserve the coalition's unity, CC21 organisers ultimately agreed to organise days of action during the first and last weekend of the COP.

Given its underlying motivations, the outside-insider character of the first day of action is fairly obvious. Preparatory discussions relating to this day of action largely focused on logistical issues, in particular with respect to the scope – international or national – and organisation of the march – themes, marching order and choreography. Ultimately, CC21 organisers agreed to organise a large demonstration in Paris open to activists and citizens from France and from neighbouring countries where domestic demonstrations were not planned.

As for the second day of action (on the last weekend of the COP), there was far less of a consensus. How do you "have the last word"? How do you use the COP's "force of attraction" to build up a global climate movement without being drawn into the negotiation process? Should the second day of action's messaging refer to the Paris outcome or not? In short, how do you construct an outside-outsider strategy in response to COP21? These issues were at the heart of the discussions within CC21 and CJA on the last weekend mobilisation (or D12).[8] A (precarious) consensus was reached around five dominant and intersecting approaches. The first approach was centred on creating a discursive space to interpret the COP outcome. Closely related to the first, the second approach sought to disrupt and delegitimise the negotiations (in particular, by surrounding and blocking the Le Bourget conference centre). The third approach focused mainly on using the COP mega-event to target big polluters (like fossil fuel companies). The fourth approach focused on promoting the movement's concrete alternatives to the climate crisis (e.g. local, sustainable food and energy systems). The fifth and final approach consisted in using the Paris conference to build up and strengthen the international climate movement for "after Paris" by attracting new members towards it and by increasing the movement's internal coherence.

When it came to realising these approaches, CC21 and CJA organisers faced a number of challenges. Firstly, organisers struggled to find targets for their direct actions in the Paris city centre. On the back of a CJA meeting in Paris in May 2015, organisers went around town looking for potential targets, and concluded that there were none. There were no fossil fuel plants inside Paris and the offices of companies located in the business district of La Défense (in the outskirts of Paris) would be closed on D12. Secondly, organisers were increasingly aware of the fact that it would be difficult to redirect the media's, the public's and potential participants' attention away from the official conference. Finally, some organisers feared that by not targeting the COP, they would be letting the negotiators off easy.

These challenges go a long way into explaining why ultimately, after having claimed that minimal attention should be paid to the official negotiations, the most ambitious of the planned D12 actions ended up directly targeting the negotiations space. At the final CC21 international meeting before the COP (in Paris, October 2015), participants agreed to organise a "Red Lines" civil disobedience action on the last day of the conference. The idea – originating from within CJA, but toned down to receive the endorsement of CC21 – was to symbolically draw red lines around the Le Bourget conference centre as negotiations were about to end. The red lines symbolised the "minimal requirements for a just and livable planet" and the idea was to force negotiators and government officials to cross them as they were leaving the conference centre. While targeting the Le Bourget space, the Red Lines action was not intended to influence the ongoing negotiations. As one organiser explained at a CC21 meeting,

> We are not demanding anything from the COP process. We are not going to negotiate with the negotiators. We are creating a counter narrative [. . .] to have the last word. And for that to happen, we need to go where the story is unfolding. And that in a way is about taking back discursive space by occupying public space through acts of civil disobedience.[9]

Nevertheless, a number of CC21 organisers and participants reacted with confusion. Had it not been their aim to break free from the COP? Should the COP not be ignored altogether? This, it turned out, was hard to achieve given the UNFCCC process's role in structuring the movement over the past two decades, and given the Paris conference's historic status. The same applied to the "convergence space" – for groups unwilling to participate in the civil disobedience action in Le Bourget – that was planned in the centre of Paris after the Red Lines action to conclude the two weeks of climate activism. Thus, the COP's formidable force of attraction that had led so many groups to converge in Paris complicated their attempts to keep a safe distance between themselves and the official conference. Despite these difficulties, however, there were some events and actions that more clearly focused elsewhere – in particular on negotiating "real" and "false" solutions to the climate crisis.

### The movement in the streets of Paris

Social movements' strategy planning processes provide important insights into why organisers privilege certain courses of action over others. However, translating plans into action is never straightforward. Movements frequently have to deal with unexpected events and challenges. In Paris, the climate movement actions surrounding the conference were heavily disrupted by the terrorist attacks that shook the city a few weeks earlier (November 13). The French president's decision to declare a state of emergency, and the accompanying protest ban, meant that all public gatherings and street rallies were either cancelled or scaled down (Wahlström and de Moor 2017).

While marches on November 29 did take place around the world, the Paris march was cancelled. Several more modest actions did still take place, however. As an alternative to the march, Avaaz collected thousands of shoes and laid them out on the Place de la République (including a pair of shoes belonging to Pope Francis). On the same day, three other CC21 affiliated organisations – Alternatiba, Attac France and Friends of the Earth France – organised a "human chain" on the sidewalk of the avenues that formed part of the original itinerary of the march. While not officially permitted, the French authorities allowed the event to take place. On the margins of the human chain and Avaaz event, action groups not associated with CC21 – in particular a French action network called "Les Désobéissants" – called on citizens to converge towards the Place de la République (the original starting place of the march) in the name of climate justice and civil rights. Between 5,000 and 10,000 people took part. While the demonstration started off relatively peacefully, it later escalated into confrontations with the police and a series of arrests.

Many more actions were staged over the course of the following days, two of which stood out in terms of their size and scope. On December 4, activists disrupted the opening of the Solutions COP21 event organised near the Champs Elysées to showcase corporate solutions to the climate crisis. Participating activists wished to highlight the "false" nature of the corporate solutions on offer. To do so, they organised "toxic tours" of the venue whereby activists informed bystanders and journalists about participating corporations' actual track records in the climate and environmental fields. The action was rapidly suspended when plainclothes police forcefully expelled activists involved in the action.

On the weekend of December 5 and 6, CC21 organised the "Peoples' Climate Forum" in Montreuil, east of Paris. Open to the general public, the forum hosted debates and discussions on a variety of climate-related topics (negotiations, agriculture, development, trade), offered information on upcoming actions and staged training sessions for activists (on civil disobedience, collective organising). Representatives from groups that were present in Le Bourget organised a number of events, in many cases urging citizens and activists to keep pressing for more transformative change. The forum's Global Village of Alternatives was an opportunity for groups to showcase their work and their concrete solutions to the climate crisis – as opposed to the false solutions being offered by corporations. The French organisation Alternatiba, through its focus on "lifestyle politics", was at the heart of this initiative (de Moor 2016). Through their grassroots approach to change, Alternatiba argues that, given the urgency of the situation, citizens cannot wait for governments to unilaterally or collectively decide to take action – especially when we consider their track record so far.

During the second week of the Paris conference, the CentQuatre, a large city-run cultural space in the 19th Arrondissement district of Paris, hosted the Zone Action Climat (ZAC, Climate Action Zone) for activists, organisers and the wider public. Like the Peoples' Climate Forum, the ZAC acted as a space for people to organise, exchange ideas and learn about climate change and climate activism. A daily "general assembly" – involving high-profile activists and specialists – was organised to address a predetermined climate-related topic. The general assembly was also a chance for activists monitoring the negotiations to report on the negotiations' progress. It was also an opportunity to share information on upcoming actions. For instance, on December 9, and on the back of the negotiations update, an organiser from 350.org called on activists to take part in the Red Lines action: "We've just heard an update about the negotiations and quite frankly, these governments have been meeting for 21 years, and they haven't figured out how to deal with climate change. It's up to us!"

After more than a week of assemblies, workshops and actions whose focus was, in many cases, largely detached from the official conference, the movement re-centred its attention and efforts towards the final day of action on December 12.

Given the state of emergency and the massive police presence in the vicinity of the Le Bourget conference centre, the big challenge for CC21 and CJA became finding a way to stage a D12 event without compromising participants' safety. While some groups continued to push for civil disobedience actions on the margins of the Le Bourget conference centre, the larger groups within CC21 were unwilling to expose their members and followers to potential police repression. Following very tight negotiations, police authorities finally authorised two public events: a Red Lines rally close to the Arc de Triomphe and a static protest under the Eiffel Tower (Figure 4.2). At both events, protesters displayed or chanted familiar slogans, such as "System change, not climate change", and "What do we want? Climate justice! When do we want it? Now!" The movement later converged under the Eiffel Tower for a second gathering. Key figures of the movement spoke, usually combining an analysis of the Paris Agreement (many, including Naomi Klein, concluding that it was weak and unambitious) with calls to keep up the mobilisations.

In sum, while efforts were made to secure a far greater degree of internal coordination than in Copenhagen, the climate movement outside Le Bourget was still shaped by internal differences. While clearly affecting the CC21's mobilisation agenda, the Paris terrorist attacks amplified pre-existing tensions. Far from forming a single outsider category, the climate movement in the streets of Paris combined both outside-outsider and outside-insider elements. While sharing a common belief in the value of civil society mobilisations, underlying understandings of the official negotiation process differed substantially from one organisation to the next. These differences notwithstanding, mobilisations in Paris highlight the climate movement's inability to fully detach itself from the official COP process. This difficulty was accentuated by the fact that, as we saw in the preceding

*Figure 4.2* Red Lines action on December 12, 2015.

Source: Climacop Collective.

section, the Paris process's success also hinged on its ability to channel and use outsider mobilisations to its advantage. Hence, while it generates momentum and draws public and media attention towards the climate crisis, the COP process and attendant strategy undermine the international climate movement's efforts to advance on its own terms.

## The "Place to B"

The Paris COP's historic status fostered the emergence of new categories of non-state actors who are active on the margins of both the official conference space and "outsider movement" (see earlier) but who ended up playing a supportive role for the official negotiations process. In this section, we offer a detailed overview of one such actor: Place to B (PtB). Launched in the summer of 2015, PtB offers a potent example of what we term an "outside-insider". While not directly engaging in the negotiations space, it nevertheless contributed to create the conditions for a "successful" outcome in Paris. As we saw with IPPI, communication played a key role in the run-up to and during the Paris COP. By offering an "ephemeral co-working space" for individuals – usually associated with the "creative industries" (design, web, architecture, cinema, games, fashion or on a more market side: consulting, marketing, advertising) – to build and circulate a narrative around the Paris COP, in particular through the Internet, PtB's raison d'être was to focus on the messaging that surrounded the climate issue and the Paris COP. In many ways, PtB shared a number of similarities with the TckTckTck-affiliated "Fresh Air Centre" in Copenhagen (COP15). In both cases, they were physically located in fashionable and cosy locations: the Huset Café in Copenhagen and the St Christopher Inn B&B in Paris. In both cases, the ambition was to produce an alternative, more inspiring and engaging coverage of the COP to that being offered by accredited media in the official COP space. Moreover, both initiatives fall into the "2.0 activism" (though their massive use of digital networks and collaborative tools is remarkable) and "3.0 activism" categories (thanks to connections with makers and fablab movements[10]). Breaking with the mainstream news coverage and narratives on climate change, both initiatives attempt to tap into the climate movement's cultural – rather than political or ideological – dimensions.

While there are important similarities between PtB and the Fresh Air Centre (e.g. addressing and mobilising roughly the same audiences), both initiatives were not formally linked. Whereas the Fresh Air Centre was connected to the climate movement through TckTckTck, PtB was a new and autonomous venture. One of the main ideological drivers behind PtB's "positive" climate narratives and low-carbon scenarios was the Climate Outreach platform, a European network of climate change communicators who believe in the power of marketing and media strategies, communication and cultural change.[11] As we will see, while presenting itself as a groundbreaking initiative, PtB's relative disconnection from prior and analogous COP-related experiments and actors paradoxically leads to the production of a very conventional climate narrative. Given PtB's "newcomer" status, its

*Figure 4.3* View inside St Christopher's Inn.

Source: Climacop Collective.

participants' personal biographies play a far greater role when it comes to situating PtB within the outsider space.[12]

According to PtB, approximately 15,000 people from seventy countries attended at least one of the numerous workshops, debates, meetings or performances organised at the St Christopher's Inn venue (Figure 4.3). The venue's daily programme of events was organised on a topical basis – technology, communication, consumption, behaviours, business, spirituality and energy, among others. Over 200 hundred activists and specialists spoke at the PtB space, including Naomi Klein, Vandana Shiva, Nicolas Hulot, James Hansen and Rob Hopkins, representing a wide spectrum of views and approaches towards the climate issue. In the "creative factory", every forty-eight hours, 141 "creatives" were set with the task of collectively imagining and producing content – drawings, comics, websites, games, designs, street gardening, guides and audiovisual productions, among others – on a particular theme (giving rise to eighteen projects).[13] In the space of two weeks, a wide variety of media contents were produced for television, radio and websites. These included reports on green innovations or ecological alternatives, interviews with climate actors and portraits of PtB participants. Through its different activities, PtB reportedly reached over 313 million people.

This wide range of activities and projects hosted in the PtB space can be interpreted as serving two overarching and interrelated goals. First, they focus on the construction of representations, meanings, symbols, concepts, images and narratives that project a non-alarmist and non-critical approach to the climate problem. Second, in doing so, they hope to reach and mobilise the widest possible audience. The (intended?) result is an overall narrative that neither refers to the UNFCCC process nor questions the technology- and market-based solutions that are associated with it.

## The role of social capital

Participants' high levels of social capital (in the Bourdieusian sense) go a long way towards explaining (1) how the PtB project was able to materialise in less than fifteen months; and (2) why, despite its alleged exteriority to both the climate negotiations and other climate outsiders, PtB can nevertheless be seen as having played an outside-insider role in Paris (Bourdieu 1980). Influential contacts in government ministries, the media, business circles, the art world, academia and think tanks were activated. In the case of the French fraction of the PtB "community", many of the participants, speakers and co-workers were already well-acquainted. The social, professional and ideological homogeneity was especially visible during the COP. In addition to contributing to the broader PtB project, many of the 613 guests in the Inn used the co-working space for professional networking purposes. Moreover, our observations point to the fact that participants used the breaks between activities to share experiences and exchange ideas and professional contacts. These exchanges fostered a sense of belonging to a shared "community of ideas and beliefs". Social capital's role in organising the PtB space and nurturing this sense of community upheld and enhanced a sense of "*entre-soi*" that was detrimental to PtB's insertion within the broader climate movement.

## A closed crossroad

PtB was never intended to engage with the official negotiations space. A short 5–20-minute recap of the ongoing negotiations was nevertheless provided during the daily two-hour talks. The speakers at the talks were very rarely involved in the negotiation process. The audience – between 50 and 100 people daily – was mostly composed of newcomers who had a limited knowledge of and/or interest in the UNFCCC – setting them apart from the more UN-savvy and experienced members of the climate movement community. Subsequently, a great number of contributors to the PtB space had no fixed opinion of the UNFCCC.

The same holds true of PtB's position with respect to the broader climate movement. While there were some limited connections – an organiser from CJA who played a central part in the organisation of the Red Lines action (see previous section) was present at PtB during the first week; the same fablab devices were used at the 104 and Saint Christopher Inn; many PtB participants took part in CC21 events such as the Global Village of Alternatives – there were no real attempts to build up strong and lasting partnerships with the climate movement. In fact, many PtB participants were critical of the confrontational approach that they felt dominated the climate movement. In addition to remaining clear of the negotiation process, many at PtB criticised the climate movement's supposed violent tactics and system-critical approach. As one representative explains, given its "deliberately broad" approach, PtB keeps at a safe distance from "the aggressive tone of certain activists". In turn, many climate movement actors either have never heard of PtB or do not regard it as a significant player in the global climate space.

For many attendees, PtB marks an entry point into the global climate space. In certain cases, participants' professional backgrounds were in polluting industries – frequently referred to as the "dark side". Their decision to take part in PtB reflected a sudden awakening and desire to find answers and take action. They wanted to give new meaning to their existence by finding a compromise between their professional aspirations and concern for the climate.

Their contributions to the PtB space reflect this desire to address the climate problem but without jeopardising the dominant social order – of which, given their high levels of social capital, they are prime beneficiaries. While one could expect these newcomers to convey new and innovative perspectives, our observations show that their limited experience actually leads them to uphold the status quo. Their discursive space is dominated by conventional practices, references and representations. They continue to value and engage in partnerships with journalists from the mainstream media. They continue to adopt conventional media logics, by drawing on audience scores to measure success.

PtB presents itself as a "non-ideological", "all-inclusive" and "neutral" space (from which only "non-ethic businesses" and "radical activists" are excluded).[14] This produces a paradoxical situation whereby PtB officially asserts its open-ended character while simultaneously cutting itself off from large sections of the broader climate community. In other words, PtB can be likened to a political crossroad that is socially closed. It is a place that is theoretically open to all but where the dominant "community spirit" tends to inhibit social diversity and limit the level of interactions with other organisations or institutions.

### An ecological reformist ethos

While presenting themselves as "apolitical" or "neutral", PtB organisers and participants are in fact promoting a very conventional approach to climate action. A rapid look at PtB organisers' biographies shows how, despite their limited experience in the international climate space, their social, professional and educational backgrounds increase their chances of adhering to the existing climate *doxa*. While recognising the need for a transition to a low-carbon society, they do not challenge the ideological underpinnings of our contemporary societies. They believe that change will happen through bottom-up, voluntary actions, as well as technological innovation and individual lifestyle changes and "eco-citizenship" (Comby 2015). They justify their approach by a form of "pragmatism" or "realism" insisting on the fact that, as one participant put it, "we cannot, in the current transition, simply switch from one model to another." Interestingly, this approach largely reflects the dominant framing inside the climate negotiations – and that would ultimately form the basis of the Paris Agreement.

As previously highlighted, involvement in PtB enables participants to align their professional aspirations with their individual attentiveness to the climate problem. They do not regard themselves as professional activists – in fact many reject the activist label – but rather as "active professionals" who aspire to jobs that serve the greater good and are self-fulfilling at the same time. Interestingly, many of them are self-employed and value the flexibility that this brings.

The PtB example signals a new approach to outsider engagement in the international climate arena – an approach that is grounded on the idea that narratives shape individual attitudes and actions, and therefore produce meaningful change. As we have seen in the first section, this focus on momentum building through the diffusion of "positive" narratives was a key feature of the insider strategy in the run-up to and during the Paris conference. Yet, far from detaching itself from it, PtB can be viewed as an outgrowth of the dominant framing of the climate problem. PtB subsequently highlights the fact that, while not actively engaging with or monitoring the UNFCCC process, certain outsiders can (inadvertently?) end up playing a supporting role for the official negotiations process. In other words, an organisation or initiative's insider or outsider status is not automatically determined by its position towards the official negotiation process or its degree of embeddedness in the global climate community. It is also shaped by the social and cultural capital of its members – social capital and cultural capital that shape their worldviews and understandings of the climate problem.

## Concluding remarks

The Paris outcome – and process that preceded it – signals a shift in climate diplomacy "from a relatively narrow focus on the UNFCCC process, to a more complex and wider discipline that now engages new constituencies and embraces broader geopolitical discussion" (Mabey, Gallagher and Born 2013, 6). Accelerated in the aftermath of COP15, this shift reflects a growing belief in international climate circles that "society as a whole, from the progressive to the conservative, right to left, engaged and disinterested, will be required to move to allow for the policy shift towards the goal of a sustainable future" (ECF 2011, 4). As our observations of COP21 demonstrate, this changing approach to climate diplomacy has produced important effects on the climate movement inside and outside the official negotiations space.

First, traditionally considered as a secondary player when compared to negotiators or climate scientists, the climate movement – but also the media, business and religious leaders – was now regarded as an essential factor of success. Initiatives like the IPPI reflect a growing awareness of the need to mobilise non-state actors so as to shape the wider climate narrative and build up momentum in the lead-up to the Paris conference. Second, through their actions in support of the official process, certain groups active outside of the negotiations space played an insider role (what we term outside-insiders). Preparatory discussions inside CC21 on the format, the timing and the messaging of actions in Paris reflect a growing attentiveness to outsider mobilisations' effects on the official process.

Third, as the CC21 example also demonstrates, a number of groups within the climate movement lost faith in the UNFCCC's ability to effectively solve the climate crisis. They subsequently attempted to distance themselves from the process while simultaneously capitalising on its "global mega-event" status and the media hype that it produces. Yet, this task was particularly difficult given that success inside the negotiation space now hinged on successful mobilisations outside of it. Fourth and finally, these changes in climate diplomacy expand the limits and scope of the outsider group. Newcomer groups like Place to B that narrowly focus on producing climate narratives and that are largely detached from the rest of the climate movement also fall into the outside-insider category.

Given the substance of the agreement, we can expect outside-insiders to play an even greater role in the post-Paris context. Indeed, now more than ever, achieving the 1.5°C target will hinge upon the climate movement's ability to mobilise public opinion in support of ambitious climate action, and to pressure national governments to act. In particular, this will require movement actors to adopt a more a nationally centred and sector-based approach – by focusing on high-emitting energy sources for instance. In view of the climate regime's increasingly decentralised character, the challenge becomes of seeing how climate movement groups are able to coordinate their actions internationally. Given its global character, the climate crisis demands a global climate movement response. The priority thus becomes of finding new, innovative and more effective ways of building up a global movement beyond COPs.

## Notes

1 https://350.org/press-release/cop21-reaction.
2 The Dutch chapter of Earth First!
3 The group became the "Climate Eight" with the arrival of CIDSE.
4 https://ciff.org/grant-portfolio/climate-briefing-service/ (accessed September 9, 2015). For more on CBS see Chapter 5.
5 While there are important similarities in terms of strategic and political views, and some overlaps in membership, CJA at COP21 and CJA at COP15 are two distinct entities. The CJA group around COP21 was looking for a name, and realising its similarities with CJA from COP15, and the fact that the latter network had ceased to exist, it adopted the latter's name.
6 CRID is a French association for the promotion of research on development-related topics.
7 There were really only two more official international CC21 meetings (one in Tunis in March 2015 and one in Paris in October 2015) where decisions were officially taken, yet in between there were several other meetings involving large international delegations.
8 D12 stands for December 12, the first day after the climate conference.
9 Observational note, October 2, 2015.
10 Associated with the Do It Yourself movements, makers and fablabs promote collaborative practices to invent new technologies, robotics, 3D printings, software and so forth.
11 http://climateoutreach.org/#.

12 The present section draws on two weeks of ethnographic fieldwork conducted by Jean-Baptiste Comby and Tania Dufner (who was hired as research assistant). A survey was circulated and thirty interviews were conducted.

13 For an example of output, see the "do-tank" project called The Pond: http://www.thepond.co.

14 The distance with these two "extremes" is not explicitly claimed but it appears as taken for granted, linked to PtB's goal and spirit.

## Bibliography

Bartley, Tim. "How foundations shape social movements: The construction of an organizational field and the rise of forest certification." *Social Problems* 54, no. 3 (2007): 229–255.

Bennett, Lance. W. "Social movements beyond borders: Organization, communication and political capacity in two eras of transnational activism." In *Transnational Protest & Global Activism*, by Donatella della Porta and Sidney G. Tarrow, 203–226. Lanham: Rowman & Littlefield, 2005.

Bourdieu, Pierre. "Le capital social: Notes provisoires." *Actes de la recherche en sciences sociales* 31 (1980): 2–3.

Carbon Pulse. *COP-21: Reaction to the Paris Climate Agreement.* December 12, 2015. http://carbon-pulse.com/13323/ (accessed February 5, 2016).

Climate Briefing Service. *CBS Briefing: Understanding Who Could Undermine a Strong Agreement in Paris.* November 4, 2015.

Comby, Jean-Baptiste. *La question climatique: Genèse et dépolitisation d'un problème public.* Paris: Raisons d'Agir, 2015.

Cox, Brendan. *Campaigning for International Justice: Learning Lessons (1991–2011); Where Next? (2011–2015).* 2011. https://www.bond.org.uk/data/files/Campaigning_for_International_Justice_Brendan_Cox_May_2011.pdf.

de Moor, Joost. "Lifestyle politics and the concept of political participation." *Acta Politica* (2016). doi: 10.1057/ap.2015.27

Dietz, Matthias. "Debates and conflicts in the climate movement." In *Routledge Handbook of the Climate Change Movement*, by Matthias Dietz and Heiko Garrelts, 292–307. New York: Routledge, 2014.

ECF. *Vision 2020: International Climate Diplomacy.* The Hague: European Climate Foundation, 2011.

Fisher, Dana R. "COP-15 in Copenhagen: How the merging of movements left civil society out in the cold." *Global Environmental Politics* 10, no. 2 (2010): 11–17.

Friends of the Earth International. *Where We Stand and Way Forward – Press Conference at COP21.* December 12, 2015. http://unfccc6.meta-fusion.com/cop21/events/2015-12-12-14-30-friends-of-the-earth-international-friend-for-the-earth-international-where-we-stand-and-way-forward (accessed January 2, 2016).

GCCA. "Annual Report 2009." *Global Call for Climate Action.* June 8, 2010. http://tcktcktck.org/files/reports/GCCA_Annualreport_2009_EN.pdf (accessed May 2, 2016).

Hadden, Jennifer. *Networks in Contention.* Cambridge: Cambridge University Press, 2015.

Hjerpe, Mattias, and Björn-Ola Linnér. "Functions of COP side-events in climate-change governance." *Climate Policy* 10, no. 2 (2010): 167–180.

Jacobs, Michael. "High pressure for low emissions: How civil society created the Paris climate agreement." *Juncture* 22, no. 4 (2016): 314–323.

Keck, Margaret E., and Kathryn Sikkink. *Advocates beyond Borders: Advocacy Networks in International Politics*. Ithaca: Cornell University Press, 1998.

Losson, Christian. "COP21: 'L'accord doit être une prophétie autoréalisatrice'." *Libération*, 17 December 2015.

Mabey, Nick, Liz Gallagher, and Camilla Born. *Understanding Climate Diplomacy: Building Diplomatic Capacity and Systems to Avoid Dangerous Climate Change*. London: E3G, 2013.

Minkoff, Debra, and John McCarthy. "Reinvigorating the study of organizational processes in social movements." *Mobilization: An International Quarterly* 10, no. 2 (2005): 289–308.

Morena, Edouard. *The Price of Climate Action: Philanthropic Foundations in the International Climate Debate*. Basingstoke: Palgrave, 2016.

Morgan, Jennifer. *Setting the Bar for Success at the Paris Climate Summit*. September 30, 2015. http://www.wri.org/blog/2015/09/setting-bar-success-paris-climate-summit (accessed October 8, 2015).

Newell, Peter. "Climate for change? Civil society and the politics of global warming." In *Global Civil Society 2005/6*, by Mary Kaldor, Marlies Glasius and Helmut Anheier, 90–119. London: SAGE, 2006.

Oberthür, Sebastian, Antonio G. M. La Vina, and Jennifer Morgan. *Getting Specific on the 2015 Climate Change Agreement: Suggestions for the Legal Text with an Explanatory Memorandum*. Working Paper. Washington, DC: Agreement for Climate Action 2015 (ACT2015), 2015.

Voorhaar, Ria. *Civil Society Responds as Final Paris Climate Agreement Released*. December 12, 2015. http://www.climatenetwork.org/press-release/civil-society-responds-final-paris-climate-agreement-released (accessed February 5, 2016).

Wahlström, Mattias, and Joost de Moor. "Governing dissent in a state of emergency: Police and protester interactions in the global space of the COP." In *Climate Action in a Globalizing World: Comparative Perspectives on Social Movements in the Global North*, by Carl Cassegård, Linda Soneryd, Håkan Thörn and Åsa Wettergren. London and New York: Routledge, 2017.

# 5 Follow the money

## Climate philanthropy from Kyoto to Paris

*Edouard Morena*

## Introduction

As an international mega-event of historic proportions, COP21 and its host city drew global attention and attracted many of the most prominent and active players in the international climate regime. In the innumerable reports, articles and studies devoted to the UNFCCC process, one group of actors involved in and around the Paris COP seems to have gone largely unnoticed: philanthropic foundations. This is fairly surprising given that foundations, in their grant-making and convening capacities, have historically supported and contributed to the UNFCCC process. In the days following the Paris COP, members of the foundation community, who traditionally tend to keep a low profile, openly stressed their role in the agreement. According to the European Climate Foundation (ECF 2016), "although we should be careful not to overstate our role, it is important to recognise that the climate philanthropy community's activities prior to and at the COP helped to lay the basis for the outcome."

The physical presence of foundation representatives in Paris during the COP offers some indications as to foundations' interest in the international climate process. An estimated 300 predominantly US foundation representatives (staff members, trustees, board members) were in Paris. The COP was an opportunity for foundations to showcase their climate-related work and to exchange ideas and views with fellow philanthropists and participants in the conference. More generally, through their presence in Paris, foundations could get a clearer sense of the current state of play in international climate negotiations.

Foundations were involved in and hosted a number of high-profile events on the margins of the negotiations space. These included showcasing projects or initiatives that had benefited from foundation support. Examples include the Climate Summit for Local Leaders, whose partners included the Children's Investment Fund Foundation (CIFF) and Bloomberg Philanthropies (which are both funders of the C40 Cities Climate Leadership Group). Events were also specifically tailored towards the foundation community. A group of foundations and foundation networks set up the COP21 Funders Initiative in mid-2015 "to help funders communicate, coordinate, and collaborate on the path to COP21" (Randazzo et al. 2015). The network played a central role in informing foundations and coordinating foundation activities during the COP (Randazzo et al. 2015). In the run-up to the COP, the Initiative organised a series of invitation-only conference calls to share and identify strategic information, updates and needs, and to support logistics around COP21.[1] During the Paris conference, and with support from the Centre Français des Fonds et Fondations (CFF), the Initiative co-hosted various climate-related events. This included a series of meetings on climate and health, women and environment, divest/invest, climate and food, and climate and refugees. Daily breakfast briefings were also organised to inform foundation representatives on the current state of play in the negotiations. External actors – NGO and business representatives, climate experts – were regularly invited to share their views at these events. Throughout the duration of the COP, the COP21 Funders Initiative also hosted social events, such as dinners and receptions with national and international personalities (Al Gore, Christiana Figueres[2] and others).[3]

Foundation representatives were well represented inside of the negotiation space as well. In their capacity as officially recognised observer organisations, a number of philanthropic foundations sent delegates to the Paris talks. This was the case of large US-based liberal foundations, like the Rockefeller Brothers Fund, the Packard, Joyce, Rockefeller, Gordon and Betty Moore, ClimateWorks and UN foundations. Representatives from the India-based Shakti Sustainable Energy Foundation, the Latin American Avina Foundation and the ECF were also represented in Le Bourget. Bringing together "foundation executives and trustees who make environmental grants", the US-based Consultative Group on Biological Diversity (CGBD) also sent a delegation to the Paris COP.[4] In addition to these foundation delegations, a handful of foundation representatives attended the negotiations through other observer organisations – both inter- and non-governmental. This was, for instance, the case of two representatives from the KR Foundation who attended the conference through the OECD and CAN-Europe delegations. Additionally, the climate lead at the UK-based CIFF attended the talks through the SouthSouthNorth (SSN) Project Africa delegation.

Capturing and interpreting foundation involvement in international climate negotiations require us to look beyond their physical presence in and around international climate conferences such as COP21. While signalling an interest, a foundation's presence in Paris reveals relatively little about its actual contribution to the international climate regime or underlying motivations. Given the fact that foundations act – at least in appearance – through their grantees, evaluating foundations' influence requires us to look at the projects, initiatives and organisations they support. In their capacity as field builders, foundations' actions – or dare I say activism – can be assessed through *what* they fund and *how* they fund as well as through their convening and supporting roles. To this end, we will begin by retracing the origins and evolution of international climate philanthropy. As we will see, far from being at its margins, foundations – and especially one group of liberal foundations – have historically been at the heart of the international climate regime. They are stakeholders in their own right, pushing for a given outcome, interacting and engaging with a variety of different actors and constantly adapting and refining their strategies along the way. As we will see, in Paris, one foundation initiative was especially revealing of the nature and degree of philanthropic involvement in international climate politics: the International Policies and Politics Initiative (IPPI).

## A brief history of climate philanthropy

Any discussion of contemporary international climate philanthropy requires us to look at the history of environmental philanthropy – and more specifically US environmental philanthropy (Spero 2010, 19). The origins of philanthropic engagement in the environmental field can be traced back to the origins of liberal philanthropy in the United States. In terms of its approach, liberal philanthropy is often credited with using science and reason to address the root causes of a given social problem. When it comes to its underlying agenda, it is usually associated with the liberal political tradition in the United States, a tradition that combines, to varying degrees, ideas of individual liberty – of speech, of religion – civil rights, pluralistic democratic systems, support for government activism but opposition to more radical reforms (Faber and McCarthy 2005, 15). In the early twentieth century and drawing on a "progressive" approach to social change, wealthy liberal philanthropists, such as Andrew Carnegie, Henry Ford and George Eastman, helped establish a variety of groups and funds in the fields of conservation and preservation (Brulle and Jenkins 2005, 151). Following in their footsteps, a group of foundations promoted a "rational use of nature through scientific management of natural resources" (Johnson and Frickel 2011, 307).

In the post-war period, and especially in the 1960s and 1970s, a handful of large liberal foundations expanded their focus towards more population-centred environmental concerns. This was a time of growing attention towards the human origins and impacts of environmental degradation. The 1970s saw the first Earth Day celebrations and the passing of around thirty environmental laws. It also witnessed the development of grassroots environmental groups whose strategies and ideologies, through their combination of environmental and social concerns, marked a fundamental departure from the larger mainstream conservationist groups that had hitherto dominated the US environmental landscape. Only a handful of large liberal foundations – including the Ford, Andrew Mellon and Rockefeller foundations – were prepared to support this increasingly diverse and politically engaged environmental movement (Ames 1981, 9, Barker 2008, 24). Given their reluctance to fund more grassroots and radical groups, the vast majority of their grant-making went to groups supporting a reformist agenda grounded on the idea that, given the right policies, environmental preservation and corporate-driven capitalism were mutually reinforcing. Given their small number, these liberal foundations exerted a disproportionate influence on the US environmental movement (Dowie 2001, 89).

From the early 1980s onwards and at a time when environmental degradation was increasingly being framed as a global problem, environmental funders, in their grant-making and convening capacities, began to actively take up the climate issue. Over the next two decades, a handful of philanthropic foundations contributed to turn global warming into a legitimate social problem in the United States while simultaneously helping to forge an international climate governance regime (Hemphill 2013, 10).

Foundations actively supported efforts to secure and coordinate civil society involvement in the international climate debate. They funded, and in some cases helped initiate, large mainstream environmental NGOs and think tanks, such as the WorldWatch Institute, WWF, Natural Resources Defense Council (NRDC), International Union for the Conservation of Nature (IUCN), World Resources Institute (WRI), Environmental Defense Fund and Conservation International, as well as research institutes, such as the International Institute for Environment and Development (IIED). They also helped to launch international NGO networks, such as the Climate Action Network (1989).

Foundations also played a field-building role by hosting a series of climate-related events and meetings. At the international level, foundations funded research, awareness raising and support for the international discussions leading to the establishment of the UNFCCC. In so doing, they contributed to strengthen the "compromise of liberal environmentalism" whereby international environmental protection and a liberal economic order are presented as mutually reinforcing (Bernstein 2002, 1). In 1987, for instance, the Rockefeller Brothers Fund, the Rockefeller Foundation and the W. Alton Jones Foundation co-sponsored two important workshops in Villach, Austria, and Bellagio, Italy, that led to the formation of the IPCC (Agrawala 1998). A third workshop in Woods Hole in 1988 laid the groundwork for the future climate convention.

Over the course of the 1992–1997 period, having actively and successfully contributed to the establishment of the UNFCCC, US foundations redirected their efforts towards the domestic level. The priority was now to get the United States to agree to an ambitious international deal. Faced with the federal government's reluctance to act and given the scale of the climate problem, certain foundations redirected their efforts towards "winnable battles" at the sub-national or sectorial level, laying the groundwork for a new "strategic" approach to climate philanthropy. Through initiatives like the Pew Charitable Trusts' Pew Center on Global Climate Change (launched in 1998), foundations increasingly targeted the business community by stressing the business case for climate action. Efforts were made to foster "a new cooperative debate on climate change" within the business community through the production of reports and the facilitation of dialogue (Spero 2010, 20).

### The rise of strategic climate philanthropy

In the process of re-evaluating their climate strategies, foundations refined the liberal philanthropic approach by making it even more "focused" and "strategic". This basically took the shape of a very targeted, results-driven and metrics-based approach to philanthropy. These new grant-making methodologies were directly inspired by corporate practices (market analysis, target setting, evaluation). Given the comparatively low levels of available assets, greater efforts were made to align and combine philanthropic actions and, where deemed appropriate, to pool funds and channel them through new specialised re-granting foundations. Strategic leverage was deemed essential given that "the philanthropic sector is tiny compared with the issues it confronts. Its grant dollars are miniscule compared with spending by the government and transactions in the private sector" (Brest and Harvey 2008, 6). Unlike other areas of philanthropic engagement – education, health care – where, given the right amount of funding, foundations can make a difference, no amount of philanthropic funding can, by itself, solve the climate problem.

The idea was to draw on philanthropy's comparative advantage when compared to the private sector or governments. As Sonia Medina from the CIFF explains, a philanthropist "can test innovative approaches, take risks, be nimble and react quickly to windows of opportunity, and is an honest broker that is not politically driven" (Medina 2015, 5). As she goes on to explain, "philanthropy can therefore use its relatively small resources to play a catalytic role to create transformational change by: opening pools of capital, being a catalyst to climate policy, helping to speed up innovation, motivating finance ministers" (Medina 2015, 5). Climate change therefore requires foundations to invest in the levers of change, rather than change itself. Given the origins of most greenhouse gas (GHG) emissions, it means creating a regulatory framework and economic environment more conducive to low-carbon business models and greater investments in clean technologies.

From the moment that foundations treat their grants as investments with expected social returns, they logically tend to adopt a more proactive approach to grant-making (Rimel 1999, 230). Instead of holding a backseat position, foundations actively contribute to the various stages of the project – from its drafting to its realisation – by offering grantees expertise, consultation, insights and direction. Grant proposals are evaluated on the basis of their ability to provide a clearly defined and ambitious goal, an evidence-based roadmap or business plan, achievable scenarios, plans for long-term financial sustainability and proof of their competitive advantage over other similar organisations and projects. As Rebecca Rimel of the Pew Charitable Trusts explains, a growing number of foundations "have begun to move beyond [their] traditional, relatively passive role as grant givers to become catalysts, brokers, information resources, and civic entrepreneurs through strategic investments" (Rimel 1999, 230). Like "traditional" liberal philanthropy, strategic philanthropy seeks to address the root causes of a given social problem rather than just its symptoms. The "newness" of this "new and improved" philanthropy (supposedly) lies in foundations' grant-making methods, interactions with grantees and greater grant oversight (Katz 2005, 123).

This new brand of strategic grant-making gave rise to a new brand of philanthropic foundations. Dubbed "the biggest foundation you've never heard of", the San Francisco–based Energy Foundation is a noteworthy attempt to translate the principles of strategic climate philanthropy into practice (Wei-Skiller 2012). Launched in 1991 through a combined promissory grant of USD 20 million from the Rockefeller Foundation, Pew Charitable Trusts and MacArthur Foundation, the Energy Foundation's ambition was to promote, through its grant-making, energy efficiency and renewable energy in the United States. By pooling their funds and channelling them through a single organisation staffed by energy specialists, the three foundations believed that they could achieve greater overall impact (Energy Foundation 2001).

As a re-granting or "pass-through" foundation, the Energy Foundation "[specialises] as a strategic intermediary, to get the money working in the field" (Energy Foundation 2001). To do so, its priority was to get policymakers to create the appropriate environment for corporate investments in energy efficiency and renewables. By privileging a sub-national approach – which, given the unfavourable national political environment, was seen as more effective – the Energy Foundation contributed to shape and push through state standards in the areas of renewable energy and energy efficiency in utilities, appliances, vehicles and construction. By the late 1990s, the Energy Foundation was regularly referred to as a model to follow by liberal philanthropists involved in the climate debate. Many of them went on to fund the foundation – Mertz-Gilmore (1996), McKnight (1998), Packard (1999) and Hewlett (2001), among others. By 1998, contributions to the Energy Foundation were in excess of USD 100 million.

### Strategically reengaging in the international climate debate

By the mid-2000s, the more favourable national political climate and renewed global momentum around climate change encouraged US climate funders to scale up their actions by reengaging in the national and international climate debates (Kimble 2012, 11–12). A group of largely US foundations – the Hewlett, Packard, Oak, Doris Duke, Joyce and Energy foundations – commissioned California Environmental Associates (CEA), a specialised consultancy firm, to draft a strategy for foundations to address the climate change problem. The result of the CEA's work was the *Design to Win: Philanthropy's Role in the Fight against Global Warming* report, published in 2007. As Nisbet explains, the report "was intended as a blueprint to guide the investment strategies of the sponsoring foundations as well as the broader philanthropic community" (Nisbet 2011, 33). For Petra Bartosiewicz and Marissa Miley, it "served as a catalyst for an unprecedented outpouring of funding on energy and climate issues" (Bartosiewicz and Miley 2013, 30).

The *Design to Win* report insists on foundations' comparative advantage over politicians who "are fixated on the next election" and corporate CEOs who "are focused on next quarters' numbers". Philanthropists, it explains, "have longer time horizons and can tolerate more risk". They "have a strong tradition of filling gaps, spurring step-changes in technology and pursuing programming that transcends both national boundaries and economic sectors. Such capacities are exactly what are needed to tackle global warming" (California Environmental Associates 2007, 5).

In addition to highlighting foundations' comparative advantages, the report also sets out a clear reductions target and identifies a series of priority areas for philanthropic engagement. So as to reach a 30-gigatonne emissions reduction by

2030, the report suggests concentrating philanthropic efforts on the regions with the highest mitigation potential: the United States, the European Union, China and India (California Environmental Associates 2007, 6). In all regions, the authors call for the establishment of cap-and-trade systems, which, they believe, "will help spark innovation and the clean technology markets needed to prevail in the long term" (California Environmental Associates 2007, 6). The authors also encourage foundations to focus their efforts on a limited number of sectors: power (through the development of solar, wind and carbon capture and storage [CCS]), industry, buildings/construction, transportation (through new standards and technologies) and forestry (through an international market for carbon off-sets) (California Environmental Associates 2007, 7).[5] They calculate that in addition to the estimated USD 200 million already invested by foundations in the climate field, an extra USD 600 million is required annually to achieve the 2030 target.

For these carefully selected sectors and regions, the authors recommend a "three-part menu of investments": "[supporting] existing NGOs with deep knowledge of local conditions and needed strategies; cultivate new organizations where necessary"; "[creating] nation-specific expertise to facilitate grant making"; and "[building] International Best Practice Centers for critical 'don't lose' sectors to accelerate the diffusion of knowledge and innovation, either by establishing new institutions or linking existing organizations in loose networks" (California Environmental Associates 2007, 8–9). In line with this mathematical framing of the climate problem was a mathematical approach to philanthropic grant-making mirroring the Energy Foundation's strategic approach.

The *Design to Win* report directly inspired a group of large liberal foundations – the Hewlett, Packard and McKnight foundations – to launch a new re-granting or pass-through foundation in 2008: the ClimateWorks Foundation (CW). Through initial pledged funding of USD 515 million, CW's purpose was to coordinate international actions so as to reach the targets laid out in the *Design to Win* report. CW funded and helped coordinate a series of regional/national re-granting foundations and sector-specific "best practice networks" (Spero 2010, 21). Bringing together policy experts and analysts, "best practice networks" were set with the task of compiling existing best policy options and promoting them in high-potential regions and sectors (ClimateWorks 2011, 12).

The original CW regional re-granting network was made up of the European Climate Foundation (ECF, launched in 2008), the Energy Foundation and the Energy Foundation China (created in 1999). In addition to making grants, they were all operating foundations, carrying out a range of awareness-raising, capacity-building, convening, lobbying and research activities. In 2009, the network was expanded to include the Climate and Land Use Alliance (CLUA) and the India-based Shakti Sustainable Energy Foundation. A Latin America Regional Climate Initiative (LARCI) was launched in 2012. Each regional foundation or initiative receives core funding from the CW and various allied foundations and redistributes all or part of the funds to local or regional NGOs and projects. The overwhelming majority of regional foundations' core funders form part of the same group of strategic and focused foundations that directly fund the CW Foundation and/or abide by the *Design to Win* strategy. As one CW representative told me, "ClimateWorks acted as the organiser, the headquarters of the system."[6]

## Foundations in Copenhagen

The months leading up to the Copenhagen climate conference witnessed a scaling-up of foundation engagement in the international climate negotiations. Although the ClimateWorks Foundation and network had a global outlook, its original approach was centred on regional or national policy actions and corporate initiatives, rather than the international climate negotiations. Soon after its creation, however, the prospect of a global, legally binding deal in Copenhagen led CW and the foundations associated with it to actively engage in the UNFCCC space. In particular, the pre-Copenhagen period was characterised by the launch of two large-scale foundation-backed initiatives: the Global Call for Climate Action (GCCA) and the ClimateWorks-backed Project Catalyst (PC). Foundations associated with CW and the *Design to Win* strategy were actively involved in both initiatives.

### *Influencing the negotiations through communications*

With an overall budget of USD 6.8 million – over 95% of which came from foundation funding – the GCCA was undoubtedly the most well-funded global climate awareness-raising campaign of 2009. Launched in the run-up to Copenhagen (2008), the GCCA's goal was to "mobilize citizens and galvanize public opinion in support of urgent climate action".[7] Bringing together over 170 NGOs, it was grounded on the idea that by joining forces around a well-oiled communications strategy and generating public momentum, non-state actors could get decision-makers to reach a fair, ambitious and legally binding agreement on climate change.

With a total contribution of USD 5 million in 2009, the Oak Foundation was by far the GCCA's main financial backer (the Sea Change Foundation coming second with USD 1.5 million). The Oak Foundation is without doubt the most active European-based foundation in the climate field. Given the origins of its founders and having also funded projects in the United States, it has the characteristic of being well connected within both European and North American funder circles. As was previously highlighted, it formed part of the handful of foundations that co-funded the *Design to Win* report in 2006. Given its strong presence in Europe, it played a major role in setting up CW's European partner foundation, the ECF in 2008 (Hughes 2008, 42).

While clearly situating itself within the liberal tradition, unlike most foundations associated with the *Design to Win* strategy, Oak values both policy work *and* capacity building. Capacity building – especially through support to NGOs – is regarded as essential to create the necessary political momentum. Furthermore, it also believed, from a very early stage, in the need to actively engage in and support the UNFCCC process. This clearly sets it apart from Hal Harvey's (ClimateWorks

CEO) more focused, national/regional and policy-centred outlook. As we shall see, Oak's more "holistic" approach to policy change had a major influence on the ClimateWorks strategy in the post-Copenhagen period.

### An elitist approach to climate diplomacy

Officially launched in May 2008 by ClimateWorks, Project Catalyst's (PC) stated purpose was "to provide analytical and policy support for the UNFCCC negotiations on a post-Kyoto international climate agreement" (Project Catalyst 2009a). Formally headed by Andreas Merkl (ClimateWorks) and coordinated by a small group of well-connected individuals with robust experience and expertise in the climate field (including representatives from the European ECF and the McKinsey consultancy firm, which was granted USD 17 million for its work on PC), PC was intended as a platform for leading climate change specialists, advocates, negotiators, envoys and ministers from around the world "to identify and estimate the costs of country-specific carbon abatement programs and to develop a financial framework for the carbon trading mechanism that would be used to cover some of the costs of these programs" (Hewlett Foundation 2009). In this respect, while signalling CW's recognition of the need to engage in the UNFCCC process and reach a global agreement, PC adopted a very elitist approach to international climate diplomacy – an approach that was grounded on the idea that the climate crisis could be solved by assembling the right people in the same room and helping them to cooperate through the provision of data and analytics. Unlike GCCA, the priority was not communication, outreach or mobilisation.

The PC team set up an informal network of approximately 150 climate negotiators, senior government officials, representatives from multilateral institutions, business executives and leading experts from over thirty countries. They were divided up into six working groups: abatement, adaptation, technology, forestry, climate-compatible growth plans and finance. McKinsey provided analytical support to each of the working groups. Through these working groups and PC more generally, the overall idea was "to provide a forum where key participants in the global discussions can informally interact, conduct analyses, jointly problem solve, and contribute ideas and proposals to the formal UNFCCC process" (ClimateWorks Foundation 2009). At its March 2009 Washington symposium, PC assembled representatives from governments,[8] think tanks and independent research organisations,[9] intergovernmental organisations (World Bank, OECD, UNEP), the UNFCCC secretariat, the business community,[10] the finance and banking sector,[11] academia,[12] large environmental NGOs and think tanks[13] and of course foundations.[14]

On the back of the symposium, PC produced a series of thematic papers and a synthesis briefing paper offering elements for a potential agreement (Project Catalyst 2009b). In line with the "building blocks" approach, the synthesis paper clearly stresses the need for policies to "create the necessary incentives and mandates" for the private sector to shift towards a low-carbon economy. According to Project Catalyst, the agreement's primary function should be to "help sustain action and ratchet up ambition over time and through political cycles" (Project Catalyst 2009b, 7). The PC team felt that in order to get countries to make the required efforts, it was necessary to set a global objective and timeline. As Andreas Merkl explains, "there's no combination of domestic and bilateral agreements that could enable this to happen. It requires a global agreement" (Hewlett Foundation 2009).

According to PC, a successful Copenhagen agreement subsequently hinged on six core elements: a long-term goal of limiting global emissions to 20Gt (or less) by 2050; developed country commitments to reduce emissions to 25%–40% below 1990 levels by 2020; developing country commitments to enact "climate-compatible growth plans"; technology innovation and deployment through various policy incentives; a dramatic scaling-up of the finance and the carbon market system in order to fund adaptation and mitigation efforts; and finally, an enduring yet flexible institutional architecture.[15]

During COP15, PC continued to be active through public events and behind the scenes activities. The fact that they were not registered as observers but through national delegations (these included Papua New Guinea, Guinea-Bissau, The Netherlands and Ghana) granted them privileged access to negotiators and government officials.

When it comes to evaluating PC's work in the run-up to and during the COP, it would appear that those involved did exert a certain level of influence on the negotiation process. As one participant in PC explains,

> There are lots and lots of ideas that emerged out of the Project Catalyst process that you could put your finger on and say that is where Project Catalyst came up with this idea – ideas shared with negotiators, with the Danish Presidency. The 100 billion [financial package], low-carbon growth plans, the ratchet mechanism [. . .] There are a number of others [. . .] The deep understanding that we could only get there if we got developing countries to carry the bulk of the mitigation challenge. Project Catalyst supported the Danish government in creating the famous Danish text.[16]

According to another former PC team member,

> Project Catalyst created a set of analytics that was pretty influential, generating a bit of "shared understanding" especially of a core "deal" around mitigation and finance. Especially the climate finance work influenced the Copenhagen outcome and post-Copenhagen finance decisions (100 billion number, creating a Green Climate Fund).[17]

While both GCCA and PC were supported by foundations associated with the *Design to Win* strategy, they point to differing understandings of how to approach the international climate negotiations. On the one hand, the Oak-funded GCCA believes in the possibility of achieving a fair, ambitious and legally binding agreement and believes that this can be achieved through well-coordinated communications campaigns and by building up the capacities of non-state actors. On the other hand, Project Catalyst steers away from the top-down approach and focuses its efforts on getting policy and business elites to commit to an ambitious long-term goal and to embark on low-carbon pathways. The Copenhagen COP's failure to deliver an agreement highlighted the limits of both approaches. As we will see in the following pages, foundations would learn the lessons from Copenhagen and come up with a new strategy – the IPPI – effectively combining elements from both the GCCA and PC approaches.

## COP21: learning the lessons from COP15

Following the Copenhagen collapse, many foundations proceeded to reassess their involvement in the climate field – and particularly in the international climate field. Copenhagen was, as the Oak Foundation puts it, a "reality check" for foundations and NGOs (Oak Foundation 2011). While they did not purely and simply abandon the climate field, many foundations drastically downsized their climate portfolios and programmes. Following an initial period of disillusionment and despair, some, within the climate funders community, attempted to make sense of *what* had happened and *why* it had happened the way it had. Having done this, a group of foundations proceeded to devise new strategies to secure a new climate regime for the post-2020 period. As we will see ahead, within the ClimateWorks community in particular, this gave rise to renewed engagement during the 2011–2015 period.

In 2011 the ClimateWorks Foundation, its funders, regional re-granting foundations, best practice networks and partners initiated a network-wide consultation to "reshape and guide the Network's efforts for the next 10 years" (ECF 2011b, 2). The Oak Foundation, which as we saw had supported the *Design to Win* report and heavily funded the GCCA, played a proactive role in this exercise. It pushed for a reorganisation of the CW network. In particular, the CW Foundation was expected to play more a coordinating and supportive role, and regional foundations were encouraged to have greater grant-making and strategic oversight. The ClimateWorks Foundation and network were also expected to "share strategies and knowledge more widely, and support more coordination among funders".[18] The idea was now to encourage foundations to align their grant-making strategies but without necessarily channelling their funds through the ClimateWorks Foundation. The hope was of broadening the climate funder community by enabling funders to align their strategies and "pick and choose" their preferred projects and initiatives. As one foundation representative explains, the ClimateWorks Foundation became "more of a coordinator rather than a direct implementer".[19]

### The European Climate Foundation's leadership role

Given its close ties to the Oak Foundation and previous involvement in PC and European and international climate diplomacy more broadly, the ECF took on a leadership role in the network's international climate diplomacy activities. The ECF felt that reaching an international climate agreement was essential for ambitious national climate action. The international climate regime, they argued, generates "momentum and confidence", contributes to "lowering financial and knowledge barriers" and enhances "transparency and accountability to domestic and international audiences" (ECF 2011a, 6). In other words, the cumulative success of domestic climate policies is contingent upon a favourable international environment (ECF 2011a, 3). "Without progress", writes the ECF, "the international arena can exert strong negative influence on domestic action. Competitiveness and carbon leakage concerns continue to matter, as do arguments about the futility of individual countries' efforts in the fact of others' inaction" (ECF 2011a, 3).

The ECF's belief in the combined virtues of bottom-up action and an overarching framework is consistent with the PC approach described earlier. The key difference relates to the ECF's suggested strategy in order to reach a climate agreement that reflects this understanding. According to the ECF, PC's – and through it ClimateWorks' – failure in Copenhagen derives from an excessively narrow and elitist approach to policy change, and a failure to harness the complexity and subtleties of international climate diplomacy. In particular, some within the ECF felt that PC was "too focused on big polluters" and that "smaller countries, vulnerable countries, ones that had a voice in Copenhagen, were not sufficiently included in the consultation process." Additionally, PC drew on a very superficial and narrow assessment of countries' respective priorities and interests. As one former ECF member of the PC team explains,

> [PC] did not really understand the North South politics as the mindset was too "pragmatic", thinking in terms of a deal of mitigation against money. It could not see the moral dimension, it did not understand the relevance of symbolic politics (like the firewall [division between Annex 1 and non-Annex 1 countries]). It was Northern at its core and therefore could not cross the North-South barrier, which would have been essential for success in creating a shared understanding of the deal.[20]

Furthermore, according to ECF, PC did not sufficiently account for the fact that "climate diplomacy has shifted from a relatively narrow focus on the UNFCCC process, to a more complex and wider discipline that now engages new constituencies and embraces broader geopolitical discussions" (Mabey, Gallagher and Born 2013, 6). By focusing almost exclusively on policy development and deployment,[21] PC underestimated the impacts of broader political factors and the role of non-state actors and the media. The initiative failed to recognise that change happens "in rather oblique and non-linear ways" and that there is a "need to pay more attention to politics and even to the polity" (Meier 2015). Subsequently, the CW network must

> move society as a whole along the political path to economic change across the world, acting to incentivize sustainable decisions and close-off the many diversions which will be both accidentally and consciously explored, slowing down progress and threatening our vitally important 2020 goals.
>
> (ECF 2011b, 5)

In effect, the ECF challenged the traditional liberal philanthropic idea that providing policy elites with impartial and scientifically backed evidence inexorably brought about transformative change. The ECF's call for greater attention to politics does not involve – at least in appearance – taking sides but rather actively engaging in the political arena through the provision of "aspirational narratives" to "all strata of society". It is grounded in the idea that "every effort to change public policy is political" (Teles and Schmitt 2011, 16). Messaging and communication subsequently become core elements of any effort to influence the policy process. Adequately communicating facts and ideas becomes just as important as producing them. The ECF's insistence on the need for "aspirational narratives" shares a lot in common with the GCCA's communications-centred and capacity-building approach. In terms of grant-making, this means coming to terms with the fact that success in the climate field requires foundations to simultaneously invest in a variety of strategies without guaranteed or easily quantifiable results.

## The International Policies and Politics Initiative (IPPI)

The Durban COP's encouraging outcome and the international community's commitment to reaching a global agreement in 2015 validated the strategy laid out by the ECF for the post-Copenhagen context. In close collaboration with Third Generation Environmentalism (E3G), the WRI and the Institut du Développement Durable et des Relations Internationales (IDDRI), among others, the ECF consulted with a variety of stakeholders over the course of 2012, including negotiators, civil society representatives and members of the foundation community. In addition to getting as many actors involved as possible, the plan was to reengage funders in the international climate space. A priority became providing funders with "a platform for philanthropic cooperation [. . .] to catalyse greater ambition on climate change by working at the intersection of national and international decision-making" (ECF 2013, 26). Early supporters of the ECF initiative include the Oak, Mercator and ClimateWorks foundations as well as the UK-based CIFF.

Having drummed up support from within the philanthropic and wider climate communities, ECF went on to launch the IPPI in April 2013. Its stated purpose was to "highlight opportunities for philanthropic collaboration, joint strategy development, resource pooling, and grant-making alignments in the arena of international policies and politics of climate change" (ECF 2014, 26). The IPPI was far more than just a platform for foundations to devise common strategies. It served as an instrument to catalyse/orient funding – either through a pooled IPPI fund or through the alignment of foundation grants with the IPPI strategy – towards a predetermined strategy, a strategy that reflected the core principles laid out by the ECF in the post-COP15 context.

While formally linked to the ECF, the IPPI platform brought together a variety of stakeholders from within the international climate community: foundation representatives, climate experts, business and NGO representatives, and negotiators. Throughout the pre-COP21 period, the IPPI team – headed by Jennifer Morgan, formerly of the WRI – orchestrated a three-part strategy consisting in: (1) a series of targeted interventions in national and international arenas to boost domestic climate action; (2) a campaign over the course of 2015 to build up momentum in the lead-up to the Paris "global moment"; and (3) the promotion of "a strong climate regime with binding elements in the second half of the decade, to ensure accelerated and coordinated action beyond 2020" (ECF 2011a, 3).

When it came to strengthening domestic action and mitigation pledges – through the intended nationally determined contributions (INDC) – the IPPI pushed through and co-funded a variety of projects aimed at increasing ambition. In particular, it promoted the "green growth narrative" through the advancement of best practices and stakeholder dialogue, as well as outreach and communication to business, economic and finance players in developed and emerging economies (Bowen and Fankhauser 2011). The IPPI was also involved in initiatives aimed at tracking and assessing national mitigation and finance actions, and building scenarios on what would be required to keep the global temperature increase below 2°C. Their purpose was as much about evaluating current efforts and pledges as building up momentum for action. It was about showing how, given the right policies, an ambitious long-term temperature target could still be achieved (even if this meant "moving the goalposts" along the way through "negative emissions"). Examples of IPPI-backed projects include the Open Climate Network–Climate Action Tracker joint initiative whose purpose was to produce an actionable assessment of the post-2020 GHG targets of eight top-emitting countries (Brazil, China, EU, India, Indonesia, Japan, Mexico and the United States). Another example is the Deep Decarbonization Pathways Project (DDPP) – co-funded by IPPI, the Gross Family Foundation, CIFF and the Deutsche Gesellschaft für Internationale Zusammenarbeit (GIZ) and co-coordinated by IDDRI and the Sustainable Development Solutions Network (SDSN).

When it comes to generating momentum for a "global moment" in Paris, members of the climate community affiliated with the IPPI orchestrated an international communications strategy that consisted in simultaneously highlighting the dangers of unmitigated climate change – by drawing on the climate science – and emphasising the economic benefits of immediate and decisive action. The idea was to "shift the public narrative around the low-carbon transition from costs and barriers to challenges and opportunities" (ECF 2014, 30). To do so, communication experts organised collective and personalised media training sessions to assist various stakeholders in their media-related activities – and in the process align and coordinate their messages. Through a loose platform, the Global Strategic Communications Council (GSCC) communications specialists delivered key messages in the climate and energy fields at both the international and national levels. Given their role in raising public awareness on the climate issue, carefully selected NGOs also benefited from IPPI support – either in kind or through strategic assistance.

When it comes to communications around the climate science, IPPI-affiliated communications experts worked closely with the IPCC to produce "digestible summaries", briefing notes, "rebuttal lines" and coordinated press interviews upon the release of the Fifth Assessment Report (AR5) in 2014 (ECF 2015). The issue for the IPPI team was making sure that the scientific community not only highlighted the dangers of unmitigated climate change but also did not undermine their efforts to promote an optimistic discourse on the feasibility of a 1.5–2°C target. During the COP21, this meant preventing members of the scientific community from undermining the progress of the negotiations.

### Climate Briefing Service: orchestrating and controlling the climate narrative

So as to more efficiently "shape the 'realm of discourse'" and better coordinate the actions and messages of a wider range of climate actors – rather than just the ECF grantees – the IPPI team, in particular through the efforts of Jennifer Morgan and Liz Gallagher, launched the Climate Briefing Service (CBS) in late 2014 (Mabey 2014). With support from CIFF, ClimateWorks, the Villum Foundation, the Hewlett Foundation, the Oak Foundation and Avaaz, the CBS's purpose was to provide real-time and ready-to-use information to selected members of the climate community and "[coordinate] voices at national and international levels to help shape the national offers as they are being drafted and the thinking around the international agreement".[22] Echoing the work of the GCCA, it also acted as a global political and communications hub in support of the overall IPPI strategy, bringing together various representatives from the international climate community (environmental and development NGOs, climate networks, campaign groups, think tanks, research organisations, foundations). Members of this "global team" regularly took part in conference calls, strategy sessions, workshops and conferences to share views, information and intelligence on policy-related issues, and collectively establish strategic priorities.

These elements of continuity notwithstanding, three important aspects distinguish the CBS from the GCCA. First of all, whereas the GCCA called for a top-down, legally binding agreement, the CBS supports a bottom-up approach involving voluntary, nationally determined mitigation commitments, an overarching long-term goal and a framework to track progress. Secondly, whereas the GCCA pushed its partners to adopt, publicise and rally behind a common brand – TckTckTck – the CBS and IPPI adopted a behind-the-scenes, unbranded approach, supplying partners with information and suggested key messaging but without ever appearing as the source of that information and messaging.[23] CBS briefing recipients were systematically reminded that they were "confidential and not for public circulation". Thirdly and finally, unlike the GCCA's open approach, the CBS is an invitation-only platform where individuals were asked to join on the basis of their potential contribution to the overarching strategy.

### Involvement in the formal negotiations process

While effective communications and campaigning fit into IPPI's holistic approach to climate diplomacy, the IPPI was also actively involved in the formal UNFCCC process. Through the work of the Agreement on Climate Transformation 2015 (ACT2015) consortium, IPPI-affiliated actors promoted a bottom-up approach centred on national voluntary commitments rather than agreed and legally binding international targets. Launched in early 2014 and coordinated by the World Resources Institute (WRI), ACT2015 presents itself as

> a consortium of the world's top climate experts from developing and developed countries that has joined together to catalyse discussion and build momentum toward reaching a global climate agreement at the forthcoming UN Framework Convention on Climate Change (UNFCCC) summit in December 2015.[24]

In particular, the ACT2015 consortium pushed for the inclusion of two long-term goals: one for mitigation and one for adaptation. Beyond committing countries, the long-term goal on mitigation "[sends] a clear signal to policy makers, businesses, investors, and the public that the low-carbon climate-resilient economy is inevitable" (Morgan, Dagnet and Tirpak 2014, 2). In line with the bottom-up approach centred on national commitments rather than agreed international targets, the consortium called for the inclusion of a provision to regularly update commitments through five-year improvement cycles in three policy areas: mitigation, adaptation and support (capacity building, finance, technology transfer and cooperation). And finally, they called for a set of robust transparency and accountability provisions "so that governments, companies, and the public have a clear understanding of what countries are doing to shift their economies, build resilience, and, in the case of developed countries, provide support to poorer countries" (Morgan et al. 2014, 5).

In an attempt to address the "Northern bias" of 2009, the IPPI sought to better account for Southern positions and involve representatives from the Global South. It funded and facilitated the launch of Southern-based think tanks with the aim of mobilising developing country actors and offering a "Southern perspective" on the climate question. In 2013, for instance, the IPPI backed the creation of the Costa Rica based Nivela, whose mission is to "challenge conventional wisdom on development using multidisciplinary analysis and reflections from the ground to spur changes in how environmental, climate and socio-economic goals are integrated in [developing countries'] pursuit of prosperity".[25]

Within the IPPI network – and consequently the CBS global team – there were individuals with close working relations with Southern negotiators and governments. Names include Bill Hare, former lead author for the IPCC and current CEO and founder of Climate Analytics, and Farhana Yamin, climate and development law and policy expert who had actively contributed, in the post-COP15 context, to the development of progressive coalitions in international negotiations, and in particular the Cartagena Dialogue for Progressive Action.

Throughout 2015 and during the Paris conference itself, the IPPI made a series of grants to support the participation of developing countries' (Peru, South Africa, among others) and developing country groupings' (LDCs, Association of Latin America and the Caribbean) participation in the climate negotiations.[26] Interestingly, ClimateWorks made a $175,000 grant to Independent Diplomat, a non-profit diplomatic advisory group, to assist the Republic of Marshall Islands in developing its strategy and communications in the negotiations.[27] During the Paris conference, the Marshall Islands spearheaded the "High Ambition Coalition", a loose grouping of Northern and Southern countries that successfully pushed through the Paris Agreement (Goodell 2016).

## Conclusion: the elephant in the room?

The adoption on the evening of December 12, 2015, of the Paris Agreement was presented as a resounding victory for international diplomacy. It was also a victory for the IPPI and the philanthropic foundations that were associated with it. By and large, the final agreement reflects many of IPPI's ideas and views: five-year cycles to ratchet up commitments, a long-term temperature goal, a framework for reporting and no binding emissions targets. Beyond the agreement's content, the IPPI network's sophisticated approach to climate diplomacy – through its orchestration of actions and interventions both inside and outside the negotiation space – greatly contributed to create the conditions for an international agreement in Paris.

Interestingly and despite their proactive role in the lead-up to Paris, many of the foundations and foundation initiatives presented in this chapter are conspicuously absent from the social science literature on international climate politics. Up to now, none of the prominent academic publications on civil society engagement have looked into philanthropic foundations' role in the international climate debate. This is surprising given the history and level of philanthropic involvement and the fact that, far from limiting themselves to an auxiliary role, foundations are genuine stakeholders in the international climate debate. It is also regrettable in view of the important questions that their involvement raises. These relate to long-standing debates on foundations' legitimacy and accountability, as well as to debates on the limits of the strategic approach to philanthropy.

## Notes

1 As we see in de Moor, Morena and Comby (this volume), this was an important part of the IPPI strategy.
2 Executive secretary of the UNFCCC.
3 http://www.centre-francais-fondations.org/cercles-themes/themes-1/climat/cop-21/cop-21-en (accessed April 5, 2016).
4 The delegation included the CGBD programme manager, three foundation representatives – Energy Foundation, Global GreenGrants Fund – and a foundation consultant on climate and energy issues.

5  The approach developed in the report largely echoes the seminal research by a group of Princeton University academics on "wedges" for $CO_2$ reduction (commonly referred to as the Princeton wedges).

6  Interview with author.

7  http://tcktcktck.org/about/ (accessed February 4, 2016).

8  Ghana, Brazil, Japan, Australia, Ireland, Denmark, Korea, Norway, Mexico, United Kingdom, Spain, Guyana, China, France, Poland, the European Commission, Russia, United States and Tanzania.

9  The Brookings Institution, The Climate Group, Potsdam Institute for Climate Impact Research, Pew Center on Climate Change, Stockholm Environmental Institute, E3G and IIED.

10  Toyota, SunEdison, Shell, Tata BP Solar, Rio Tinto, WBCSD and World Economic Forum.

11  Deutsche Bank, C-Quest Capital, Merrill Lynch and International Finance Corporation.

12  Renmin University, Cornell University, Tsinghua University and LSE.

13  NRDC, WWF, The Nature Conservancy and WRI.

14  ClimateWorks Foundation, European Climate Foundation, Hewlett Foundation, Packard Foundation, McKnight Foundation, Energy Foundation and Summit Foundation.

15  The paper was presented on June 6 at a side event organised at the Bonn climate negotiations. Speakers included Professor Tom Heller (Stanford University, ex-co-chair of the IPCC) and Dr Bert Metz (fellow at the European Climate Foundation and ex-co-chair of the IPCC).

16  The interviewee is referring here to an initiative by the Danish government to produce a proposal for the outcome of COP15 "on the basis of which the presidency could engage in bilateral negotiations at the level of heads of state" (Meilstrup 2010, 124–125).

17  Email exchange with author.

18  http://www.climateworks.org/about-us/our-history/ (accessed November 3, 2015).

19  Interview with author.

20  Email exchange with author.

21  By targeting the regulators and policy elites who are responsible for setting the rules for industry, transport, appliances, building and natural resource use.

22  https://ciff.org/grant-portfolio/climate-briefing-service (accessed September 9, 2015).

23  One only needs to go on the CBS website to get a sense of its unbranded communications approach. http://www.cbs-climate.org.

24  About ACT 2015.pdf.

25  http://www.nivela.org/updates/a-brief-introduction-to-nivela/en (accessed February 9, 2016).

26  http://www.climateworks.org/portfolios/grants-database (accessed April 4, 2016).

27  Ibid.

## Bibliography

Agrawala, Shardul. "Structural and process history of the Intergovernmental Panel on Climate Change." *Climatic Change* 39 (1998): 621–642.

Ames, Edward. "Philanthropy and the environmental movement in the United States." *The Environmentalist* 1 (1981): 9–14.

Anheier, Helmut K., and Regina List. *A Dictionary of Civil Society, Philanthropy and the Non-Profit Sector*. London: Routledge, 2005.

Barker, Michael. "The liberal foundations of environmentalism: Revisiting the Rockefeller-Ford connection." *Capitalism Nature Socialism* 19, no. 2 (2008): 15–42.

Bartosiewicz, Petra, and Marissa Miley. *The Too Polite Revolution: Why the Recent Campaign to Pass Comprehensive Climate Legislation in the United States Failed*. 2013. https://www.scholarsstrategynetwork.org/sites/default/files/rff_final_report_bartosiewicz_miley.pdf.

Bernstein, Steven. "Liberal environmentalism and global environmental governance." *Global Environmental Politics* 2, no. 3 (2002): 1–16.

Brest, Paul, and Hal Harvey. *Money Well Spent: A Strategic Plan for Smart Philanthropy*. New York: Bloomberg Press, 2008.

Brulle, Robert J., and Craig Jenkins. "Foundations and the environmental movement: Priorities, strategies and impact." In *Foundations for Social Change: Critical Perspectives on Philanthropy and Popular Movements*, by Daniel Faber and Debra McCarthy, 151–173. Lanham, NJ: Rowman & Littlefield, 2005.

California Environmental Associates. "Design to Win: Philanthropy's Role in the Fight against Global Warming." *ClimateWorks*. August 2007. http://www.climateworks.org/wp-content/uploads/2015/02/design_to_win_final_8_31_07.pdf (accessed October 4, 2015).

ClimateWorks. *2011 Annual Report*. Annual Report, San Francisco: ClimateWorks Foundation, 2011.

ClimateWorks Foundation. *The Business Case for a Strong Global Deal*. Copenhagen: Copenhagen Climate Council, 2009.

Dowie, Mark. *American Foundations: An Investigative History*. Cambridge, MA: MIT Press, 2001.

ECF. *Annual Report 2012*. The Hague: European Climate Foundation, 2013.

ECF. *Annual Report 2013*. The Hague: European Climate Foundation, 2014.

ECF. *Annual Report 2014*. The Hague: European Climate Foundation, 2015.

ECF. *The Paris Agreement on Climate Change: A Perspective on the Implications for the Role of Philanthropy*. The Hague: European Climate Foundation, 2016.

ECF. *Vision 2020: International Climate Diplomacy*. The Hague: European Climate Foundation, 2011a.

ECF. *Vision 2020: A Synthesis Document on the Strategic Input of the ECF to the V2020 Process*. The Hague: European Climate Foundation, 2011b.

Energy Foundation. *10 (Energy Foundation 2000 Annual Report)*. Annual Report, San Francisco: Energy Foundation, 2001.

Faber, Daniel, and Debra McCarthy. *Foundations for Social Change: Critical Perspectives on Philanthropy and Popular Movements*. Lanham, NJ: Rowman & Littlefield, 2005.

Goodell, Jeff. *Will the Paris Climate Deal Save the World?* January 13, 2016. http://www.rollingstone.com/politics/news/will-the-paris-climate-deal-save-the-world-20160113?page=6 (accessed January 16, 2016).

Hemphill, Bonnie. *Funding the Next Chapter of the Climate Movement*. New Haven, CT: Yale School of Forestry & Environmental Studies, 2013.

Hewlett Foundation. *What's Next in the Battle against Climate Change*. July 1, 2009. http://www.hewlett.org/newsroom/news/whats-next-battle-against-climate-change (accessed May 5, 2016).

Hughes, Róisín. "Climate philanthropy in Europe: Raising the bar." *Effect*, Spring 2008: 42–43.

Johnson, Erik W., and Scott Frickel. "Ecological threat and the founding of U.S. national environmental movement organizations, 1962–1998." *Social Problems* 58, no. 3 (2011): 305–329.

Katz, Stanley N. "What does it mean to say that philanthropy is 'effective'? The philanthropists' new clothes." *Proceedings of the American Philosophical Society* 149, no. 2 (2005): 123–131.

Kimble, Melinda. *Changing Climates: Philanthropy, Environmental Policy, and Climate Change.* Global Philanthropy Issue Brief, Center for Public & Nonprofit Leadership, Georgetown University, Washington: Georgetown University, 2012: 22.

Mabey, Nick. "E3G 10th Anniversary Speech." *E3G.* July 2, 2014. http://e3g.org/docs/ E3G_10th_Anniversary_speech_Nick_Mabeyv2.pdf (accessed September 8, 2015).

Mabey, Nick, Liz Gallagher, and Camilla Born. *Understanding Climate Diplomacy: Building Diplomatic Capacity and Systems to Avoid Dangerous Climate Change.* London: E3G, 2013.

Medina, Sonia. "Presentation – Practical approach to climate finance: View from the donors (CIFF's experience)." *Generalitat de Catalunya.* May 28, 2015. http://canviclimatic. gencat.cat/web/.content/home/politiques/acords_internacionals/conferencies_de_les_ parts__cop/COP21_Paris/Climate-finance-CExpo_CIFF_Sonia-Medina.pdf (accessed April 9, 2016).

Meier, Johannes. *Response to "Strategic Philanthropy and Its Discontents".* April 27, 2015. http://ssir.org/up_for_debate/strategic_philanthropy_and_its_discontents/meier (accessed March 9, 2016).

Meilstrup, Per. "The runaway summit: The background story of the Danish Presidency of COP15, the UN climate change conference." *Danish Foreign Policy Yearbook 2010* (2010): 113–135.

Morena, Edouard. *The Price of Climate Action: Philanthropic Foundations in the International Climate Debate.* Basingstoke: Palgrave Macmillan, 2016.

Morgan, Jennifer, Yamide Dagnet, and Dennis Tirpak. *Elements and Ideas for the 2015 Paris Agreement.* Washington, DC: Agreement for Climate Transformation 2015 (ACT 2015), 2014.

Nisbet, Matthew. *ClimateShift: Clear Vision for the Next Decade of Public Debate.* School of Communication, American University, Washington DC: American University, 2011.

Oak Foundation. *2010 Annual Report.* Annual Report, Oak Foundation, 2011.

Project Catalyst. *Overview.* 2009a. https://web.archive.org/web/20091103064847/http:// www.project-catalyst.info/index.php?option=com_content&view=article&id=51&Ite mid=59 (accessed May 5, 2016).

Project Catalyst. *Towards a Global Climate Agreement.* Synthesis Briefing Paper, 2009b.

Randazzo, Mark, Paige Brown, Marilena Vrana, Rachel Leon, Robin Millington, Mathilde Mansoz, and Nicolas Krausz. "Invitation to Join COP21 Funders Initiative." *EDGE Funders.* July 2015. http://www.edgefunders.org/wp-content/uploads/2015/07/COP- 21-Funders-Initiative.pdf (accessed November 15, 2015).

Rimel, Rebecca. "Strategic philanthropy: Pew's approach to matching needs with resources." *Health Affairs* 18, no. 3 (1999): 228–233.

Rockefeller Brothers Fund. *Annual Report 1988.* New York: The Rockefeller Brothers Fund, 1989.

Rockefeller Brothers Fund. *Annual Report 1993.* New York: The Rockefeller Brothers Fund, 1994.

Spero, Joan E. *The Global Role of U.S. Foundations.* Foundation Center, 2010.

Stiftung Mercator. *2012: Zahlen, Daten, Fakten.* Annual Report. Essen: Stiftung Mercator GmbH, 2013.

Teles, Steven, and Mark Schmitt. "The elusive craft of evaluating advocacy." *Stanford Social Innovation Review*, May 2011.

von Moltke, Konrad. *Turning up the Heat: Next Steps on Climate Change*. Pocantico paper N°1. New York: Rockefeller Brothers Fund, 1995.

Wei-Skiller, Jane. "The biggest foundation you've never heard of." *Alliance Magazine*, December 2012.

# 6 The partial climatisation of migration, security and conflict

## Lucile Maertens and Alice Baillat

### Introduction[1]

In March 2011, protests erupted in Damascus, Syria, followed by five years of civil war that is forcing millions of people to flee their country. Severe droughts during the years before the conflict challenged the livelihood of rural populations and led to forced displacements. Ill-equipped urban areas then received vulnerable populations that had been left without governmental support. In this fragile situation, climate disruptions contributed indirectly to the uprising, as Malm observed (2014, 31): "As for Syria, it is now common knowledge that the exceptional drought – and the Assad regime's utter failure to tackle it – loomed large in the mélange of miseries that finally made the country boil over." While the conflict in Darfur, Sudan, was once considered the prime illustration of a "climate conflict", multiple studies have now highlighted the contribution of global food crises and environmental degradation to the Arab Spring and the Syrian conflict.

In the immediate run-up to COP21, several developments contributed to attracting more attention towards the climate-security-migration nexus. For months, European countries had faced a major migrant and refugee crisis, as well as a surge in the activity of extreme rights groups. Two weeks before the conference, Paris was hit by a coordinated terrorist attack that directly affected the organisation of COP21. In this context, French president François Hollande's opening statements at the Leaders Event also stated that climate change would cause conflicts, migrations and threats to human security.

Set against this broad contextual backdrop, our chapter explores how migration, security and conflict issues – at that time probably the most acute issues covered by international media – entered the climate negotiations. It aims to assess both why and how political leaders, civil society members and experts aspired to include migration and conflict in the climate talks. Focusing on the political outcomes, it also evaluates the implications of and resistance to the merging of these meta-problems of contemporary international relations.

Empirically, the chapter provides a snapshot of the summit, based mainly on the discourse of political leaders and the content of the meeting's side events. While we do not purport to explore the negotiation process in detail, we aim to study the general framing of issues, including at the political level and in the scientific community and civil society. To do so, we examine statements by heads of state during the Leaders Event (available on the UNFCCC's website[2]) as examples of how migration and conflict are typically framed, vis-à-vis climate change. We also analyse the different drafts of the Paris Agreement to track the evolution of these issues in the negotiated text. Direct observation of the nego-tiations, of side events pertaining to migration, security and conflict, of on-site exhibitions and of events that were organised outside the blue zone complete the analysis. Finally, we present results of interviews conducted with key informers during and after COP21.

Our chapter is intended to fill both an empirical and theoretical gap. First, it brings new elements to an ongoing scholarly debate by focusing on the most recent climate summit. This complements Detraz and Betsill's (2009) work on security in the climate negotiations. It also provides new empirical examples on the discourses of climate security analysed by McDonald (2013) and von Lucke, Wellmann and Diez (2014), and of climate-induced migration examined by McAdam (2011) and Oels and Methmann (2015). Second, it uses the concept of climatisation to shed new light on the ways that migration, security and conflict are brought into the climate arena. Instead of focusing on how climate change has been constructed as a security issue – that is the "process of securitisation" (Buzan, Wæver and De Wilde 1998, Trombetta 2008, Rothe 2012), meaning that climate change should be tackled with security policies – rather we look at how migration, security and conflict are framed as issues relevant to the climate convention – namely the process of *climatisation*.

Derived from the concept of environmentalisation, seen as "the adoption of a generic environmental discourse by different social groups, as well as the concrete incorporation of environmental justifications to legitimate institutional, political and scientific practices" (Acselrad 2010, 103), the process of climatisation relies on the definition of a given issue as being relevant to climate policies. In the case of migration and security, climatisation is not a way that "new phenomena are being constructed and exposed to the public sphere", but rather that "old phenomena are renamed" (ibid.) as relevant to the climate field. In continuation of Oels's (2012) work on climatisation of the security field, this chapter analyses how migration, security and conflict were incorporated into COP21. It looks at how the climatisation of such issues participates in the globalisation of climate negotiations – that is to say, penetration of the climate arena by multiple global issues. The introduction of new issues can affect negotiations and thus deserves our attention. In the case of migration, security and conflict, we also highlight the tensions that arise when such meta-problems of international relations are attracted to the climate arena.

In this chapter we address four main issues. We begin by discussing the geneal-ogy of links between climate change, migration and conflict, and of their con-sideration within the previous COP meetings (first section). We show that the climatisation of migration, security and conflict constitutes a tool to dramatise and humanise climate change, while it also shines light on issues unrelated to climate change (second section). We then observe that in the climate debates of COP21, security and conflict were less climatised than was migration, and that a shift was apparent from human security towards conflict (third section). Finally, we show how resistance from actors, along with limitations inherent to the nature and organisation of the climate regime itself, acts as a barrier to the climatisation of migration, security and conflict (fourth section).

## Climate change as a security threat: from environmentalisation to climatisation

Throughout the 1970s and 1980s, concern grew about the relation between environment and security, starting with the first official mention of "environmental security" in the 1987 Brundtland Report *Our Common Future* (Barnett 2010, 125). In the United States, government agencies and the military conducted multiple research projects in the late 1980s, and in the aftermath of the Cold War, the environmental threat became a new enemy to justify military budgets (ibid.). After a temporary dip post-9/11, the 2000s saw renewed official attention to the possible links between climate change and security: researchers who formerly worked on environment and security shifted towards climate and security (Barnett 2013, Dalby 2014); the Pentagon published its first report on climate change and security (Schwartz and Randall 2003); and the Council of the European Union followed in 2008 (McAdam 2011), with the UN secretary general close behind in 2009. Two dominant narratives can be identified in those documents: (1) the role of climate change in causing conflicts, and (2) the threat that climate change poses to various dimensions of human security (food, health, etc.) (Trombetta 2008, Oels 2012, McDonald 2013, von Lucke et al. 2014). The security implications of climate change have also been discussed at the UN Security Council in 2007 and 2011 and in an Arria-Formula Meeting in 2013. While the secretary general has defined climate change as a "threat multiplier" (UNSG 2009), in 2011 he qualified it as "a threat to international peace and security".[3] Yet member states have been unable to reach a resolution on this, especially as the G77 refused placing the Security Council in charge of universal development issues, such as climate change (Maertens 2015a). Since then, multiple studies have examined the role of climate change in triggering conflicts and in threatening the daily livelihood of the most vulnerable populations.

The relationship between environment and migration also emerged in scientific and institutional arenas during the 1980s. While there is no universal definition of environmentally induced migration, the term usually pertains to any people who are forced to move, temporarily or permanently, within or beyond the borders of their country of origin, due to a sudden onset of disaster or gradual environmental degradation (Foresight 2011). There is also a strong link between human movement and security concerns, with migration being framed as both a consequence of environmentally related conflicts and as a trigger of future conflicts over natural resources (Gemenne 2011). However, there is little empirical evidence that migration triggered by environmental and climatic changes may lead directly to violent conflicts (Foresight 2011). The fact that climate-induced migration can have multiple causes is also becoming recognised, with the environment being just one among many other political, social and economic factors that can trigger migration (Mayer, Boas, Ewing, Baillat and Das 2013). Regardless, as climate change became widely perceived as a threat to global security since the 2000s, migration continued to be securitised as one of the main examples of climate risk (McAdam 2011). Alarmist scenarios have thus spread in climate debates, predicting that millions of "climate refugees" worldwide will destabilise international peace. However, this securitisation of climate-induced migration as a threat to national and international security has been criticised as counterproductive and xenophobic, leading to restrictive immigration policies in Western countries (Oels and Methmann 2015). Competing discourses then began to reframe climate-induced migration as a threat to *human* security – shifting attention to individuals, away from states – or in some cases, as an adaptation strategy that can help to reduce people's vulnerabilities (Bettini 2014). While migration and security issues continue to be discussed independently to some extent at climate conferences, they continue to be framed mainly as being interrelated, both within and beyond climate negotiations. It is thus relevant to handle them together in this chapter.

In the context of the United Nations Framework Convention for Climate Change (UNFCCC), migration, security and conflict were brought into the debates long before COP21. Specifically, discussions of climate and security have focused on a human security perspective. With few exceptions, the environmental security discourse (i.e. viewing the environment as a *threat* to human security) dominated the debate until 2009, compared to the environmental conflict discourse (i.e. viewing the environment as a *cause* of conflict) (Detraz and Betsill 2009). The UNDP report on human development has defined human security this way: "It means, first, safety from such chronic threats as hunger, disease and repression. And second, it means protection from sudden and hurtful disruptions in the patterns of daily life" (UNDP 1994, 23). Based on an apocalyptic notion of climate change as the enemy that humanity should oppose (Rothe 2012, 249), UNFCCC debates focused on how climate change would threaten the daily human life. This diverted attention to the vulnerabilities of developing countries, instead of highlighting threats to national security of the most developed countries (Oels 2012). Now, attention could be shifting towards the environmental conflict view, climate change being considered as a threat to national and international security instead of human security.

Attempts to put migration issues on the UNFCCC agenda (mainly by NGOs, experts and the most vulnerable states) are seen as "part of a clear process to invest the international debate with a greater sense of urgency" (Brown, Hammill and McLeman 2007, 1144). While early discussions of climate change emphasised non-human impacts (e.g. ecosystem disruption, species loss, resource degradation) that were somewhat abstract for public understanding, the climate refugee image embodies the "human face of climate change" and places people at the centre of the climate debates (Ollitrault 2010, Gemenne 2011). Migration issues officially entered into the negotiations with the Cancun Adaptation Framework. Parties are encouraged

> To enhance action on adaptation [. . .] by undertaking, inter alia [. . .] Measures to enhance understanding, coordination and cooperation with regard to climate change induced displacement, migration and planned relocation, where appropriate, at the national, regional and international levels.
>
> (UNFCCC 2010, 4)

Since the 2012 Doha decision that encouraged further understanding of how climate change affects human mobility, migration and displacement issues have been included in discussions of "loss and damage". This term refers to impacts that occur despite adaptation and mitigation efforts; the most vulnerable developing countries introduced it to climate debates, to address their fear that existing measures are insufficient to prevent extreme climate change impacts.[4]

## Sounding the alarm: migration and security as tools to attract attention

While climatising migration, security and conflict contributes to the dramatisation and humanisation of climate change, it also shines light on migration and security issues unrelated to climate change. This reciprocal instrumentalisation reveals the strategic dimension of discourses that associate climate change with migration and conflict.

### Dramatising and humanising climate change

As outlined earlier, the first mention of climate-induced migration in the climate debates was aimed at highlighting the urgency and scope of the climate challenge. Likewise, the framing of climate change as a threat to human and national security is an alarmist message that this serious phenomenon should be a global priority. During COP21, almost every head of state has described climate change as a "threat", "danger", "risk", "challenge" or an "urgent" matter. Similarly, many statements have portrayed climate change as life-threatening, with the potential to disrupt the livelihoods of vulnerable populations. For instance, the president of Guinea-Bissau called it one of the main concerns on the global agenda of human security,[5] while the president of Djibouti suggested that people will be unable to survive in East Africa and the Middle East if nothing is done about rising temperatures.[6]

Further, the climatisation of migration, security and conflict has been used during the summit to urge for a global response to climate change:

> [Climate change] threatens our national security and economic prosperity, it has negative impacts on food security and the efforts to eradicate poverty and it is one of the causes of migration. In order to protect and save our planet and

preserve natural resources for future generations, we must seek the answer to this pressing challenge together right here and now.[7]

This was also the main message from a July 2015 debate at the UN Security Council about issues facing small island developing states, where the secretary general and other speakers called for a general agreement in Paris.[8] Likewise, during a side event on climate-induced migration that also highlighted human security and conflicts, a member of the Swedish government concluded the conference by underlining that the "single most important measure is to decrease greenhouse gas emissions".[9] Finally, during a demonstration on the weekend prior to the conference, numerous civil society organisations used the expression "climatic state of emergency" to draw attention to the urgency of climate change, echoing the state of emergency called by the French government following the attacks on 13 November 2015. As placed alongside posters that promoted a "climate of peace" (see Figure 6.1), such headlines revealed the juxtaposition of narratives during the summit.

During COP21, the mentions of migration in the leaders' statements were also used to humanise climate change. They showed that climate-induced migration is real and underway, and stressed the specific needs of the most

*Figure 6.1* Activists holding a banner that reads "Climatic State of Emergency. For a climate of peace."

Source: Authors.

vulnerable countries. First, by focusing on climate-induced displacement, the Climate Vulnerable Forum highlighted a key challenge of its members, requesting that it be included in international efforts to address loss and damage as follows: "Establish a climate change displacement coordination facility to help coordinate efforts to address the displacement of people as a result of the extreme events as well as slow onset impacts of climate change".[10] Placing the issue of displacement and migration among one of nine action areas under the work programme of the Warsaw International Mechanism for loss and damage was among the main demands of developing countries during COP21.[11] In climate negotiations, these countries have pressed for recognition of their specific vulnerabilities and needs via inclusion of loss and damage as a third pillar of the UNFCCC, alongside mitigation and adaptation. Second, while the president of the Marshall Islands insisted that climate change and sea level rise threaten the sovereignty of his country,[12] the prime minister of Tuvalu also used the registry of state survival, implying that climate change threatens the security of his country, and then concluded, "Let's do it for Tuvalu. For if we save Tuvalu we save the world."[13]

The alarmist approach is not new; however, the balance between that and an optimist approach reveals evolution over recent years of the climatisation of migration, security and conflict. Indeed, continuing the positive narrative developed at the Earth Summit Rio+20 in 2012 with the motto "The future we want", most heads of state emphasised both the threat of climate change and the opportunity of COP21. While representatives of Australia and Sweden focused their statements on economic opportunities, Romania (like Belgium) demonstrated this shift towards a more balanced narrative:

> Climate change can therefore be considered an important threat multiplier and should be tackled accordingly. Unless we act now, the impact will quickly become unmanageable, with irreversible consequences for humanity and our environment.
>
> Acting on climate change also offers opportunities. We are convinced that, by focusing our efforts towards low-carbon economies, we will become more competitive, create new jobs and better address both the energy and climate security challenges we are all facing today.[14]

Similarly, while the official French government video to promote COP21 started with a dire warning, it then stated solutions and opportunities.[15] The conference's setting also reflected this balanced duality of threat and opportunity. A large picture placed at the entrance to the conference meeting room contrasted the despair of a dying tree with the hope of a child. Thus, the heads of state's statements during the Leaders' Event demonstrate a contrast between "stories of decline" and "stories of control" (Stone 2012). As Stone argues,

> stories of control offer hope, just as stories of decline foster anxiety and despair. The two stories are often woven together, with the story of decline serving as

the stage set and the impetus for the story of control. The story of decline is meant to warn us of suffering and motivate us to seize control.

(Stone 2012, 168)

### COP21 *as a tribune: staging issues of migration and security*

Bringing migration and conflict into the climate debate is also highly instrumental and opportunistic: COP21 as a mega-event constitutes a tribune to shine light on important global issues that may not be connected to climate change.

Regarding migration, two examples of leaders' statements show how its intro-duction to negotiations intends to raise awareness of migration issues unrelated to climate change. First, while speakers from Algeria, Antigua and Barbuda, Cape Verde and Papua New Guinea mentioned the prospect of "climate refugees", those from Greece and Jordan highlighted the current refugee crisis they are facing without discussing its link to climate change. King Abdullah II of Jordan called his country a "safe haven for refugees fleeing regional violence", reminding the audience that Jordan was now "hosting 1.4 million Syrian refugees – one for every five Jordanians".[16] Similarly the prime minister of Greece, while advocat-ing for "political priority to the need to prevent climate change displacement risk", stated that his country "is experiencing an unprecedented refugee crisis and human despair".[17] In both cases, leaders used the forum of COP21 to draw atten-tion to what they considered as their most urgent problems – that is the migration crisis. Second, Sao Tome and Principe's statement emphasised the conditions of economic migrants, noting that young people face discrimination in rich coun-tries, and denouncing the way developed countries welcome economic migrants fleeing despair.[18] Other international security and conflict issues were also show-cased at COP21. Besides terrorism, which was mentioned by most heads of state in tribute to victims of the 13 November Paris attacks, two other security issues unrelated to climate change were placed on the agenda. (1) The president of Ukraine condemned Russia by stating his "country became the object of hybrid warfare" and by calling for attention to "the issue of environment protection under the conditions of conflicts".[19] While denouncing environmental damage from war, this also raised attention of the conflict in Ukraine, including Russia's responsibility. The vice-president of Iran also accused "some powerful political lobbies", "the arm (sic) industries" and "the oil cartels" of contributing to global warming, further asking "the UN system to initiate an assessment on the carbon footprints of wars, conflicts, insecurity and terrorism".[20] (2) Similarly, during the "Climate Change Planning in Conflict Settings Case of State of Palestine" side event, a speaker from the Swedish development agency in Jerusalem explained why countries in conflict are most vulnerable to climate change, because they lack institutions and/or control over their territory to enable adaptation to cli-mate change.[21] Most presentations shared this conclusion about Palestine: the main challenge for adapting to climate change would be occupation. By focusing on climate adaptation, the event raised awareness about occupation. Both issues were also on the agenda of the May 2016 second session of the UN Environment

Assembly in Nairobi. While Ukraine managed to create consensus for approval of its draft resolution on "Protection of the Environment in Areas Affected by Armed Conflict",[22] no agreement was reached on a draft resolution proposed by Morocco and the Arab Group on Gaza.[23] Far from the usual focus on human security, COP21 saw a shift towards a stronger focus on conflict in the climate convention's debates; this can be explained by the international context in which the meeting took place, marked by the Syrian conflict and European refugee crisis, along with the Ukrainian and other crises.

Climatisation thus constitutes a political tool that is instrumentalised by some countries both to alert about climate change and to showcase issues of security and migration with no clear link to climate change. This dynamic illustrates the tension between the globalisation of climate and climatisation of the world: the climate sphere has become so powerful that it draws in multiple issues that become reframed as climate issues, like migration and conflict – that is the process of *climatisation*. However, that reframing considerably expands the range of negotiations by including topics beyond the realm of climate change – that is the process of *globalisation*. Notably, such processes are not uniform. On the contrary, different issues seem to become climatised to different degrees, rendering the globalisation of climate a highly uneven process.

## The uneven globalisation of climate

In studying the case of migration and conflict, we argue that the success of climatisation can be measured by the degree of inclusion of those issues in the climate debates. Our assessment indicates that the case of migration has been climatised successfully, while the climatisation of conflict remains in the early stages.

### The successful climatisation of migration

The relatively large number of side events[24] and cultural manifestations[25] organised during this period in Paris, whether fully or partly dedicated to climate-induced migration, demonstrates a sustained interest in bringing this issue into the climate change debate. Yet there has been a distinct shift in how the issue is tackled: the nexus of climate, migration and security has been contested in recent years, but COP21 witnessed a revival of alarmist narratives, as seen in the leaders' statements.[26] The ongoing migration crisis in Europe definitely heightened political interest in this issue. Two elements further contributed to this process and were mentioned frequently in side events. First, the International Displacement Monitoring Centre's (IDMC) *Global Estimates* report of July 2015 revealed that disasters forced more than 19.3 million people in 100 countries to flee their homes in 2014 (IDMC 2015). The Advisory Group on Climate Change and Mobility quoted that report in its recommendations to address human mobility in the Paris Agreement (Advisory Group 2015).[27] Second, 109 states endorsed the Agenda for the Protection of Cross-Border Persons in the Context of Disasters and Climate Change at the Nansen Initiative Global Consultation in October

2015, which also facilitated the inclusion of human mobility in COP21 discussions. Overall, the content of side events demonstrated that while the problem of climate-induced migration had been well defined and noted in previous COPs, focus had now shifted to potential solutions. Thus, the linkage of climate change and human mobility was barely contested at COP21, a form of consensus that materialised for instance in the space sharing, in the exhibition area of the conference, by the UN refugee agency (UNHCR) and the International Organization for Migration (IOM), despite their past oppositions (Gemenne 2011). Such broad acceptance fosters the increasing climatisation of migration.

Migration issues are mentioned twice in the Paris Agreement. The preamble states,

> Acknowledging that climate change is a common concern of humankind, Parties should, when taking action to address climate change, respect, promote and consider their respective obligations on human rights, the right to health, the rights of indigenous peoples, local communities, migrants.
>
> (UNFCCC 2015, 2)

In the COP Decision on Loss and Damage, Paragraph 50

> also requests the Executive Committee of the Warsaw International Mechanism to establish, according to its procedure and mandate, a task force to [. . .] develop recommendations for integrated approaches to avert, minimize and address displacement related to the adverse impacts of climate change.
>
> (Ibid., 7–8)

Although the final text does not specify how the "task force" will operate, the mere mention of displacements confirms the trend towards climatisation of migration issues, and simultaneously towards the globalisation of climate negotiations. It also demonstrates the growing strength in climate negotiations of the most vulnerable countries, which succeeded at keeping displacement in the final text, despite reluctance by the most industrialised countries.

### From human security to conflict

Traditionally, security debates in the climate arena focused on human security; COP21 revealed a shift, as questions of conflict became more central.

Among the seven classical dimensions of human security – economic, food, health, environmental, personal, community and political – (UNDP 1994, 25–26), during COP21 food security was the most visible. Numerous heads of state used the expression in their opening statements, and food security was the main angle for talk about security in the conference's official side events. It was even adopted as a buzzword, with the four side events that had "security" in their titles being about food security, and among all thirteen side events that mentioned security in their titles or descriptions, twelve were about food security while one was about energy security.[28] Three of four exhibits listed on the UNFCCC's web-site concerned food security and indigenous people, agriculture practices in the Andes enhancing food security, and food security under climate change, which was organised as part of the One UN initiative. This framing of food security as a climate issue was successful, in the sense that food security was included in the preamble of the Paris Agreement.[29] However, while the mention focused on food production, the innovation at COP21 was less about human security than about framing it in terms of state security and conflict.

A new development at COP21 was that the links between climate change and conflicts were more visible than in previous conferences, such as in this passage from French president Hollande's opening statement:

> Let's be aware of the seriousness of the threat to the world's equilibrium. Global warming is predicting conflicts like clouds predict a storm. It causes migrations that displace more refugees than wars do. States may not be able to satisfy the vital needs of their populations given the risk of famine, massive rural exodus and confrontation over access to water.[30]

Contrary to Detraz and Betsill's (2009) analysis for the period 1992–2008, the environmental conflict discourse that frames climate change as a cause of conflicts was present during COP21. About fifteen heads of state mentioned tensions, con-flicts and wars in their statements. President of the European Commission Juncker stated that climate change could destabilise entire regions and create conflicts over access to resources.[31] US president Obama mentioned "political disruptions that trigger new conflict" among the possible effects of climate change,[32] and the president of Chad alluded to tensions among communities that result from desertification and droughts.[33] Some also linked climate change to terrorism: the prime minister of Luxembourg explained how precarious conditions caused by cli-mate change facilitate the recruitment of young generations by non-state actors, such as ISIS, Al Qaida, Boko Haram and Al Shabaab.[34] Before the summit, the French Ministry of Defence organised an international conference on climate and defence, presented as part of the preparations for COP21.[35] Security, in the classical sense, was also discussed during side events dedicated to climate-induced migration. For instance, citing the roles of the food crisis in the Arab Spring, and of droughts in the Syrian conflict and in Darfur, the scholar Jürgen Scheffran discussed possible interactions between climate and conflict, with climate change being one among many factors.[36] In another side event dedicated to the Nansen Initiative on displacements in the context of disasters and climate change, a gov-ernment representative of Uganda explained how climate impacts on the liveli-hood of pastoralists contribute to conflicts.[37] A conference on migration, climate and security was also organised in the *Espaces Générations Climat*, and another entitled "War, Peace and Climate: Will Climate Conflicts Be the Conflicts of Tomorrow?"[38] took place at the Grand Palais in Paris. A long-standing observer of the climate conferences noted that COP21 was the first where national secu-rity and conflicts were so visible on the climate agenda, especially given media attention over the situation in Syria.[39] In other words, the international context affected the COP21 discussions and contributed to a relative climatisation of conflicts. The unfolding of future conferences will reveal whether that was merely a context-specific process or the beginning of a new framing of the issue.

Considering the failed securitisation of climate change at the Security Council, which was unable to achieve a consensus among member states to include the issue in its jurisdiction (Maertens 2015a), the introduction of international security and conflict into the climate debates can be understood as an attempt to identify the most relevant political arena for discussing the actual security implications of climate change. Yet in terms of policy outcomes, the discursive climatisation of conflicts has not yet succeeded, as no formal document officially recognises the links between climate change and conflicts. This discrepancy necessitates better understanding of factors that may prevent issues from entering formal negotiations even if they are highly climatised in public debate.

## The limits of climatisation

The moves to frame new issues as being relevant to the climate debate and to include them in climate negotiations face multiple forms of resistance. These resistances are discussed first, before we analyse institutional limits to climatisation. Indeed, if the globalisation of the climate can slow down the negotiation process, then the nature of the climate convention does not facilitate complete introduction of other mega-problems, such as migration and conflict.

### Resistance

Climatisation of migration, security and conflict during COP21 faced great opposition of three types: political, scientific and ethical. The first type of opposition relates to the structure of international relations and global governance. On one hand, migration and security are part of the exclusive jurisdiction of states. While the G77 and China opposed the introduction of climate change into the Security Council agenda (Maertens 2015a), protecting their sovereignty might also make some states reluctant to include migration and security in climate negotiations. For example until the fifth IPCC report, states refused to include a chapter on human security in the report of Working Group II despite recommendations by the secretariat and experts (Maertens 2015b, 183). Similarly, during the question-and-answer session of a side event on climate change planning in Palestine, we asked if security framing was perceived as an efficient tool to facilitate governmental negotiations. A member of one NGO replied in favour of using security framing to raise attention. Yet after the event, a representative from Sweden disagreed, arguing that it actually complicates the negotiations.[40] On the other hand, the absence of strong global governance structures for international migration is a result of states' desires to keep control over their borders (McAdam 2011). For this reason, Dina Ionesco of the IOM recalled that until now, international migration and asylum policies have remained largely blind to environmental and climate factors.[41] Although migration can be debated within the UNFCCC, resulting decisions would not differ from the general governance approach to international migration that relies on soft law mechanisms. Unsurprisingly, the Nansen Initiative followed this tradition, as a bottom-up and state-led consultative process. Likewise, the Security Council agreed only on a presidential statement, without binding implications that would have allowed it to fully assess the complex ramifications of climate change and international security. In other words, political factors prevent the creation of climate policies on migration and security.

Secondly, opposition comes from scientific reluctance to climatise migration and conflicts. Despite growing interest in climate-induced migration and the links between climate change and security, vivid academic debates question the chain of causality and the risk of simplifying the relationship (Mayer et al. 2013). Indeed, the complex relationship between climate change and migration on one hand, and between climate and conflict on the other, limits the climatisation process, as the environment is rarely the sole factor triggering migration or conflict and researchers aspire to avoid oversimplification (Foresight 2011). For example the audience at a side event on migration, climate and security blamed the speakers for not mentioning conflict in their presentations. The organisers justified this reduced attention on security by saying everything was connected; one speaker called climate change a meta-problem, with environmental, economic and social causes of wars being inextricably linked.[42]

Another factor hampering the climatisation of migration, security and conflict within climate negotiations is that such an inclusion has important ethical implications. Researchers have criticised the securitisation of climate change as a way to conceal political responsibilities for conflict, such as the role of the Sudanese government in Darfur (Hartmann 2013). The climatisation of migration and conflict might thus cause depoliticisation of the triggers of conflict and migration.[43] Finally, others fear that drawing attention to climate-induced migration might position the world's most vulnerable populations as a threat to developed countries: "peripheral instabilities are in part symptoms of climate change, but they are not the cause of the contemporary transformation. Confusing cause and effect here may be politically convenient for xenophobic politicians" (Dalby 2014, 6).

### The slowness and isolation of climate negotiations

The chapters of this book illustrate how climate is being "globalised" via inclusion of more and more issues in climate debates. However, the slowness and isolation of formal talks under the UNFCCC's umbrella reduce its capacity to incorporate meta-problems like migration and conflict into the negotiations.

For instance, the climatisation of migration succeeded and brought this issue into the negotiations. Yet there are limits to the COP21 outcomes on migration; many questions remain open about timing, membership and accountability of the Task Force (Randall 2016). Furthermore, the final document mentions only displacement, a focus that could narrow the Task Force's scope to just forced migration, effectively excluding discussions on migration as an adaptation strategy.

While the socio-economic consequences of climate change received more attention at COP21 than previously, some major factors limit the ability of climate negotiations to address those challenges. First, the discrepancy or "schism" between the slow pace of the negotiating process versus the fast pace of climate change (Aykut and Dahan 2015) makes the Climate Convention out of phase with the challenges of developing countries, such as internal movements, food insecurity and urban tensions. If the Task Force requires at least a decade of implementation before any concrete action, clearly it will be unable to tackle current climate-related displacement and migration. Likewise, addressing conflict can require urgent measures decided at special meetings and a rapid negotiation process – that is actions that do not follow an annual calendar.

Second, the UNFCCC is too isolated from other international regimes (e.g. those that govern energy, international trade or development) and is paralysed by competing interests (Aykut and Dahan 2015). The Advisory Group on Climate Change and Migration observed that the UNFCCC can be a good arena for drawing attention to cross-cutting issues, such as migration and conflict, and it can trigger the development of alternative and complementary solutions (Advisory Group 2015, 4). For instance, Walter Kälin noted that the Nansen Initiative emerged as an outcome of the Cancun Adaptation Framework (Paragraph 14[f]).[44] Nonetheless, the UNFCCC has shown a weak ability to connect different frameworks – ranging from development to adaptation, disaster risk reduction and humanitarian aid – and different scales, that are needed to provide a coherent international response to climate-induced migration (Mayer et al. 2013). In 2015, several international conferences tackled migration and climate change, directly or indirectly: the 12th COP of the United Nations Convention to Combat Desertification addressed for the first time the question of migration and land rehabilitation; the Sendai Conference on Disaster Risk Reduction included discussions on post-disaster mobility and the role of migration in reducing risk and vulnerability; the United Nations Sustainable Development Summit strengthened the link between migration and development even if it did not draw a clear link between migration and climate change (Ionesco, Mokhnacheva and Gemenne 2016); and the Nansen Initiative provided a new framework with the adoption of the Agenda Protection. However, it is unclear how these different international processes relate to each other and might reinforce each other's work. Similarly, as mentioned previously, while security-based narratives are mobilised with the aim of fostering ambitious action on climate change, they can also undermine cooperation. Like for migration, security policies require a large number of actors from multiple sectors with opposing interests, including national security agencies, ministries of defence, military actors and the arms industry. Yet, the UNFCCC lacks capacity and the mandate to include all the actors required to properly address meta-problems like migration and conflict. Thus, the slow pace of climate negotiations and isolation of the UNFCCC from other political arenas partly explain the limited inclusion of migration, security and conflict in formal negotiations that are designed primarily to solve climate change as a meta-problem on its own.

## Conclusion

Aimed at evaluating the use of migration, security and conflict as "climatised objects" during the Paris summit on climate change, this chapter identified continuities and ruptures in the treatment of these issues compared to previous climate conferences. Discourses related to migration and security emerged simultaneously in the climate negotiations during the 2000s, which underscored the urgency of climate change. COP21 witnessed continued use of climatisation as a tool for alert, instrumentalised to shed light on climate change and sometimes also on issues completely unrelated to climate. In an international context marked by a European refugee crisis, the Paris attacks and the Syrian conflict, COP21 demonstrated the notable shift from a human security focus towards attempts to climatise conflict.

Yet, our analysis also shows that these issues are climatised to varying degrees. For the issue of migration, successful climatisation led to the inclusion of climate-induced migration in the official negotiations. For security and conflict, the reframing of international security as a climate issue had no direct impact on climate talks. On the contrary, we observed resistance to including these meta-problems within the Climate Convention. Some actors stressed the risks of depoliticising the causes of migration and conflict. In other words, the Paris conference illustrated the tension between the powerful attraction of the climate arena for political discussions and the inability of the formal negotiation process to include a growing number of issues. Climatisation has become the strongest form of environmentalisation, yet other sectors resist inclusion in the Climate Convention. The competition among these meta-problems will continue with the election of the next UN secretary general, with among the candidates Christiana Figueres, former executive secretary of the UNFCCC, and António Guterres, former UN high commissioner for refugees. The newly elected secretary general will be able to influence the international agenda by focusing on one specific international problem, or by stressing the complex interconnection of meta-problems in current international relations.

## Notes

1 For their invaluable feedback on earlier versions of the chapter, we are particularly grateful to the editors of the book and Matt McDonald.
2 http://unfccc.int/meetings/paris_nov_2015/items/9331.php.
3 Security Council, in a Statement, Says 'Contextual Information' on Possible Security Implications of Climate Change Important When Climate Impacts Drive Conflict, SC/10332, 20 July 2011.
4 Interview with Dr Saleemul Huq, Paris, 27 November 2015.
5 Statement by the President of Guinea-Bissau, José Mário Vaz, "Leaders' Event", COP21, Paris-Le Bourget, 30 November 2015.
6 Statement by the President of Djibouti, Ismaïl Omar Guelleh, "Leaders' Event", COP21, Paris-Le Bourget, 30 November 2015.
7 Statement by the Prime Minister of the Czech Republic, Bohuslav Sobotka, "Leaders' Event", COP21, Paris-Le Bourget, 30 November 2015.

8  *Issues Facing Small Island Developing States 'Global Challenges' Demanding Collective Responsibility, Secretary-General Tells Security Council,* Official meetings coverage, SC/11991, 30 July 2015.

9  "Prepare and Adapt: Climate Change and Human Mobility in Paris and Beyond", side event, 2 December 2015.

10  Manila-Paris Declaration of the Climate Vulnerable Forum, CVF/2015/1, 30 November 2015.

11  Interview with Dr Saleemul Huq, Paris, 27 November 2015.

12  Statement by the President of the Republic of the Marshall Islands, Christopher J. Loeak, "Leaders' Event", COP21, Paris-Le Bourget, 30 November 2015.

13  Statement by the Prime Minister of Tuvalu, Enele S. Sopoaga, "Leaders' Event", COP21, Paris-Le Bourget, 30 November 2015.

14  Statement by the President of Romania, Klaus Iohannis, "Leaders' Event", COP21, Paris-Le Bourget, 30 November 2015.

15  COP21/CMP11 Official video, https://www.youtube.com/watch?v=cQ4EYieWsTU.

16  Statement by King Abdullah II of Jordan, "Leaders' Event", COP21, Paris-Le Bourget, 30 November 2015.

17  Statement by the Prime Minister of Greece, Alexis Tsipras, "Leaders' Event", COP21, Paris-Le Bourget, 30 November 2015.

18  Statement by the Prime Minister of Sao Tome and Principe, Patrice Emery Trovoada, "Leaders' Event", COP21, Paris-Le Bourget, 30 November 2015.

19  Statement by the President of Ukraine, Petro Poroshenko, "Leaders' Event", COP21, Paris-Le Bourget, 30 November 2015.

20  Statement by the Vice-President of the Islamic Republic of Iran, Massoumeh Ebtekar, "*Leaders' Event*", COP21, Paris-Le Bourget, 30 November 2015.

21  "Climate Change Planning in Conflict Settings Case of State of Palestine", side event, 5 December 2015.

22  Resolution from the United Nations Environment Assembly of the United Nations Environment Programme, "Protection of the Environment in Areas Affected by Armed Conflict", UNEP/EA.2/L.16/Rev.2, 26 May 2015.

23  IISD Reporting services. http://www.iisd.ca/unep/unea2.

24  Several side events were organised in the Blue Zone and the *Espaces Générations Climat* – for example Fondation Nicolas Hulot's event called "Migration, Climate and Security" (4 December 2015) and one by the governments of Norway and Switzerland (as chairs of the Nansen Initiative) entitled "Prepare and Adapt: Climate Change and Human Mobility – in Paris and Beyond" (2 December 2015).

25  Among others, the IOM photo exhibition "Entwined Destinies: Migration, Environment and Climate Change" in the National Museum of Immigration in Paris (24 November 2015 to 17 January 2016), and the Cartier Foundation's art exhibition "Exit" at the Palais de Tokyo (25 November 2015 to 10 January 2016).

26  Interview with Dr François Gemenne in Paris, 19 January 2016.

27  The Advisory Group is composed of experts and international organisations (e.g. the UNHCR, IOM, UNU-EHS, UNDP and NRC/IDMC). It was created after COP16 in Cancun to provide technical support to UNFCCC parties on human mobility in the context of climate change.

28  UNFCCC website, side events archives, https://seors.unfccc.int/seors/reports/archive.html.

29  "*Recognizing* the fundamental priority of safeguarding food security and ending hunger, and the particular vulnerabilities of food production systems to the adverse impacts of climate change" (UNFCCC 2015, 21).

30 Statement by President of the French Republic, Francois Hollande, Opening of the "Leaders' Event", COP21, Paris-Le Bourget, 30 November 2015 (translated by the authors).

31 Statement by the President of the European Commission, Jean-Claude Juncker, "Leaders' Event", COP21, Paris-Le Bourget, 30 November 2015.

32 Statement by the President of the United States of America, Barack Obama, "Leaders' Event", COP21, Paris-Le Bourget, 30 November 2015.

33 Statement by the President of Chad, Idriss Deby Itno, "Leaders' Event", COP21, Paris-Le Bourget, 30 November 2015.

34 Statement by the Prime Minister of Luxembourg, Xavier Bettel, "Leaders' Event", COP21, Paris-Le Bourget, 30 November 2015.

35 http://www.defense.gouv.fr/dgris/la-dgris/evenements/conference-climat-et-defense-quels-enjeux-14-octobre-2015/conference-internationale-climat-et-defense-14-octobre-2015.

36 "The Importance of Social Science Research for Understanding Climate Change Induced Migration", side event, 1 December 2015.

37 "Prepare and Adapt: Climate Change and Human Mobility in Paris and Beyond", side event, 2 December 2015.

38 Translated from French.

39 Interview with Dr François Gemenne, Paris, 19 January 2016.

40 "Climate Change Planning in Conflict Settings Case of State of Palestine", side event, 5 December 2015.

41 "Migrations, climat et sécurité", conference organised by the Fondation Nicolas Hulot pour la Nature et l'Homme at *Espaces Générations Climat*, 4 December 2015.

42 Ibid.

43 "The Importance of Social Science Research for Understanding Climate Change Induced Migration", side event, 1 December 2015.

44 "Migrations, climat et sécurité", conference organised by the Fondation Nicolas Hulot pour la Nature et l'Homme at *Espaces Générations Climat*, 4 December 2015.

## Bibliography

Acselrad, Henry. "The 'environmentalization of social struggles': The environmental justice movement in Brazil." *Estudos Avançados* 24, no. 68 (2010): 103–119.

Advisory Group. *Human Mobility in the Context of Climate Change, UNFCCC – Paris COP21 Recommendations from the Advisory Group on Climate Change and Human Mobility*. Geneva: UNHCR, 2015.

Aykut, Stefan C., and Amy Dahan. *Gouverner le Climat? 20 ans de négociations internationales*. Paris: Presses de Science Po, 2015.

Barnett, Jon. "Climate change and security." In *A Changing Environment for Human Security: Transformative Approaches to Research, Policy and Action*, by Linda Sygna, Karen O'Brien and Johanna Wolf, 34–45. London: Routledge, 2013.

Barnett, Jon. "Environmental security." In *The Routledge Handbook of New Security Studies*, by Peter Burgess, 123–131. New York: Routledge, 2010.

Bettini, Giovanni. "Climate migration as an adaptation strategy: De-securitizing climate-induced migration or making the unruly governable?" *Critical Studies on Security* 2, no. 2 (2014): 180–195.

Brown, Oli, Anne Hammill, and Robert McLeman. "Climate change as the 'new' security threat: Implications for Africa." *International Affairs* 83, no. 6 (2007): 1141–1154.

Buzan, Barry, Ole Wæver, and Jaap De Wilde. *Security: A New Framework for Analysis*. Boulder, CO: Lynne Rienner, 1998.

Dalby, Simon. "Rethinking geopolitics: Climate security in the anthropocene." *Global Policy* 5, no. 1 (2014): 1–9.

Detraz, Nicole, and Michelle Betsill. "Climate change and environmental security: For whom the discourse shifts." *International Studies Perspectives* 10 (2009): 303–320.

Foresight. *Migration and Global Environmental Change*. London: Crown Copyright/The Government Office for Science, 2011.

Gemenne, François. "How they became the human face of climate change: The emergence of 'climate refugees' in the public debate, and the policy responses it triggered." In *Migration and Climate Change*, by Etienne Piguet, Antoine Pécoud and Paul De Guchteneire, 225–259. Cambridge: Cambridge University Press, 2011.

Hartmann, Betsy. "Climate chains: Neo-Malthusianism, militarism and migration." In *Interpretive Approaches to Global Climate Governance: (De)constructing the Greenhouse*, by Chris Methmann, Delf Rothe and Benjamin Stephan, 91–104. London: Routledge, 2013.

IDMC. *Global Estimates 2015: People Displaced by Disasters*. Geneva: Internal Displacement Monitoring Centre and Norwegian Refugee Council, 2015.

Ionesco, Dina, Daria Mokhnacheva, and François Gemenne. *Atlas des migrations environnementales*. Paris: Presses de Sciences Po, 2016.

Johnstone, Sarah, and Jeffrey Mazo. "Global warming and the Arab Spring." *Survival* 53, no. 2 (2011): 11–17.

Kelley, Colin P., Shahrzad Mohtadi, Mark A. Cane, Richard Seager, and Yochanan Kushnir. "Climate change in the Fertile Crescent and implications of the recent Syrian drought." *Proceedings of the National Academy of Sciences of the United States of America* 112, no. 11 (2015): 3241–3246.

Maertens, Lucile. "Changement climatique au Conseil de sécurité: reconfigurations du débat Nord-Sud." *INFORMATIONS et Commentaires – Le développement en questions* 172 (2015a): 17–24.

Maertens, Lucile. *Quand le Bleu passe au vert: La sécurisation de l'environnement à l'ONU*. PhD Dissertation in Political Science and in Social Sciences, Sciences Po Paris & University of Geneva, 2015b.

Malm, Andreas. "Tahrir submerged? Five theses on revolution in the era of climate change." *Capitalism Nature Socialism* 25, no. 3 (2014): 28–44.

Mayer, Benoît, Ingrid Boas, Jackson Ewing, Alice Baillat, and Uttam Kumar Das. "Governing environmentally-related migration in Bangladesh: Responsibilities, security and the causality problem." *Asian and Pacific Migration Journal* 22, no. 2 (2013): 177–198.

Mazo, Jeffrey. *Climate Conflict: How Global Warming Threatens Security and What to Do about It*. London: IISS, 2010.

McAdam, Jane. "Environmental migration." In *Global Migration Governance*, by Alexander Betts, 153–188. Oxford: Oxford Press University, 2011.

McDonald, Matt. "Discourses of climate security." *Political Geography* 33 (2013): 42–51.

The Nansen Initiative. *Global Consultation Conference Report*. Geneva, October 12–13, 2015.

Oels, Angela. "From 'securitization' of climate change to 'climatization' of the security field: Comparing three theoretical perspectives." In *Climate Change, Human Security and Violent Conflict: Challenges for Societal Stability*, by Michael Brzoska, Hans Brauch, Günter Jürgen Scheffran, Peter Michael Link and Janpeter Schilling, 185–205. Berlin: Springer, 2012.

Oels, Angela, and Chris Methmann. "From 'fearing' to 'empowering' climate refugees: Governing climate-induced migration in the name of resilience." *Security Dialogue* 46, no. 1 (2015): 51–68.

Ollitrault, Sylvie. "De la sauvegarde de la planète à celle des réfugiés climatiques: l'activisme des ONG." *Revue Tiers Monde* 4, no. 204 (2010): 19–34.

Randall, Alex. *Briefing: After the Paris Climate Talks – What Next for Migration and Displacement?* 2016. http://climatemigration.org.uk/tag/cop21/ (accessed June 15, 2016).

Rothe, Delf. "Security as a weapon: How cataclysm discourses frame international climate negotiations." In *Climate Change, Human Security and Violent Conflict*, by Jürgen Scheffran, Michael Brzoska, Hans Günter Brauch, P. Michael Link and Janpeter Schilling, 243–258. Heidelberg: Springer, 2012.

Schwartz, Peter, and Doug Randall. "An Abrupt Climate Change Scenario and Its Implications for United States National Security." *Report to the Pentagon*. 2003. http://stephenschneider.stanford.edu/Publications/PDF_Papers/SchwartzRandall2004.pdf (accessed September 17, 2016).

Stone, Deborah. *Policy Paradox: The Art of Political Decision Making*. 3rd edition (1st edition, 1988). New York: W.W. Norton, 2012.

Trombetta, Maria Julia. "Environmental security and climate change: Analyzing the discourse." *Cambridge Review of International Affairs* 21, no. 4 (2008): 585–602.

UNDP. *Human Development Report 1994*. New York: Oxford University Press, 1994.

UNFCCC. *Adoption of the Paris Agreement*. FCCC/CP/2015/L.9/Rev.1, United Nations Framework Convention on Climate Change, 2015.

UNFCCC. *Decision 1/CP.16. The Cancun Agreements: Outcome of the Work of the Ad Hoc Working Group on Long-Term Cooperative Action under the Convention*. FCCC/CP/2010/7/Add.1, United Nations Framework Convention on Climate Change, 2010.

UNSG. *Climate Change and Its Possible Security Implications*. Report of the Secretary-General, A/64/350, September 11, 2009.

von Lucke, Franziskus, Zehra Wellmann, and Thomas Diez. "What's at stake in securitising climate change? Towards a differentiated approach." *Geopolitics* 19, no. 4 (2014): 857–884.

# 7 Climate change, a new "buzzword" for the "perpetual present" of development aid?[1]

*Aurore Viard-Crétat and Christophe Buffet*

## Introduction

Climate change issues appeared on the international agenda at a moment when development aid was being questioned on its ability to generate deep and effective change. Concepts such as "participation", "civil society", "capacity building", "ownership" or "empowerment" proliferated in international aid policy, but they soon appeared as a succession of mere "buzzwords". While each term initially referred to relatively precise framings with the potential to upset the political order, these concepts eventually lost their meaning once they were progressively mainstreamed. Put in perspective amid the history of development concepts and practice, this succession of buzzwords serves as a "perpetual present" of development agencies: they contribute to renewing promises for generating future change, and erasing the power, politics and continuous failures of development aid .

In this chapter, our aim is to show that, in a similar way, the growing awareness that emissions should be reduced and climate change impacts should be simultaneously managed has created an opportunity to revive the traditional development and humanitarian agenda. Two important cases will be discussed: climate change adaptation, and forest policies grouped under the concept of Reducing Emissions from Deforestation and forest Degradation (REDD+). Though responding to very different issues and framings, both fields are symptomatic of a classical cycle of renewal and survival of aid. While potentially involving deep transformations (political, institutional, conceptual, etc.), in practice they mainly constituted a lever for the symbolic re-enchantment of the international aid system, without reaching all their promises to address climate change challenges. By retracing the political history of these two issues, we examine how traditional development aid networks and financing channels have been central to shaping and steering the way they are addressed, and, ultimately, to containing their subversive potential. In this process, our analysis of COP21 illustrates how the climate change issue supports a perpetuation of "business as usual" development aid organisational routines, agendas and power relationships.

## Adapting to climate change or to potential contestations?

Prior to becoming an important point of negotiation during COP21 in Paris, the concept of adaptation was a progressive scientific and political construction within the climate regime. In this section, we sketch this trajectory and underline the core issue of funding that has been the most contentious part of the negotiations: based on the literature and our analysis of the Paris Agreement, we examine four different dimensions of funding for adaptation (i.e. framing, amounts, channels and repartition) to enlighten the large absorption of climate justice issues that has occurred through "traditional" official development aid.

### From a taboo to an imperative

Whereas the concept of adapting to climate impacts was mentioned as early as the Climate Convention in 1992, the steps stipulated initially in the Berlin Mandate (1995) to support adaptation measures and facilitate their implementation were imprecise. At that time, negotiators hoped that reduction efforts could be timely, and the temporality of potential impacts remained unclear (Burton, Huq, Lim, Pilifosova and Schipper 2002).

Moreover, adaptation suffered from a taboo until the late 1990s, for reasons related both to contentious international relations and different framings opposing "adaptationists", "limitationists" and "realists" (Schipper 2006). People in the first group were in line with a Darwinist perception that human and natural systems demonstrate a long history of "natural" adaptation to environmental change. In that sense, adaptation measures were neither necessary nor desirable, insofar as they could be counterproductive. Conversely, "limitationists" feared that adaptation might divert attention from the core issue of reduction. They considered adaptation as "an unacceptable, even politically incorrect, idea" (Burton 1994, 14). "Realists", however, succeeded in progressively breaking down this taboo of adaptation by relying on scientific arguments: due to inertia of the Earth's system, impacts of climate change were already unavoidable, regardless of reduction efforts, and "natural" adaptation would be inadequate to address their expected magnitude.

Successive IPCC reports supported the "realist" framing and contributed to setting adaptation as a pillar of negotiations. The third IPCC report (2001), the first with an entire chapter dedicated to adaptation, went along with the decision to launch the Adaptation Fund the same year at COP7 in Marrakesh. In the IPCC's fourth report (2007), reduction and adaptation appeared as two sides of the same coin: it became necessary to both avoid the unmanageable and manage the unavoidable. On the back of this report, in the same year the COP13 Bali Roadmap placed adaptation as one of the pillars of negotiation. The fifth IPCC report then affirmed that "climate impacts could slow down or reverse past development achievements, hinder global efforts on poverty reduction, and lead to human and environmental insecurity, displacement and conflict, maladaptation, and negative synergies" (Burkett et al. 2014, 179).

Twenty years of successive geopolitical compromises at COPs have thus led to a proliferation of entangled structures under the climate convention umbrella, dealing with research, policy advice, work programmes and capacity building about adaptation (UNFCCC 2013). This institutional proliferation is a part of an "adaptation plumbing" whose capacity for coordination, transparency and effectiveness is coming more and more under question (Smith et al. 2011, Caravani, Nakhooda, Watson and Schalatek 2012, WRI, Oxfam and ODI 2013).

### Adaptation funding: when charity crowds out justice and compensation

A key issue that cuts across this progressive construction is funding. The Climate Convention stipulates that wealthy countries grouped in Annex I are committed to supporting countries considered to be "particularly vulnerable". Article 4.8 sets out a vague list of countries (coastal territories, small island states, disaster-prone countries, among others) that have "specific needs and concerns [. . .] arising from the adverse effects of climate change and/or the impact of the implementation of response measures." This commitment leads to two highly polarised perspectives, setting Annex I and non-Annex I countries in opposition.

Following a "polluter-pays" principle, Southern countries demand that adaptation funding should be proportional to the damage sustained due to climate impacts. The Alliance of Small Island States (AOSIS), Africa and V20[2] groups epitomise this position, turning IPCC reports into values: climate models showing that those less responsible for climate change will be the most affected imply a fundamental climate injustice. In fact, climate justice was initially conceived as a "right to develop" for less wealthy countries, within debates about a fair allocation of $CO_2$ emissions in the atmosphere being perceived as a common good of humanity (Agarwal and Narain 1991). From the mid-2000s, climate justice increasingly refers to a "third era of climate change" (Huq and Toulmin 2006) that takes into account injustice from differentiated responsibilities, from physical processes that unevenly distribute impacts around the globe, and from an unequal distribution of wealth, capacity and power that contributes to vulnerabilities; this situation may exist among different countries, or among different populations within a country (Adger, Paavola and Huq 2006).

A core concept of adaptation, as discussed in COPs, is the principle of "additionality". Initially mentioned in the 1992 Climate Convention, this notion recognises that for Southern countries, climate change represents a new risk and a burden that jeopardise their development efforts. It has been reiterated consistently through COP agreements, in order to affirm that adaptation funding from Northern countries should be additional to "traditional" development aid funding – even though the official objective to provide 0.7% of their GDP for development assistance remains largely unmet.

While some developed countries officially recognise additionality and their overall responsibility for climate change, they persistently refuse to apply the polluter-pays principle to adaptation. Four main reasons explain their intransigence. First, in contrast to reduction discussions that can draw on clear indicators (such as tonnes of $CO_2$ emissions), adaptation efforts have suffered from lack of a common metric. Second, questions about the effectiveness and timing of adaptation measures slowed down the discussions: how and when to use funds to adapt remained unclear for years. Third, Northern countries feared that adaptation might become a "bottomless pit" due to potentially daunting financial liability (Burton et al. 2002). Though quite complex and subject to a wide array of methodologies (Chambwera et al. 2014), this latter point related to cost assessments of climate impacts was progressively confirmed: a reference point was established by a World Bank study that estimated adaptation would cost least developed countries $70 billion to $100 billion per year from 2010 to 2050. That amount is staggering, considering that it equals more than half of the current overall development aid from OECD members ($137 billion in 2014). Fourth, a major cause of Northern countries' reluctance to provide funds has been their doubts about the "absorption capacities" of Southern countries, meaning their risks of corruption in the politically correct terminology of aid. Though mentioned sparsely in official statements, this argument is overwhelming in more informal discussions with negotiators – that is with the implication being, how could a country's taxpayers be expected to feed corrupt foreign governments with "climate compensations" while their own domestic situations are in crises?

As a consequence, "solidarity" emerged as a key framing to wrap up adaptation into a positive narrative that would be acceptable to Northern negotiators. By blurring the legal responsibilities and liabilities of the main emitters, it sought to anchor adaptation in the imaginary notion of Northern countries sharing a part of their wealth. In that sense, adaptation would be an extension of charity and development aid, rather than compensation, and thusly Northern countries' taxpayers would be no longer polluters but instead generous donors helping poor people to face a changing climate whose cause is blurred.

In the run-up to COP21, Southern countries indicated that adaptation funding would constitute a crucial issue for them to accept a deal. In order to contribute to a "positive agenda", and perceived as a condition for reaching an agreement, it was essential for Northern countries to demonstrate that current funding levels were in line with previous pledges: an important outcome of the COP15 conference in Copenhagen (2009) had been a pledge by Northern countries to jointly mobilise $100 billion annually by 2020, "to address the needs of developing countries" (FCCC/CP/2009/11/Add.1, 7). This amount was supposed to come from public and private sources, to be "balanced" between adaptation and reduction, and to flow "significantly" through a newly set-up Green Climate Fund.

### COP21: a milestone for adaptation, or an adjournment of core issues?

Before the Conference, France and Peru had mandated the OECD to assess current flows of climate finance. The Climate Policy Initiative think tank was set with the task of drafting the report. Their report "Climate Finance in 2013–14 and the USD 100 Billion Goal" concluded that the current flow of climate finance was $62 billion (OECD 2015). Notwithstanding numerous precautions about its findings and explicit statements about methodological gaps, the report stirred deep controversies.

On one side, negotiators or actors from Northern countries that supported the "positive agenda" strategy were quick to praise the report and conclude that this amount was encouraging. On the other side, it faced fierce critics, especially from the Indian Ministry of Finance, which qualified it as "deeply flawed and unacceptable" (GoI-MoF 2015, 10).

The report specified some reasons to be unsatisfied with the current situation: only 16% of climate finance flows (less than $10 billion) are devoted to adaptation, far from a "balance" with reduction support. Moreover, the Ministry underlined that the report made no distinction between grants and loans, whereas the latter are actually reimbursed by beneficiary countries. Other criticisms made by India were consistent with numerous other reports and academic analyses: the additionality of adaptation is highly under question, with some projects being counted as both development aid and adaptation. This double counting has been long denounced (Stadelmann, Roberts and Huq 2010), including in other OECD reports (Caruso and Ellis 2013), though not in the 2015 report. The lack of a common and robust methodology shared among donor countries led to variable attributions of the projects, and many projects have been recategorised with major biases: a study of the OECD database and its 5,201 projects that are officially considered "adaptation related" showed that two-thirds were actually over-coded (AdaptationWatch 2015). Finally, the Indian Ministry of Finance adopted a hardline position, by estimating that adaptation finance was actually just $2.2 billion, if only the seventeen specifically adaptation-dedicated funds were taken into account – an amount far from the commitments made in Copenhagen (around $50 billion per year by 2020). It must be noted that this commitment fell far below the needs of least developed countries, which a World Bank study (2010) estimated to be as high as $100 billion per year, or even higher according to other estimates (UNEP 2016).

Three main challenges emerge from these discussions: the lack of a common methodology for assessing climate funds, the channels used to direct this money and its allocation towards countries identified as the "most vulnerable". The question is, to what extent did COP21 respond to these challenges?

The Paris Agreement may represent important progress on methodology, by mandating the Subsidiary Body for Scientific and Technological Advice (SBSTA) to propose a new approach by 2018. This decision constitutes a reinforcement of the Climate Convention and its multilateralism, and overcomes critics about the OECD's legitimacy to assess funding levels. However, a potential agreement on the metrics could lead to higher political tensions about the discrepancy between pledges and actual funding – even more so since the $100 billion target has been reaffirmed by 2020 and is now considered as a floor after 2025.

The channelling of climate finance also remains a contentious issue. In spite of dedicated funds under the aegis of the Climate Convention (e.g. Adaptation

Fund, Global Environment Facilities, Least Developed Countries Fund, Special Climate Change Fund, Green Fund), major flows generally go through "traditional" providers of development aid (Caravani et al. 2012, AdaptationWatch 2015). Adaptation has been more or less mainstreamed within United Nations agencies (UNDP, UNEP, FAO), multilateral development banks (World Bank, Asian Development Bank), bilateral cooperation agencies from many countries (UK, Sweden, Norway, Denmark, USA, France, etc.), many NGOs (CARE, Oxfam, ActionAid, etc.) and the Red Cross/Red Crescent movement.

Among those actors, the World Bank has come to hold a prominent a position in the field of climate finance, both as a trustee aiming officially at ensuring transparency, accountability, efficiency and effectiveness, and through its own programmes, such as the Pilot Programme for Climate Resilience. Unsurprisingly then, the World Bank affirmed that current financial instruments were "technically adequate" (Klein and Möhner 2009), in spite of Southern countries' complaints about the World Bank's high fees, long time frames and the complexity of its appraisal process, or its potential encroachment on their national policies.

The Paris Agreement did not significantly change this finance architecture: the Adaptation Fund (whose resources come mainly from a 2% tax on Clean Development Mechanisms) remains affected by the collapse of the price of carbon. That fund is still dependant on punctual pledges to save it; at a side event in Paris, many members of Northern countries confirmed their support. Eight years after its announcement in Copenhagen, the Green Climate Fund is finally operational and yet no mechanism was agreed upon in Paris to provide it with sufficient and predictable funding beyond the current collective and punctual pledge of $9.1 billion.

Finally, research over recent years has addressed the fair allocation of funds based on countries' vulnerabilities. There has been hope that a scientific vulnerability index could soften political conflicts among countries trying to establish their vulnerability so as to maximise and capture new resources. However, the construction of such indices was inevitably subject to normative choices (Klein 2009). Far from being a tool for minimising conflict this led to mistrust between parties; each country suspected others of favouring indices that would promote their self-interest (Füssel 2010). As a consequence, climate finance mainly flows via traditional development aid geopolitics – or, for Climate Convention funds, via the capacity of "vulnerable" countries to elaborate complex files (Adaptation-Watch 2015).

Overall, it appears that the geopolitical balance of power is what led adaptation funding; roughly, it followed and revived the pre-existing development aid system in terms of framing, amounts, channels and even repartition. Paradoxically, though, this continuity is accompanied by a parallel institutional proliferation under the umbrella of the Climate Convention, and by an imperative of adaptation that has prompted Southern countries to prove themselves "climate-finance–ready" through national adaptation plans.

The same pattern is true at the local scale: both the literature and side events of projects presented during COP21 indicate that current practices correspond to incremental adaptation, defined by the IPCC as adaptation actions with the central aim of maintaining the essence and integrity of a system towards the impacts of climate change. Those side events also demonstrate a focus on techno-centred approaches that favour large infrastructure and often fail to tackle root causes of vulnerability; they have been anchored in uneven development pro-cesses that the IPCC underlined, such as multidimensional inequalities due to social, economical, cultural, political or institutional marginalisation (IPCC 2014). Concepts such as "reformist" or "transformative" adaptation, whose aims are to change the fundamental attributes of a system in response to climate and to emphasise the evolution of socioeconomic and environmental determinants of vulnerability (Pelling 2011, Kates, Travis and Wilbanks 2012, O'Brien 2012), remain to be implemented.

In this sense, COP21 essentially showed continuity with the status quo, in spite of some progress towards more transparency and accountability of climate finance. That leaves doubts about whether the current adaptation regime is up to the challenges. Though it follows different paradigms, we observe that the situation is quite similar to the pattern of development aid related to the issue of deforestation.

## Saving the forest or the international forest cooperation sector?

Our second case study illustrates how an institutional innovation – namely REDD+ – arose and generated important momentum, promising for a while to renew international policies aimed at protecting and economically valorising for-ests in the Global South. We will examine how, while the intrinsic limits and risks of this idea were highlighted very early on in the process, the momentary success of REDD+ relied more on immediate interests and constraints than on its real likelihood for future implementation. Debating, experimenting, preparing and financing this new mechanism quickly became a great opportunity for diverse communities of experts linked with the development aid system to develop their activities. A snowball effect made REDD+ inescapable in international debates, while its development on the ground was characterised by a significant dilution of the initial concept towards diverse schemes and encountered the typical structural limits of forest development aid programmes. COP21 was symptomatic of this tension and confirmed that the cycle of REDD+'s success is about to decline: the REDD+ concept was successfully promoted inside the Paris Agreement by some Southern forest countries that hoped to keep benefiting from this financial manna, whereas side events and corridor discussions seemed to be clearly distanced from the initial concept, or people seemed disinterested and instead were focused on other approaches.

### Genealogy of a political success story

Initiated under the Climate Convention, REDD+ was aimed at valuating forest ecosystems for their carbon stocks. The idea was in line with the Kyoto Protocol

and associated debates: to offset their surplus of greenhouse gas emissions, industrialised countries could (as part of their commitment to reduce emissions between
2008 and 2012) purchase carbon credits on the open market from projects that
reduce emissions in Southern countries. The REDD+ concept was officially proposed in 2005 to expand the carbon trading mechanism and include efforts to
combat deforestation for the post-2012 agreement (UNFCCC 2005). Regardless of the diversity of approaches that were further developed and debated, the
central concept remained the same: project leaders or states that would maintain
or increase carbon stocks in the forests of the South could claim financial compensation, depending on how many tonnes of carbon emissions would have been
avoided in the process.

REDD+ emerged as an innovative, pragmatic solution within a context of relative disenchantment about international forest and climate policies. After many
years of growing political attention on global forest depletion, and following the
failure to sign a convention on forests at the Rio Earth Summit in 1992, the only
official result of the international cooperation regime on forestry was a non-binding
agreement of limited effectiveness (United Nations 1992). Since then, beyond
multilateral negotiations, there was significant investment for forest protection,
particularly through development assistance. However, such funds that typically
support the first few years of a project are generally known to be insufficient for
initiating long-term changes in practice. A financial mechanism based on the sale
of carbon credits has thus been encouraged as a means of longer-term funding.

Meanwhile, results of the Kyoto Protocol were also proving inadequate to address
climate change. The notion of avoided deforestation had been rejected from subsequent negotiations in 2001, particularly due to pressure from environmental NGOs
denouncing a loophole for emissions by the industrial North. Given the urgency
and increasing difficulty of achieving commitment to ambitious and binding goals
beyond 2012, adding deforestation to the fight against climate change became a
pragmatic solution. Different agendas related to forests, climate change and development converged and crystallised around a win-win discourse that involved governmental and intergovernmental institutions, environment and development
NGOs, the private sector, and other actors. Due to the UN's constraint of having
to integrate diverse, sometimes conflicting viewpoints and interests, the concept
of REDD+ became a kind of promise for an "all-inclusive" sustainable development mechanism. Compensation for avoided carbon emissions would not only
address climate change but also, almost automatically, protect a long-term suite
of forest ecosystem services (including biodiversity), and provide income for local
and indigenous populations. More generally, it would develop the economies of
the countries involved.

What drove this momentum, despite the conflicts that until then had defined
international forest governance? The success of REDD+ depended on previous
active and strategic efforts from several actors to promote deforestation as an
activity eligible for the carbon market.

When the REDD+ concept arose, numerous forest actors were frustrated
because action against deforestation was excluded from the Clean Development

Mechanism. Moreover, other forest activities that were included in the Kyoto Protocol – that is different kinds of reforestation – did not generate the interest anticipated. Ever since carbon markets were discussed, diverse private initiatives had already tried to show that it was possible to finance forest protection by valorising their carbon stocks as an ecosystem service. Some of them, such as the Noel Kempff Climate Action Project launched in 1996 in Bolivia, or the Wildlife Works Kasigau Corridor REDD+ Project launched in 1998 in Kenya, were later portrayed as success stories to promote REDD+. In each project, the component of technical innovation was crucial to building REDD+'s credibility – for instance the deployment of advanced satellite tools (used to verify the accuracy of carbon measurements) or the first certification of carbon credits from REDD+ activities.

The World Bank was also one of the early promoters of forest carbon marketing – for example by supporting think tanks, such as the Ecosystem Marketplace, and then by experimenting with it. In 2002, the Bank launched the BioCarbon Fund, intended to "explore projects with a component of avoided deforestation" (Noble 2003, 7), which had been excluded from the Kyoto Protocol one year earlier. The fund played the role of both broker and certifier of carbon credits that were purchasable by governments and businesses in the North. The rhetoric of "exploration", which was repeated for the voluntary markets (Hamilton et al. 2007), tended to shroud the political reasons for excluding deforestation from the Kyoto Protocol with technicalities, presenting them as surmountable in the future. In this way, a partnership around the BioCarbon Fund developed a methodology in 2004 for monitoring carbon in the forests of Madagascar (Bidaud Rakotoarivony 2012). That project, which was subsequently renamed "REDD+", was held up as a forest carbon success story by the stakeholders who started it.

A new step was reached with the idea of reducing the risks of plain displacement of deforestation by considering reduction of deforestation at a national scale, instead of at a project scale. Then called "compensated reduction", this proposal was first made in 2003 at the margins of the Milan climate conference by a coalition of NGOs from Brazil and the United States (Santilli, Moutinho, Schwartzman, Nepstad, Curran and Nobre 2003). The Environmental Defense Fund, an American NGO, had a long-standing commitment to promote "cap and trade" as a solution to environmental problems, a tool it had already promoted to the Bush Sr. administration for the 1990 Clean Air Act, and later to the Clinton administration for the Kyoto Protocol (Fialka 2011). Beyond the work of disseminating their concept in international political and scientific arenas, they efficiently lobbied the Brazilian government, which has always been hostile to international negotiations on Southern forests, by citing the Southern countries' sovereignty, their right to development and the historical responsibility of industrialised countries for climate change (Moutinho, Martins, Christovam, Lima, Nepstad and Crisostomo 2011). While remaining opposed to market financing, Brazil began to consider climate negotiations on forestry as an opportunity to assert itself as a major political, scientific and technical player, and therefore accepted reopening the debate on including deforestation in the Climate Convention (Carvalho 2012).

An analogous idea, then called "RED", was promoted officially in 2005 by Costa Rica and Papua New Guinea in the name of a coalition of forested Southern countries. Diverse interests crystallised quickly around this proposition: some countries asked for an enlargement of the principle to benefit from it, and RED progressively became REDD+ to include reduction of forest degradation and other activities, such as reforestation and afforestation. Above all, vigorous debates appeared in multiples venues and involving many communities of forest actors (scientists, think tanks, NGOs, international and national development aid institutions, consulting firms, etc.); such discussions considered how to implement the concept concretely, measure avoided forest emissions, guarantee the environmental and social integrity of the mechanism, ensure a fair distribution of expected benefits and address numerous other questions about how it would work.

### An "aid-ification of REDD+" or a "REDD-ification of aid"?

Many advocates of REDD+ have used a "trade-not-aid" rhetoric (Angelsen, Brown et al. 2009), stating that this mechanism was expected to offer Southern "stakeholders" (in the international development jargon) access to the carbon market and thus enable them to break away from traditional development aid programmes. Nevertheless, this objective was expected to require a preliminary phase of "capacity-building" that would have to be funded by the usual providers of development aid. This would involve preparing a strategy, setting up a dedicated team for public administration, training national experts, developing technology transfer programmes, organising representation for "civil society" and developing "pilot" projects – all supported by development aid, international NGOs and private consultancies. Consequently, while the post-2012 Climate Convention framework remained unsettled, preparation of the REDD+ mechanism began quickly through numerous pilot projects, via a "learning by doing" approach.

For every category of players, and according to the constraints of each of their activities, REDD+'s success turned into both an opportunity and a near imperative, since it became difficult not to get involved in its global "snowball" effect. Development aid donors supported this dynamic enthusiastically. They found in REDD+ an opportunity to vivify or renew their programmes dealing with the emblematic environmental concern that deforestation represents, to promote their country's expertise and to disburse funds easily. Indeed, this innovative context justified why they financed mostly research, training and technology partnerships instead of deep institutional reforms. Moreover, the newness of REDD+ allowed detrimental effects (e.g. fictitious emission reductions, misuse of power against local communities, bureaucratic patronage, waste of public money due to a lack of coordination between donors) to be seen as technical mistakes that would be overcome in the future, and not as abuses or evidence of development aid's systemic limits, even if some of these difficulties re-emerge in every new approach. It also emphasised a collective learning process that was in perfect sync with the Paris Declaration on Aid Effectiveness. In this process, the World Bank succeeded in building on its previous initiatives to position itself as a central player. Consequently, multilateral and bilateral funds were launched (e.g. Forest Carbon Partnership Facility coordinated by the World Bank) to prompt countries of the South to engage in the REDD+ process. Finally, far from the initial promise of market funding, almost 90% of all REDD+ financing has come from public sources, most of it related to preparedness activities (e.g. research on remote sensing tools to monitor deforestation, training for Southern experts, establishing national teams and negotiations with civil society and donors) rather than to true impacts on deforestation rates (Norman and Nakhooda 2014).

These financial flows opened a promising market of expertise for all types of organisations linked with forestry and development aid, whether they be private consulting companies, NGOs, think tanks or public research institutes. Similarly, Southern networks of civil society organisations and public administrations quickly became involved and expected direct and indirect benefits. Thus, as a strong economic, strategic and professional opportunity, the REDD+ mechanism progressively became an obligatory passage point for policies and strategies of forest stakeholders in the Global South. Also, the Climate Convention began to stand as the main arena where forestry issues were addressed, despite the existence of numerous other initiatives and the fact that REDD+ transpires increasingly outside it. REDD+ became a bandwagon that everyone jumped on, particularly experts and scientists (McDermott, Levin and Cashore 2011). As such, its political success depended on the immediate opportunities that its preparation represented for the broader international network of development aid, while its future implementation remained uncertain and many stakeholders were doubtful about the long-term benefits. In contrast, few concrete projects are aimed at directly reducing deforestation, and existing ones generate significant difficulties in the field and have had trouble selling any carbon credits obtained.

This central role of development aid in the preparation of REDD+ has been described in retrospect as a regrettable "aid-ification of REDD+" (Seymour and Angelsen 2012, Angelsen 2013), explaining its progressive fall into disfavour. According to this analysis, the deferment of a global climate agreement until after 2012 prevented the rapid launch of a forest carbon market and allowed the dynamics of the aid system to compromise the effectiveness of REDD+. This analysis is biased, however, insofar as it neglects the decisive role that interests within the aid system played in the success of REDD+. This is attested by the early investment of the World Bank, and indeed of the whole range of public and private organisations connected to the development aid system, in promoting forest carbon markets first, and then the REDD+ itself. These networks did not wait for REDD+ to be legitimated to invest in it. They would certainly not have responded to the REDD+ concept with such engagement if they had not seen in it an immediate means to renew or expand their activities. It may thus be more apt to describe this shift as a "REDD-ification" of development aid, as numerous actors in the aid system were involved in preparation of this mechanism, and adjusted their vocabulary, their practices, their projects, their metrics, their network and so forth to draw as much benefit as possible from this nebulous system. The entire

community of practice (Brown and Duguid 1991, Wenger 2000) in forest cooperation was thus changed by its engagement with this concept.

### REDD+ at COP21: between inertia, readjustments and detachment

Since the emergence of the REDD+ concept, the COPs, and particularly the
associated side events, have played a decisive role in the alignment of immediate interests that enabled the constitution of a community of REDD+ experts
around the formation of debates and the preparations for this mechanism. These
were moments of intense emulation, where all of the actors involved met, negotiated contracts, communicated on their activities and learned about the latest
developments on the subject (projects, publications, vocabulary). Underneath
a show of determination to debate and share experience, interests intrinsic to
the development aid system and the accompanying expertise played a dominant
role. The very participation of experts from the South is often dependent on aid
programmes. This decisive role played by the immediate interests of the development community is also fostered by the format of the side events: a time slot to
give a presentation or a stand cost several thousand euros, an investment that
must be profitable for organisations in terms of communication and visibility,
be they public or private, for-profit businesses or scientific institutions. These
meetings often seem more like showcases for high-level figures or for the various
participating groups to promote their activities, distribute their publications and
so forth than actual discussions. Time for debate is often highly limited, or even
completely absent, and the general tone is accommodating.

COP21 was unmistakably symptomatic of the evolution of the attention given
to REDD+ and of power relations within the aid system. There were numerous
signals that the concept was in a period of transition, as a portion of the actors
involved continued to hope to be able to surf on the wave of REDD+ while others
were already saying behind the scenes that "REDD is dead" (Fletcher, Dressler,
Büscher and Anderson 2016). Today, REDD+ seems to be solidly institutionalised
and stabilised as, in principle, negotiations on it within the Climate Convention
were brought to a close in June 2015. However, long-term financing for the compensation of potential emissions reductions, particularly by means of carbon markets, remains highly uncertain (Conservation International 2013, GCP; IPAM;
FFI; UNEP F. I. 2014, Turnhout et al. 2016). Official communications on the
subject give voice to a mixture of perspectives: some continue to present REDD
as "one of the most attractive solutions", while others ask, "those who say that
REDD has failed: what are the alternatives?"

In this ambiguous context, at COP21, Southern forest countries whose preparations for REDD+ are already well underway, grouped together in the Coalition of
Rainforest Nations, fought for REDD+ to be mentioned in the Paris Agreement.
The side events were also used to challenge donors to continue to support REDD+
and to keep the related promises. Thus for example a Cameroonian official who
was preparing to speak at a side event, seeing the Australian minister of the environment attempting to slip away immediately after opening the session, rushed to

the microphone and urged him to listen: "I will not lose the chance [. . .] REDD is important for us in these negotiations, I want to draw your attention, we want to see REDD in the text." The opportunity seemed all the more significant for the fact that, at a side event centred on forests in Central Africa, several speakers emphasised the absence of Northern partners from the room, as both the panel and the audience consisted almost exclusively of Africans. This did not prevent them from recalling that donors must face their responsibilities, notably towards civil society in often undemocratic societies: "Some people have risked their lives to get us here [. . .] The partners have to finish what they started."

While the official justification for reluctance to include REDD+ in the agreement was that doing so was unnecessary as REDD+ was already validated in the Climate Convention, more strategic factors linked to the development aid system emerged in corridor discussions. According to some accounts, the formal inclusion of the REDD+ mechanism in the Paris Agreement would anchor it more firmly in UN procedures, where the balance of power between beneficiary and donor countries is more favourable to the former than in the World Bank, which is currently the leader in this area, or in bilateral negotiations. Some Northern representatives suspected that a motive behind this programme was the desire of consultants working with the countries in the Coalition of Rainforest Nations to open up professional prospects for themselves within the United Nations. Officials of these countries explained, in their turn, that they feared that donors wished to maintain their current prerogatives or to progressively let REDD+ drop without compensating forest countries for their efforts. "It's not that the funding is taking time to arrive", a Congolese representative complained, "it's that it's not coming at all." Certain donors renewed their funding commitments in Paris, notably Norway, the principal funder of REDD+, but the total amounts fall far short of requirements, and their distribution is highly unequal across continents and countries.

This ambiguous situation seems to have affected even the emblematic country of Brazil, despite the comparatively high levels of support that it has enjoyed: some speakers at side events emphasised that progress in the fight against deforestation is independent of the labyrinthine dynamics of REDD+, while others recalled that REDD+ projects were collapsing due to lack of demand for carbon credits, leading to a resurgence of both deforestation and local social tensions. Moreover, some Northern experts recognised behind the scenes that the future of international forest governance will probably not take place by way of REDD+, even if the term itself persists.

For the Paris Agreement, a compromise was ultimately found, with REDD+ integrated not as a "mechanism" but as a "framework", a less formal term. Regardless of whether these allegations and counter-allegations about the intentions of different actors are justified, their expression demonstrates how crucially the specific incentives and interests of the development aid system figure in the negotiations, and show that engagement in favour of REDD+ is increasingly in doubt.

The credibility of REDD+ as it was initially promoted thus seems to be declining. But, as in the case of other temporary conservation "fads", its decline has not been clear-cut (Redford, Padoch and Sunderland 2013): instead such concepts are progressively replaced or integrated into other approaches, in a permanent process of repackaging of old approaches. New buzzwords, notably the "landscape" approach, have come to the fore, in side events and in the literature abundantly distributed there, as well as in the initiatives launched by aid institutions in order to maintain their leadership position (e.g. the World Bank's Initiative for Sustainable Landscapes). One example is the name change of the Forest Day organised each year alongside the COP, which initially focused on REDD+ and which was recently merged with the Rural and Agriculture Day to become the Global Landscape Forum. REDD+ is also sometimes recycled in promotions for the sustainable production of products such as cacao, in an approach that seems to give new impetus to certification. This confusion has sometimes been recognised, as when an advisor to the Governors' Climate and Forests Task Force confessed that "Maybe we should not use the term REDD+ to avoid confusion, it's part of a broader agenda." In any case, expansion into new conceptualisations involving a constantly increasing range of dimensions complicates the task of concretely implementing REDD+ (Turnhout et al. 2016).

Although it has been promoted recently as being innovative (Climate Focus 2015), the results-based finance for REDD+ seems to have revived the ambitions of the 2005 Paris Declaration on Aid Effectiveness in a new format, where contractualisation is based on tonnes of non-emitted carbon. This coexistence of a certain continuity of vocabulary (ownership, conditionalities, efficiency) with a rhetoric of innovation shows how the process of "collective amnesia" of aid institutions has been playing out once again around REDD+ (King and McGrath 2004), allowing these institutions to make a show of renewal and thereby to relegitimate themselves in a cyclic fashion without questioning previous failures in depth. And, as happened in the initial crystallisation of enthusiasm for REDD+, the arrival of new ideas intended to overcome its limitations led to a need for ever more pilot projects, technical and scientific debates and so forth – once again feeding the whole chain of aid experts, who, like a "digestive tract" (Sogge 2003, 96), must transform formal policies into applicable ones, and who live on the proceeds from subcontracting of new waves of funding.

## Conclusion

In the case of adaptation and REDD+, COP21 was consistent with previous climate conferences in the sense that both topics were constructed with few considerations for previous systemic failures and limits of development aid policies. REDD+ and adaptation thus appear to contribute to a re-enchantment of aid policies through renewed promises of massive new financial flows, technical and methodological innovations, and political developments (including participation, empowerment, gender and traditional knowledge, among others). So far, while these promises are largely unmet, we observe a pervasiveness of traditional aid actors, most notably the World Bank which reasserted itself as a pivotal player.

Nevertheless, although adaptation and REDD+ are far from being able to fulfill their respective promises, they have produced other positive effects and dynamics in the climate regime. Buzzwords are not just a matter of rhetoric. They produce new imperatives for aid-receiving countries that are expected to set up "climate-ready" adaptation and REDD+ national strategies – even if, in fact, those strategies are often largely "inspired" by international consulting firms, thus prolonging a lack of ownership of those countries over their own policies, which has long been criticised within development aid spheres. In this sense, the climatisation of aid contributes to the entrenchment of existing power relations. More problematically, it fails to address the very core of uneven and unsustainable development processes, and ignores the associated proliferation of risks. Beyond COP sessions, this trend can also be observed at the national level: Southern decision-makers may also "climatise" local disasters – and thus blame Northern countries – so as to distract attention from their own responsibilities.

Now that adaptation and REDD+ have been largely mainstreamed, and their limitations have become obvious, it is striking to observe the reinvestment in them that is already underway, with new buzzwords generating a new cycle of promises: the "landscape" approach in REDD+ aims largely at integrating agriculture, forest and livelihood issues, while "resilience" could reconcile development, climate and disaster risk reduction. Discussions continue in order to define the precise meaning of those two terms. A new cycle of promises has thus begun.

## Notes

1 This chapter is based on ethnographical observations conducted during COP21, and on broader research conducted for our respective PhD theses; more elements of the theoretical work and the empirical data supporting these analyses are presented in Buffet (2015) and Viard-Crétat (2015).

2 In reference to G20, the Vulnerable Twenty (V20) is an informal group comprising Afghanistan, Bangladesh, Barbados, Bhutan, Costa Rica, Ethiopia, Ghana, Kenya, Kiribati, Madagascar, Maldives, Nepal, Philippines, Rwanda, Saint Lucia, Tanzania, Timor-Leste, Tuvalu, Vanuatu and Vietnam.

## Bibliography

AdaptationWatch. *Toward Mutual Accountability: The 2015 Adaptation Finance Transparency Gap Report*. Policy Briefing: AdaptationWatch, 2015.

Adger, W. Neil, J. Paavola, and S. Huq. "Toward justice in adaptation to climate change." In *Fairness in Adaptation to Climate Change*, by W. Neil Adger, J. Paavola, Saleemul Huq and M. J. Mace, 1–19. Cambridge, MA: MIT Press, 2006.

Agarwal, Anil, and Sunita Narain. *Global Warming in an Unequal World: A Case of Environmental Colonialism*. New Delhi: Center for Science and Environment, 1991.

Angelsen, A. *REDD+ as Performance-based Aid: General Lessons and Bilateral Agreements of Norway*. Research Paper, World Institute for Development Economic Research (UNU-WIDER), 2013.

Angelsen, A., S. Brown, C. Loisel, L. Peskett, C. Streck, and D. Zarin. *Reducing Emissions from Deforestation and Forest Degradation: An Options Assessment Report*. Meridian Institute, Prepared for the Government of Norway, 2009.

Bidaud Rakotoarivony, Cécile. *Le carbone qui cache la forêt: La construction scientifique et la mise en politique du service de stockage du carbone des forêts malgaches*. PhD Dissertation under the direction of Marc Hufty. Geneva: IHEID, 2012.

Brown, John Seely, and Paul Duguid. "Organizational learning and communities-of-practice: Toward a unified view of working, learning, and innovation." *Organization Science 2*, no. 1 (1991): 40–57.

Buffet, Christophe. *L'adaptation au changement climatique: Construction, cadrages et acteurs, des arènes globales de négociations aux populations vulnérables du Bangladesh*. PhD dissertation under the direction of Amy Dahan. Paris: EHESS, 2015.

Burkett, V. R., A. G. Suarez, M. Bindi, C. Conde, R. Mukerji, M. J. Prather, A. L. St. Clair, and G. W. Yohe. "Point of departure." In *Climate Change 2014: Impacts, Adaptation, and Vulnerability. Part A: Global and Sectoral Aspects. Contribution of Working Group II to the Fifth Assessment Report of the Intergovernmental Panel of Climate Change*, by C. B. Field, V. R. Barros, D. J. Dokken, K. J. Mach, M. D. Mastrandrea, T. E. Bilir, M. Chatterjee, et al., 169–194. Cambridge, UK: Cambridge University Press, 2014.

Burton, Ian. "Deconstructing adaptation . . . and reconstructing." *Delta 5*, no. 1 (1994): 14–15.

Burton, Ian, Saleemul Huq, Bo Lim, Olga Pilifosova, and Emma Lisa Schipper. "From impacts assessment to adaptation priorities: The shaping of adaptation policy." *Focus on North/South and Developing Countries 2*, no. 2–3 (2002): 145–159.

Caravani, Laura, Smita Nakhooda, Charlene Watson, and Liane Schalatek. *The Global Climate Finance Architecture*. London: Overseas Development Institute, Heinrich Böll Foundation, 2012.

Caruso, Randy, and Jane Ellis. *Comparing Definitions and Methods to Estimate Mobilised Climate Finance*. Climate Change Expert Group Papers, OECD/IEA, 2013.

Carvalho, Fernanda Viana de. "The Brazilian position on forests and climate change from 1997 to 2012: From veto to proposition." *Revista Brasileira de Política Internacional 55* (2012): 144–169.

Chambwera, M., G. Heal, C. Dubeux, S. Hallegatte, L. Leclerc, A. Markandya, B. A. McCarl, R. Mechler, and J. E. Neumann. "Economics of adaptation." In *Climate Change 2014: Impacts, Adaptation, and Vulnerability. Part A: Global and Sectoral Aspects. Contribution of Working Group II to the Fifth Assessment Report of the Intergovernmental Panel of Climate Change*, by C. B. Field, V. R. Barros, D. J. Dokken, K. J. Mach, M. D. Mastrandrea, T. E. Bilir, M. Chatterjee, et al., 945–977. Cambridge, UK: Cambridge University Press, 2014.

Climate Focus. *Results-based Finance for REDD+: Emerging Approaches. REDD+ Expert Dialogue 7*. Climate Focus and KFW, 2015.

Conservation International. *REDD+ Market: Sending Out an SOS*. 2013.

Cornwall, Andrea, and Karen Brock. "What do buzzwords do for development policy? A critical look at 'participation', 'empowerment' and 'poverty reduction'." *Third World Quarterly 26*, no. 7 (2005): 1043–1060.

Fialka, John J. *How a Republican Anti-pollution Measure, Expanded by Democrats, Got Rooted in Europe and China*. E&E News, 2011.

Fletcher, Robert, Wolfram Dressler, Bram Büscher, and Zachary R. Anderson. "Questioning REDD+ and the future of market-based conservation: Fletcher et al." *Conservation Biology 30*, no. 3 (2016): 673–675.

Füssel, Hans-Martin. "How inequitable is the global distribution of responsibility, capability, and vulnerability to climate change: A comprehensive indicator-based assessment." *20th Anniversary Special Issue* 20, no. 4 (2010): 597–611.

GCP; IPAM; FFI; UNEP F. I. *Stimulating Interim Demand for REDD+ Emission Reductions: The Need for a Strategic Intervention from 2015 to 2020.* Global Canopy Programme, Oxford, UK; the Amazon Environmental Research Institute, Brasília, Brazil; Fauna & Flora International, Cambridge, UK; and UNEP Finance Initiative, Geneva, Switzerland, 2014.

GoI-MoF. *Climate Change Finance, Analysis of a Recent OECD Report: Some Credible Facts Needed.* Climate Change Finance Unit, Department of Economic Affairs, Ministry of Finance, Government of India, 2015.

Hamilton, K., R. Bayon, G. Turner, and D. Higgins. "State of the voluntary carbon markets 2007: Picking up steam." Ecosystem Marketplace, New Carbon Finance, Washington, DC and London, 2007.

Huq, Saleemul, and Camilla Toulmin. *Three Eras of Climate Change.* London: International Institute for Environment and Development, 2006.

IPCC. *Climate Change 2014: Impacts, Adaptation, and Vulnerability. Part A: Global and Sectoral Aspects. Contribution of Working Group II to the Fifth Assessment Report of the Intergovernmental Panel on Climate Change [Field, C.B., V.R. Barros, D.J. Dokken, K.J. Mach, M.D. Mastrandrea, T.E. Bilir, M. Chatterjee, K.L. Ebi, Y.O. Estrada, R.C. Genova, B. Girma, E.S. Kissel, A.N. Levy, S. MacCracken, P.R. Mastrandrea, and L.L. White (eds.)].* Cambridge, UK: Cambridge University Press, 2014.

Kates, R. W., W. R. Travis, and T. J. Wilbanks. "Transformational adaptation when incremental adaptations to climate change are insufficient." *Proceedings of the National Academy of Sciences* 109, no. 19 (2012): 7156–7161.

King, K., and S. McGrath. *Knowledge for Development? Comparing British, Japanese, Swedish and World Bank Aid.* London: Zed Books, 2004.

Klein, R.J.T. "Identifying countries that are particularly vulnerable to the adverse effects of climate change: An academic or a political challenge?" *Carbon & Climate Law Review* 3, no. 3 (2009): 284–291.

Klein, R.J.T., and Anita Möhner. "Governance limits to effective global financial support for adaptation." In *Adapting to Climate Change: Thresholds, Values, Governance*, by W. Neil Adger, Irene Lorenzoni and Karen O'Brien, 465–475. New York: Cambridge University Press, 2009.

Lewis, David. "International development and the 'perpetual present': Anthropological approaches to the re-historicization of policy." *The European Journal of Development Research* 21, no. 1 (2009): 32–46.

McDermott, Constance L., Kelly Levin, and Benjamin Cashore. "Building the forest-climate bandwagon: REDD+ and the logic of problem amelioration." *Global Environmental Politics* 11, no. 3 (2011): 85–103.

Moutinho, Paulo, Osvaldo Stella Martins, Mariana Christovam, André Lima, Daniel Nepstad, and Ana Carolina Crisostomo. "The emerging REDD+ regime of Brazil." *Carbon Management* 2, no. 5 (2011): 587–602.

Noble, Ian. "The World Bank's BioCarbon Fund." *Australasian Emissions Trading Forum Review*, February/March (2003): 6–7.

Norman, M., and S. Nakhooda. *The State of REDD+ Finance.* Center for Global Development, Washington, DC, 2014.

O'Brien, K. "Global environmental change II: From adaptation to deliberate transformation." *Progress in Human Geography* 36, no. 5 (2012): 667–676.

OECD. *Climate Finance in 2013–14 and the USD 100 Billion Goal.* A Report by the Organisation for Economic Co-operation and Development (OECD) in collaboration with Climate Policy Initiative (CPI), 2015.

Pelling, Mark. *Adaptation to Climate Change: From Resilience to Transformation.* London: Routledge, 2011.

Redford, Kent H., Christine Padoch, and Terry Sunderland. "Fads, funding, and forgetting in three decades of conservation: Editorial." *Conservation Biology* 27, no. 3 (2013): 437–438.

Santilli, M., P. Moutinho, S. Schwartzman, D. Nepstad, L. Curran, and C. Nobre. *Tropical Deforestation and the Kyoto Protocol: A New Proposal.* Paper presented at COP 9, UNFCCC, December 2003, Milan, Italy, 2003.

Schipper, E. Lisa F. "Conceptual history of adaptation in the UNFCCC process." *Review of European Community & International Environmental Law* 15, no. 1 (2006): 82–92.

Seymour, F., and A. Angelsen. "Summary and conclusions: REDD+ without regrets." In *Analyzing REDD+: Challenges and Choices*, by A. Angelsen, M. Brockhaus, W. Sunderlin and L. Verchot, 317–334. Bogor: CIFOR, 2012.

Smith, Joel B., T. Dickinson, J.D.B. Donahue, I. Burton, E. Haites, R.J.T. Klein, and A. Patwardhan. "Development and climate change adaptation funding: Coordination and integration." *Climate Policy* 11, no. 3 (2011): 987–1000.

Sogge, D. *Les mirages de l'aide internationale: Quand le calcul l'emporte sur la solidarité.* Paris: Editions Charles Léopold Mayer, 2003.

Stadelmann, Martin J., Timmons Roberts, and Saleemul Huq. *Baseline for Trust: Defining 'New and Additional' Climate Funding.* London: Briefing, IIED, 2010.

Turnhout, Esther, A. Gupta, J. Weatherley-Singh, M. J. Vijge, J. de Koning, I. J. Visseren-Hamakers, M. Herold, and M. Lederer. "Envisioning REDD+ in a post-Paris era: Between evolving expectations and current practice: Envisioning REDD+ in a post-Paris era." *Wiley Interdisciplinary Reviews: Climate Change* (2016). doi:10.1002/wcc.425

UNEP. *The Adaptation Finance Gap Report 2016.* United Nations Environment Programme (UNEP), Nairobi, 2016.

UNFCCC. *Conference of the Parties.* Eleventh session. Montreal, 28 November to 9 December 2005. Item 6 of the Provisional Agenda. Reducing Emissions from Deforestation in Developing Countries: Approaches to Stimulate Action, 2005.

UNFCCC. *The State of Adaptation under the United Nations Framework Convention on Climate Change: 2013 Thematic Report.* UNFCCC, 2013.

United Nations. *Report of the United Nations Conference on Environment and Development (Rio de Janeiro, 3–14 June 1992) Annex III: Non-Legally Binding Authoritative Statement of Principles for a Global Consensus on the Management, Conservation and Sustainable Development of all Types of Forests.* A/CONF.151/26 (Vol. III), 1992.

Viard-Crétat, Aurore. *La déforestation évitée: Socio-anthropologie d'un nouvel or vert. Entre lutte contre le changement climatique et aide au développement, du laboratoire guyanais à l'expertise forestière au Cameroun.* PhD dissertation. Paris: EHESS, 2015.

Wenger, E. "Communities of practice and social learning systems." *Organization* 7, no. 2 (2000): 225–246.

World Bank. *Economics of Adaptation to Climate Change – Synthesis Report.* Washington, DC: The World Bank, 2010.

WRI, Oxfam, and ODI. *The Plumbing of Adaptation Finance: Accountability, Transparency and Accessibility at the Local Level.* Working Paper, Washington, DC, 2013: 32.

# 8  Objectifying traditional knowledge, re-enchanting the struggle against climate change

*Jean Foyer and David Dumoulin Kervran*

Weather forecasting by pastoralists, fire management and control over their terri-tory by residents of tropical forests, sophisticated water management and selection of drought-resistant seeds by peasants in arid zones, nomadic adaptation strategies, observations of ice by inhabitants of the Arctic, locally adapted strategies for pre-dicting and surviving cyclones in coastal regions or on islands – these are just a few examples of traditional knowledge and practices that are passed down from genera-tion to generation, and that could be mobilised in order to better understand and combat climate change. Yet and until recently, traditional knowledge was practi-cally absent from climate change discussions and this regardless of its longstanding presence in other UN arenas, such as the Convention on Biological Diversity, the World Intellectual Property Organization (WIPO), UNESCO and the Food and Agriculture Organisation (FAO). The Paris Agreement has changed this situa-tion. Its preamble recognises "the rights of indigenous peoples" and the possibility for some cultures to conceptualise "biodiversity" as "Mother Earth". Further, it includes an explicit reference to traditional knowledge in its adaptation section:

> Parties acknowledge that adaptation action [. . .] taking into consideration vulnerable groups, communities and ecosystems and should be based on and *guided by the best available science and, as appropriate, traditional knowledge, knowledge of indigenous peoples and local knowledge systems*, with a view to inte-grating adaptation into relevant socioeconomic and environmental policies and actions, where appropriate.
>
> (Paris Agreement, Article 7.5)

This paragraph tells us several important things. First, given that traditional knowledge[1] entered the climate regime through the growing attention towards adaptation, its evolution is closely linked with that concept. Traditional rural peoples have not participated in the general diagnosis of "global climate change", but they are now recognised as knowledgeable observers regarding the assess-ment of its impacts and identification of adaptation strategies. Second, this new legitimacy given to traditional knowledge forms part of a broader trend in climate governance since Copenhagen: bottom-up, situated approaches have replaced top-down efforts (see introduction). Third, this development is striking in that

Article 7.5 signals an alignment between Western scientific knowledge and traditional knowledge to guide "programmes and public policies" for adaptation. This alignment is rather unexpected, to say the least, as political actions within the climate regime are supposed to be based on a different set of global "sound" sciences, as synthesised mainly by the IPCC.

The low profile of knowledge considered as useful and the high "epistemic selectivity" (Vadrot 2014) of the climate arena have been strongly criticised. Indeed, climate knowledge has been largely dominated by disciplines from the natural sciences, such as earth systems science, atmospheric chemistry, physics, (paleo)geology, glaciology and climatology, which are rooted mainly in Western countries and involve heavy instrumentation (satellites, calculators, etc.). And, when social scientists have been invited to comment on climate change, again the results were mostly global models, and under the influence of one key discipline: economics. This domination of complex and abstract models and global metrologies like "global mean temperature" or "tonne of carbon" has been criticised (Miller 2004, Hulme 2010) for its tendency to "flatten the world" and to erase differences in human experiences, understandings, epistemologies, values and meanings of climate change (Pielke and Sarewitz 2005, Salick and Ross 2009, Bellier 2013, Beck et al. 2014). This decoupling from the direct experience of climate change also blurs the territoriality and temporality of the problem and makes its political translation more difficult (Jasanoff 2010). Finally, the hegemony of global and abstract knowledge is strongly correlated to an equally exclusive political order (Jasanoff 2004).

Hence, some authors are calling for a repolitisation and reterritorialisation (Aykut and Dahan 2015) of climate governance, which will demand better inclusion of traditional and local knowledge in the assessment of climate change (Ford, Vanderbilt and Berrang-Ford 2012, Ford et al. 2016). In this context of contestation in the global arena, the discursive and political category of "traditional knowledge" functions as an "inverted image", in that it is mainly defined and used in direct contrast to the mainstream definition of global, top-down sound science and governance.[2] This strong opposition differs greatly from how the academic disciplines of science and technology studies (STS) and anthropology portray the complex relationship between science and traditional knowledge (Agrawal 1995, Ellen, Parkes and Bicker 2000, Hastrup and Skrydstrup 2015). However, this "purified" opposition, even if sketchy, has resonated with collective imaginaries during COP21.

How does the climate regime affect the traditional knowledge category, and conversely, how does the inclusion of traditional knowledge affect the climate regime? Using the "translation" concept (Latour 2005), we argue that this cross-translation process results from a kind of metaphoric exchange. The price for this climatisation is an *objectification* of traditional knowledge through politics and science – an objectification that enables different sets of actors to advance their agendas while at the same time providing additional *symbolic capital* (Bourdieu 1994) to climate governance. This technocratic arena is hence "re-enchanted"[3] through narratives that give it a little something extra.

Methodologically, our analysis draws on the on-site ethnographic observation of almost thirty events at COP21, where traditional knowledge was discussed, in a systematic review of academic and grey literature (from UN bodies and NGO reports) and in interviews with key actors who promote traditional knowledge. Theoretically, we combine various analytical frameworks with a strong construc-tivist perspective, inspired by STS and political anthropology. Clearly, we are not talking about the form of traditional knowledge "on the ground", as "clas-sical" ethno-scientists or anthropologists do. Rather, in line with the anthro-pology of international institutions (Müller 2013), anthropology of indigenous performance on the UN stage (Bellier 2013) and analyses of the use of knowl-edge and worldviews as political resources (Blaser 2009), traditional knowledge is seen here as a category of global governance (Brosius 2006) with a strong political dimension (Agrawal 2002, Dumoulin 2003, Nadasy 2005). As Manuela Carneiro da Cunha (2009) did for the concept of culture, we can distinguish "traditional knowledge" as an ex-situ discursive and reflexive category, separate from traditional knowledge as a practice that is directly observable and per-formed in situ. Yet between the grassroots communities and the international arenas, the category of traditional knowledge is mediated and politicised (Alex-iades 2009) via various chains of translation by very different actors – including indigenous peoples themselves, academics, development brokers and country delegates – with different meanings and political objectives (Brosius 2006).

The first part of our chapter deals with the climatisation of traditional knowl-edge, by analysing the work and interactions of the main spokespersons (indig-enous people, scientists, parties to the UNFCCC) in the run-up to and during COP21. According to their interests and agendas, and in order to align with global climate debates, these spokespersons perform two processes of politicisation and scientisation of the traditional knowledge category. In the second part, we explore the effects of traditional knowledge "narratives" upon the climate change regime, and their ability to re-enchant it through new storytelling, actors and solutions.

## Political and scientific climatisation

We first aim to explain why traditional knowledge has recently gained such high visibility in the climate arena, and to answer some basic questions, such as "Who speaks for traditional knowledge in a global conference like COP21? With what kind of political agenda? How does its climatisation influence this knowledge?" To do so, we will illustrate how the different agendas of indigenous peoples' organisations, scientists and states tend to have two main impacts on traditional knowledge: *politicisation*, when its defence is a way to transform the power structure among actors, and *scientisation*, when this defence is focused more on epistemic and management issues. These two modes of climatisation are main-tained together but are prioritised differently by the key players, especially indig-enous peoples' organisations and scientists advocating for traditional knowledge, who have built a long-lasting partnership. Some states must also be considered as spokespeople for this kind of knowledge. We will see that their participation in *climatising* traditional knowledge has been crucial but inspired by different political strategies that influenced the way they framed it.

### Rights first? The politicisation of traditional knowledge

The salience of traditional knowledge in the climate arena – and the fact that indigenous peoples now have their authorised representatives present there – was not always evident. It is the result of a complex and open political process, leading to the specific "translation" that appears in the Paris Agreement. The emergence of traditional knowledge in the climate arena has depended crucially on the emergence of a strong "indigenous peoples" actor, engaged in "competitive knowledge claims about nature" (Goldman et al. 2011, 3) and able to speak for all indigenous peoples, despite the heterogeneity of the realities covered by this expression. The main claim of the indigenous peoples' global movement has always been specific collective rights, as defined and promoted in the UN declaration on the rights of indigenous peoples since 2007.[4] Their agenda is clearly political, involving: first, more rights for indigenous peoples, and second, the recognition of traditional knowledge. Two main impulsions in 2007/08 and 2013/14 reorganised the place of indigenous actors, the place of traditional knowledge in their agenda, and their relationship with parties and bodies of the Climate Convention.

The years 2007/08 were a fundamental time due to the confluence of various elements, beginning with the formation of a centralised indigenous institution within the climate arena, known as the "indigenous caucus" or International Indigenous Peoples' Forum on Climate Change (IIPFCC). In 2001, the secretariat had already given indigenous representatives the status of "observer organisations" (along with NGOs, farmers, women, business, etc.), which initiated a promising process of interaction that had a low profile until 2007. Conceived as the head of the "major group", the Indigenous Caucus strives to build up common positions, draft statements, proposals and recommendations. Another element was the rapidly growing importance of adaptation and REDD+ (Reducing Emissions from Deforestation and Forest Degradation) issues that brought new saliency to local actors, and particularly to tropical forest organisations (see Viard-Crétat and Buffet, this volume). Adaptation and REDD+ opened new windows of opportunity for indigenous land claims, as well as for specific funding to implement a new local "information system" for measurement, reporting and verification (MRV) of forest carbon. Also, the issue of "ecosystem-based adaptation" intensified relations among biodiversity's actors and the Convention on Biological Diversity (CBD) process, in which traditional knowledge issues were more familiar. The last one among these converging trends was the first mention of traditional knowledge by the IPCC in its fourth assessment report in 2007, as well as its inclusion in the "Bali Action Plan", a roadmap released by the UNFCCC. This evolution ultimately led to the adoption of the 2010 Cancun Adaptation Framework (CAF) a few years later, wherein the formula "*adaptation strategies based on and guided by the best available science and, as appropriate, traditional and indigenous knowledge*" (decision 1/CP.16) gained official recognition.

Concurrent with this evolution inside the climate arena, the climate problem gained recognition inside indigenous arenas: in 2008, the UN Permanent Forum on Indigenous Issues held its first specific session on indigenous peoples and climate change, followed by a global summit, the first global report and handbook on the same issue and a global indigenous declaration in 2009. Various regional and national meetings around COP15 in Copenhagen marked the diffusion of climate issues into the global ecosystem of indigenous organisations. Climatisation of traditional knowledge had thus been launched.

The years 2013/14 marked the beginning of a new mobilising cycle in climate talks – with a clearer traditional knowledge perspective – that led to the Paris Agreement. The Subsidiary Body for Scientific and Technical Advice (SBSTA) asked for a special report on the use of indigenous knowledge in assessment and adaptation, which led to ad hoc meetings with high participation of indigenous organisations. That initiative, along with parallel, enhanced discussion mechanisms with "friendly states" and the release of the second volume of the fifth IPCC report on adaptation, formed building blocks for raising awareness among parties about the importance of traditional knowledge. This "knowledge turn" of the adaptation work programme is coherent with other existing initiatives on local adaptation (i.e. risk reduction); it can be viewed as a strategic way of using this knowledge for innovative adaptation strategies, and disconnecting it from participation, prior consent or rights. Indigenous organisations intensified their mobilisation and maintained their position of putting rights first, but advancing traditional knowledge in the UNFCCC followed closely after that on their agenda. The first "Indigenous Pavilion" within the COP20 official space in Lima gave material and symbolic visibility to this newcomer in climate negotiations, and all the official side events and mobilisations around the conference demonstrated this new importance of indigenous peoples' organisations.

COP21 marked a high point regarding the visibility of indigenous peoples. Each day the *caucus* gathered some sixty delegates in the "blue zone", while more than 200 indigenous representatives travelled to the conference and took part in its various events. The caucus played a proactive role in pushing for indigenous wording in the draft agreement, and comprised working groups that conducted intense advocacy activities throughout the COP. Indigenous organisations also organized and took part in numerous side events with high participation. The most visible and active organisations were coordinated by historical indigenous platforms, such as the Forest Peoples Programme, the International Alliance of Indigenous and Tribal Peoples of the Tropical Forests (IAITPTF), the Coordinadora de las Organizaciones Indígenas de la Cuenca Amazónica (COICA) and the Asia Indigenous Peoples Pact (AIPP). All of these groups entered the climate arena after an engagement within the tropical forest/biodiversity arena. Their framing is aligned with their main interest in the REDD+ programme and modes of funding, often turning traditional knowledge into a claim for good (and cheap) management and monitoring of forests for carbon storage.

Within the "*Espaces Générations Climat*", the Indigenous Peoples Pavillion was the largest and it attracted high-level media coverage. During the two weeks that it operated, a full programme of daily cultural events, press conferences and panel discussions created an opportunity to showcase, perform and explain indigenous identities of regions around the world.[5] In that display, references to traditional knowledge via mentions of IPCC assessments and other scientific reports were used as a mark of legitimacy. Support for traditional knowledge and indigenous rights was also constructed through the lobbying of state delegates and journalists, and alliance building with other civil society actors, like women, human rights groups, trade unions and farmers. For the indigenous movement itself, that mobilisation in the climate arena has revived a broader dynamic of mobilisation at the global level, after the intense period culminating in the UN declaration on indigenous rights at the end of the 2000s. Hence, climate is one of the international arenas in which indigenous peoples are the most invested. There are, however, strong limitations to this "rights first" position of the Indigenous Caucus. Indigenous peoples lack a specific institutional working group in the COP process, which is still profoundly state-centred (Schroeder 2010, Ford et al. 2016). At the national level, they also lack dedicated funding, and national adaptation plans mention traditional knowledge infrequently (Maillet and Ford 2013).

Several Northern European states, Peru, Mexico and the Philippines have supported indigenous peoples with financial and political resources and by relaying their demands in climate negotiations. But discussions on the draft proposal of the Paris Agreement also showed that these states were looking to impose a specific framing, which disconnects knowledge from rights, against the will of indigenous organisations.[6] The main driver of this kind of support for traditional knowledge could be a desire to re-enchant the climate arena without paying the higher political cost of backing indigenous peoples' rights. In a sense, the reference to traditional knowledge in the adaptation operative section of the Paris Agreement – while indigenous rights are mentioned only in the weaker preamble section – reflects a form of compromise between a "rights first" versus a "knowledge first" approach.

Evo Morales's Bolivia and Bolivarian Alliance states (Bolivia, Ecuador, Venezuela, Cuba, Nicaragua, etc.) represent another way of politicising traditional knowledge. Since the end of the 2000s, "Rights of Nature" and "Mother Earth", two important components of Bolivarian states' phraseology and constitutions, became the dominant framework for numerous organisations in Latin America, but also for broader international coalitions,[7] and hence those terms appeared in the preamble of the COP Decision in Paris. Like the Indigenous Peoples' Caucus, these diplomatic voices insist on the link between traditional knowledge and criticism of the dominant political order. But unlike that argument, Bolivia's demands for the recognition of traditional knowledge in global fora are not focused on the struggle for indigenous peoples' rights, but rather they aim to mobilise civil society. The country organised two widely publicised "Conferences of the Peoples on Climate Change and the Rights of Mother Earth" in Tiquipaya, Cochabamba, in 2010 and 2015, which forged an international coalition, and their conclusions are supposed to dictate the agenda of Bolivarian states for climate negotiations. However, the flagrant contradictions between this international discourse on one hand and persistence "on the ground" of extractivist and anti-indigenous politics on the other point to a primarily instrumental use of indigenous themes and framings. They are mobilised to criticise powerful "Western" states that are viewed as destroying nature and the peoples, and to build an anti-capitalist block. That is why we label this more rhetorical celebration of "Pachamama" and vague reference to "saberes ancestrales" as a process of "hyper-politicisation" of traditional knowledge.

In this first section, we have portrayed different ways that traditional knowledge has been translated and used by different actors to respond to their political agendas. Traditional knowledge is objectified, as it is considered in climate arenas not so much for what it means on the ground but as a political instrument. A second kind of objectification corresponds to the scientific translation of traditional knowledge to fit UN formats.

## Lost in normalisation: the scientisation of traditional knowledge

Anthropologists and scientists from related disciplines have also played a role as spokespersons for traditional knowledge in the climate change arena. While they were not very visible during the conference itself, they are key players, acting as an "epistemic community" (Haas 1992, Hajer 1995) that defends the value and legitimacy of traditional knowledge.

The first step in the construction of this epistemic community occurred in the early 2000s, when a growing body of anthropological studies documented how climate change affects Arctic peoples. Bestowing great importance on the role of indigenous knowledge for resilience and integration with scientific knowledge, studies of Inuit communities opened new paths for a growing field of research. It was not until the end of the decade, however, that these topics began to emerge in the climate arena (Salick and Byg 2007, Macchi et al. 2008, Salick and Ross 2009). The globalisation of this epistemic community intensified in 2011 with a conference in Mexico co-organised by the IPCC, and also a new institutional publication by UN University and UNESCO that presented a broad overview of "traditional knowledge and climate change". More recently, a growing body of literature is produced by a small cluster of scholars, collating early studies of the Arctic with publications on traditional knowledge and tropical forests, as well as texts on monitoring, risk reduction or agricultural resilience.[8] Frequent co-citations and cross-participation of experts in global meetings and committees indicate the solidification of this new epistemic community. Its core is constituted through the climatisation of actors constituted initially in the biodiversity/forests arena (Dumoulin 2003).

This epistemic community developed a strong partnership with indigenous peoples' organisations, and are advocating for a very rich version of traditional knowledge that is connected with indigenous rights. Such "epistemic advocacy" (Hayden 2003) is grounded on the recognition of a diversity of ways of knowing and living in the world. A case in point is a small UNESCO programme called LINKS

(Local and Indigenous Knowledge Systems), which has a long involvement in the promotion of traditional knowledge. It represents a way of recycling and regenerating a "bio-cultural" framing at the crossroads between biodiversity studies by ecologists and cultural diversity studies by ethno-scientists. The lead officer of the programme, D. Nakashima, embodies this intense global advocacy, based on his multi-positionality (i.e. institutional memberships in UNESCO, CBD, IPBES, IPCC, etc.) and alliances with like-minded funders (e.g. Christensen Fund, IWGIA, the Norwegian and Swedish governments) and indigenous peoples' organisations (Tebtebba, etc.).

A key contribution has been the production and showcasing of the UNESCO report *Weathering Uncertainty: Traditional Knowledge for Climate Change Assessment and Adaptation* (Nakashima, McLean, Thulstrup, Castillo and Rubis 2012). This is the first science-based official report offering a global overview: it reached a broad international audience (and was quoted extensively in this emergent field), and helped to synthesise contributions from different actors into a common agenda. LINKS-UNESCO experts intensified their advocacy in the climate arena, through discussions with authors of the IPCC's fifth assessment report, through broader networking activities and then via participation in a long series of events surrounding the preparation for COP21 and the Paris Agreement (e.g. the IPCC, SBSTA, intersession meetings, ad hoc meetings). A climax of this activism was the organisation, days before the COP, of a large conference "Resilience in a Time of Uncertainty: Indigenous Peoples and Climate Change" at UNESCO's headquarters in Paris on 26–27 November 2015, followed by a meeting that aimed to finalise the common agenda of indigenous organisations, and another between indigenous organisations and states to prepare the coming Paris Agreement. LINKS advocacy gives privilege to knowledge and science, by institutional culture and strategy; it also promotes a pragmatic inclusion of traditional knowledge, by presenting it as applied solutions, best practices and methodologies, with a plea for integration between scientific and traditional knowledge (see the second section). However, they do not defend a kind of "dis-embedded flying knowledge", but see the recognition of traditional knowledge as a first step on the way to a larger transformation of the climate arena that would make it more receptive to demands of indigenous peoples.

The IPCC has been a central target of this intensifying advocacy for traditional knowledge. However, the appearance of traditional knowledge in IPCC reports has been a very slow process. The fourth assessment report is the first to contain a reference to the issue, yet it made "*only scarce mention of indigenous peoples, and then only in polar regions and merely as helpless victims of changes beyond their control*" (Salick and Ross 2009, 137). It was not until the fifth assessment report, released in 2014, that a move towards the recognition of traditional knowledge could be observed. Within the pool of IPCC authors and reviewers, experts with this kind of knowledge are still extraordinarily scarce,[9] which hampered how it has been captured. The report contains no specific chapter on traditional knowledge, but reveals a strong growth in scattered keywords related to indigenous issues, and includes specific sections, such as "Indigenous Peoples" and "Local and Traditional Forms of Knowledge" (12.3.2 & 3 of Volume 2), in regional chapters.

Nevertheless, this growing body of references on traditional knowledge within such a prestigious scientific publication constitutes strong leverage for all indigenous actors who are fighting for more recognition. The epistemic community continues the advocacy by favouring broader coverage of traditional knowledge in the next IPCC AR6, and by calling for an alignment with other existing climate change assessments for the Arctic region or for the United States.

Still, when mainstream climate scientists show interest in traditional knowledge, it is typically about an issue where they identify a "knowledge gap", and about traditional knowledge that could be "validated" by science. This "consecration" in IPCC reports is a costly translation process, alterations that have been aptly described by Agrawal as "scientisation" in the case of traditional knowledge (Agrawal 1995). First, it is depoliticised, as a vast majority of such references are vague, and knowledge holders are quoted among a list of vulnerable communities without reference to "indigenous peoples" as actors with specific rights. Traditional knowledge is presented in isolation from any broader historical, political and ethical background, and even its links to expropriation and land claims are missing. Second, the challenging epistemic "otherness" of this kind of knowledge is lost through normalisation. References are punctual (e.g. one empirical observation of a specific event) and traditional knowledge is presented mainly as a source of new data. The complexity and diversity of indigenous knowledge systems, and the holistic and spiritual nature of this knowledge, are not adequately captured (Ford et al. 2016).

This scientisation of traditional knowledge has created a strong push for its presence in the new Paris Agreement, because it is an easy way for mainstream scientists and states to give some recognition to indigenous issues, and to renew climate discourses, without actually having to share power, to extend rights or to affect the dominant epistemology.

Scientisation and politicisation are both efficient modes of climatisation. While opening two opposite paths, they give traditional knowledge access to the climate arena (see Figure 8.1). Both are processes of translation, emerging from actors' interactions, and performed through different operations (e.g. mobilisations, lobbying and publication of articles, books and reports). In fact, as is true for many other global categories, understanding the role of traditional knowledge in global climate politics is interesting not so much by what it pretends to do but much more by what it enables different actors and institutions to do. More than fighting against climate change, it allows indigenous actors to continue their historical struggle for their rights, control over their territory and recognition as peoples; it allows outsider states to pretend to fight against capitalism; it allows UN institutions to renew their concepts and legitimise themselves through the acknowledgement of marginalised categories of actors; and it allows different communities of scientists to requalify and legitimise their research agendas.

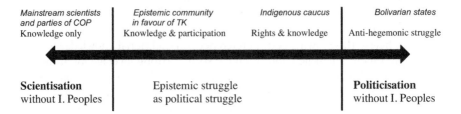

| Mainstream scientists and parties of COP<br>Knowledge only | Epistemic community in favour of TK<br>Knowledge & participation | Indigenous caucus<br><br>Rights & knowledge | Bolivarian states<br><br>Anti-hegemonic struggle |
|---|---|---|---|
| **Scientisation**<br>without I. Peoples | Epistemic struggle<br>as political struggle | | **Politicisation**<br>without I. Peoples |

*Figure 8.1* The climatisation of traditional knowledge, according to the principal actors.
Source: Authors.

## Re-enchanting the struggle against climate change

The reverse translation movement corresponds to the impact of the recognition of traditional knowledge upon the climate arena. It took the form of new climate narratives that gained momentum and reached a broader audience during COP21. In line with constructivist environmental discourse analysis (Hajer 1995, Nadasdy 1999), we will now analyse the two main narratives about traditional knowledge and climate change that we observed there: the "resilient victim-hero" and the "integration narrative". Both have been used by a large array of spokespeople, and they participate in re-enchanting the struggle against climate change by offering new storytellings, new positive actors, new bottom-up solutions and even other visions of nature.

### The "resilience narrative": when victims become heroes

Regarding the press coverage of COP15 in Copenhagen, Roosval and Tegelberg (2013) argued that indigenous peoples have been misframed as victim-heroes. Paying special attention to traditional knowledge, we want to deepen here the analysis of the victim-heroes category and to show how it renewed the broader resilience narrative (Folke 2006, Cannon and Müller-Mahn 2010) at COP21. For us, this narrative is not just a politically blind misrepresentation by the media, as Roosval and Tegelberg argued, but also a powerful tale with strong symbolical and political dimensions, produced largely by indigenous representatives themselves. We will show that traditional knowledge plays a very important part in this narrative that combines denunciation of the impact of climate change with a proposed set of solutions. If this discourse is not exactly new,[10] it was certainly actualised and widely legitimised during COP21.

Throughout the two weeks of the conference, indigenous peoples presented themselves as the first witnesses of climate change, because they have directly experienced it. Then, after the scientific alert of the IPCC, comes the alert of indigenous peoples based on stories of that experience. Melting of Arctic ice floes for the Inuit, melting of glaciers for indigenous peoples from the Himalaya, problems of drought, access to water and loss of agricultural land for the Maya in Guatemala, desertification for Peul pastoralists in Chad: these are but a few of the striking examples shared to demonstrate how indigenous peoples form the front line for climate change effects, despite the fact that they scarcely contributed to the phenomenon. This discourse about a situation of unfair vulnerability enables them to also embody climate injustice,[11] and gives them legitimacy to request funds, resources and other help from the international community.

This general discourse about indigenous peoples combines their simultaneous roles as witness, whistle-blower and victim. First, there is some empirical evidence that climate change has indeed caused dramatic impacts on indigenous peoples' livelihoods, with wide-ranging effects on their cultures and even on the validity of traditional knowledge. In Kayapo's territory in Amazonia, the disappearance of certain insect species (e.g. cicadas, bees, butterflies) because of increasing temperatures also represents the disappearance of important time and space markers for indigenous peoples there: "Now we are disorientated, if we lose our way in the forest, we don't know anymore how to get back home" (Kayapo representative, 11 December 2015, translation by the authors). The seasonal cycles of the rainforest seem to be perturbed, and hence so does their entire culture. From territory control to rituals, including human health, climate change seems to be exacting a very high cultural impact.

Yet this discourse about climate change affecting traditional knowledge is marginal, compared to the one that presents traditional knowledge as a new set of solutions in the fight against climate change. In this narrative, indigenous peoples appear to be active providers of solutions rather than passive subjects "suffering" from climate change, and traditional knowledge is precisely the element that allows resilience – that is it enables the transition from victim to a positive status of problem-solver.

The narrative was present during the conference "Resilience in a Time of Uncertainty: Indigenous Peoples and Climate Change" just before the opening of COP21, co-organised by UNESCO and the National Museum of Natural History of France (MNHN), in partnership with Tebtebba and various national and international institutions.[12] The text that presented the event offers a perfect summary of this narrative:

> For over 350 million indigenous peoples, climate change impacts are expected to be early and severe due to their location in high risk environments. To face these challenges, indigenous peoples are mobilizing their in-depth knowledge of the territories which have been the source of their livelihoods for generations. This indigenous knowledge operates at a much finer spatial and temporal scale than that of science, and includes understandings of how to cope with and adapt to environmental variability and trends. Indigenous knowledge can thus make an important contribution towards climate change action on adaptation and mitigation (e.g. REDD+) and in recent years this has been formally recognized by IPCC and UNFCCC.
>
> (UNESCO 2016, para. 2)

This quote clearly insists on the specific features of traditional knowledge: its scale compared to that of science; its pragmatic and practical dimension to adapt to changing environmental conditions; and its "actionability" in policies against climate change. Nevertheless, beyond the repetition of this general narrative, concrete examples of it and of how traditional knowledge could be mobilised in the fight against climate change were not very visible during this conference, or in general during the COP. We heard many brief references, such as weather forecasts in Inuit or African pastoralist territories, fire management in communities within forests and strategies for the conservation and recovery of native seeds that are resistant to the effects of climate change in Peru. Even if the short format of side events does not enable in-depth discussion of specific traditional knowledge or concrete projects based on it, throughout all of the different events that we attended, we have noted that any references to traditional knowledge as solutions were mostly elusive and rhetorical.

Another variation of the victim-hero narrative originated from the claims by indigenous peoples for other ways of composing the world and conceiving nature through shamanism and its "ecology". This spiritual dimension and the ability to bring that knowledge to "Western people" are the core building blocks of this variation that we have termed "supernatural ecology". Invited by the Ile de France Region for various events during the COP, representatives of the Quichua People from Sarayacu (Ecuadorian Amazonia) were very active in diffusing this kind of message with their Living Rainforest ("Selva Viviente") initiative (see Figure 8.2). Felix Santi, president of the community of Sarayacu, stated firmly,

> We came from the remote land of Ecuador, upset by the situation of indigenous people, connected with the guardians of the forest, with a connection to the cosmic world. Climate change affects all the living beings that live on this little planet, the Earth. Sarayacu elaborated its living plan and its proposal: Living Rainforest (Selva Viviente), Kawsak Sacha. Sarayacu's proposal is a space where we apply the ancestral knowledge. Our Yachak, our wise men, interact with the beings who protect the water, the mountains and the forest [. . .] The main objective is to reach a clear recognition by the Ecuadorian state of this space as a sacred bio-cultural heritage, free from oil exploitation. Our call to the international community is to become aware of the necessity to maintain the Kawsak Sacha, the living rainforest.
>
> (Felix Santi, 1 December 2015, translation by the authors)[13]

In this statement, we find a fascinating mix of claims about alternative worldviews through endogenous categories, environmental and ethical proposals to the Western world, classical indigenous territorial claims, and appropriation of international categories, such as climate change and bio-cultural heritage. The presence of this narrative at COP21 is quite ambiguous, since it is at the same time an opportunity for indigenous peoples to explain and expose their radically different manner of conceiving nature, and a way for the institutions that invite them (in this case, the Ile de France Region) and more generally the UNFCC

*Figure 8.2* Representatives of the Quichua People from Sarayacu in the *Espaces Générations Climat.*

Source: Authors.

arena to benefit from their symbolic capital in order to re-enchant discourses about climate change.

Beyond its rhetorical dimension and performative effect on the climate change arena, this narrative of the strongly resilient victim-hero must be interpreted as a new example of the "inversion of stigma" (Goffman 1963) for the formerly "archaic" peoples, echoing even a Christ-like redemption, as suffering is transformed through salvation.

### The "integration narrative": a dialogue of knowledge and innovations

The second important narrative that was perceptible throughout COP21 presents traditional knowledge and scientific knowledge as complementary approaches to fighting climate change. This narrative tends to blur the divide between traditional knowledge and science to establish new ways of co-managing the environment.

Examples of collaborations between indigenous peoples and scientists were showcased at different occasions during the conference. For instance Hindou Oumarou Ibrahim, representative of the Peul people of Chad and responsible for the Indigenous Caucus at COP21, described a project wherein pastoralist nomads had invited cooperation with meteorologists: "This is when those scientists realized the vastness of indigenous knowledge about the environment. This experience has valorised our knowledge and led to an evolution in contemporary research."[14]

According to this perspective, indigenous knowledge is more than merely traditional and local; it can contribute new data and perspectives to modern science, and thus participate in designing innovative adaptation strategies. This narrative is a clear departure from the usual "scientised" conception of traditional knowledge as a stable set of cognitive elements. It enables the actors that use it to concur with the dominant narrative, whereby modern science aims at innovation for resource management.

Another potent example of the integration perspective was presented during a side event in the Pavilion of Peru: three scientists[15] and two indigenous representatives presented a project about a network of living laboratories known as the Indigenous Peoples Biocultural Climate Change Assessment Initiative (IPCCA).[16] The IPCCA is a global network of nine projects in North and South America, Asia, Africa and Europe that promotes a methodology for local climate change monitoring based on participatory mapping and workshops for dialogue between scientists and indigenous people. Most of the presentations related to conservation of agrobiodiversity, including the need to conserve local seeds and crops to adapt to climate change. This trend indicated a form of reconversion of the more classical discourse about traditional knowledge and crop biodiversity in ethnobotany, and in international fora, such as the FAO.

The goal for a network of different local, living laboratories is to develop a long-term, global picture of climate change in indigenous communities. The integration narrative rejects not only a fixed vision of tradition in indigenous knowledge but also its reduction to locality. As Alejandro Argumedo explained, "colonialism reduced us to the local" (personal interview, 3 December 2015), while in reality, knowledge of the ancient Inca empire for instance entails a much wider perspective and is linked to far-reaching capacities of measurement and planning. According to this vision, traditional knowledge is (whether combined with scientific knowledge or on its own), if not global, at least extends much further than the local.

Another oft-discussed issue has been "indigenous REDD+", and more specifically one of its pillars, "indigenous MRV", which entails measuring, reporting and verification. It is a kind of reappropriation by indigenous peoples of the official UN-REDD MRV mechanism and it is based on the local and real-time monitoring of climate change by indigenous peoples themselves. It combines one of the most traditional activities of Amazonian indigenous peoples – control over their territory – with high-tech tools, such as cellular phones, GPS, satellite images and drones. As Henderson Rengifo, president of the Peruvian Amazonian indigenous organisation AIDESEP noted,

> With time, the climate jargon is always stronger. Nevertheless the so-called Indigenous Monitoring, Reporting and Verifying for us is nothing but a form of governance and vigilance of our territory, that is to say what we have

always been doing all along our history, but this time with technological tools that enable us to do it better.[17]

Indigenous MRV, sometimes illustrated by the paradoxical image of indigenous people managing drones, is another strong example of the integration narrative in which global scientific knowledge and techniques are combined with on-the-ground local knowledge.

The integration narrative is not new. It has structured the co-management discourse that is already established in conservation science and policies, and it allows actors from this sector to recycle their perspectives in climatic terms. Through supposedly better environmental management while empowering indigenous people, this win-win narrative is of course highly welcome and audible in international arenas, such as climate conferences: it offers new discursive spaces based on a reconciliation between globality and locality, tradition and modernity, high and low-tech, and dialogue of cultures. Nevertheless – from the question of the commensurability between radically different epistemologies, to the difficulty of implementing that view in concrete projects; from the monolithic vision of both science and traditional knowledge to the implicit relations of power embedded in such practices – the integration narrative has also inspired academic debate (Bohensky and Mahru 2011) and provoked critique (Nadasdy 1999, Nadasy 2005). By implying a dialogic movement of indigenisation of scientific knowledge, along with a scientisation of traditional knowledge, the integration discourse is a highly ambiguous project. Its climatisation opens a new chapter for this sort of practice and debate.

## Conclusion: how the global category of traditional knowledge creates productive misunderstandings

Having characterised the politics and narratives of traditional knowledge observed during COP21, let's return to our initial question about how the climate change regime and traditional knowledge affect one another.

Beginning with the climatisation of traditional knowledge, climate change has been the foundation for recycling and requalifying various arguments coming from other UN arenas (e.g. CBD, FAO). It has also expanded the traditional knowledge category, since new regions (e.g. the Arctic, arid Africa, the Pacific Islands) and new epistemic practices (weather forecasting, water management, early warning systems, etc.) were included. Specific to the climate change arena, these regions and practices were absent in the arenas where traditional knowledge was initially staged, and where it was framed mainly in terms of intellectual property rights. Moreover, we have shown that this climatisation process is based on different forms of "politicisation" and "scientisation", both of which are used by different actor groups, according to their interests and agendas, as privileged means to enter climate arenas. Political instrumentalisation to serve pre-established agendas, or standardisation of traditional knowledge to make it legible (Scott 1998) for management in the UN apparatus, is the main side effect of this process, which corresponds *in fine* to an objectification of culture (Carneiro da Cunha 2009). It therefore widens the rift between the global category of traditional knowledge and the extreme diversity of empirical practices it is supposed to describe.[18]

Inversely, the introduction of traditional knowledge in the climate regime has contributed to renew and re-enchant the struggle against climate change. This re-enchantment is the result of an array of convergent effects: new storytelling with new "exotic" figures, such as the resilient "victim-hero", and new practical and grounded options that counterbalance and complement scientific abstraction. In some cases, like in the supernatural ecology narrative, it even introduces magical dimensions and other ontologies in dominant representations of climate change. However, this re-enchantment remains weak, since traditional knowledge is still a very marginal topic in climate talks. Furthermore, there is clearly a very long way to go from this global emergence of traditional knowledge as the golden bullet for adaptation to climate change to its concrete integration within adaptation programmes, as shown by existing experiences in biodiversity conservation projects (Bohensky and Mahru 2011).

The dialogical movement of climatisation of traditional knowledge and the inclusion of traditional knowledge in climate talks can then be described as a kind of symbolic exchange between scientific and political objects on one side and symbolic force and capital on the other. Traditional knowledge "needs" to be objectified by political instrumentation and scientific standardisation in order to penetrate the climate arena, as it must respond to different interests and fit the recognised UN format. In the exchange of this access, traditional knowledge delivers its symbolic power and lends the climate change arena a "supplement d'âme" – that is a human face of courage and wisdom.

This exchange is ambiguous. If it can be interpreted as yet another example of the domination of the Western world over indigenous cultures, it can also constitute an instrument of visibility and empowerment for indigenous peoples that grants them better access to legitimacy, funding or rights. Whatever the case, traditional knowledge appears as a global category because of its capacity to unite many different realities related to widely divergent political agendas. Based on a fundamental semantic ambiguity, it ultimately generates what Marshall Shalins called a productive misunderstanding through "worlds of semantic compromise whose dialectics both bypass and reaffirm symbolic incompatibilities in confrontation" (Albert 1993, 369). By putting the narratives and the politics of traditional knowledge side by side, we have shown that it is precisely these epistemological, cultural and political misunderstandings that help us to understand the rise of traditional knowledge as a global category.

## Notes

1 We are conscious that these distinctions among traditional, local and indigenous knowledge represent a battlefield for semantic struggles with potentially important political consequences, as with all processes of stabilisation of international categories. For example some would say that "Indigenous people knowledge" undermines the existence

of Peoples (with an s) with collective rights, "traditional knowledge" negates the potential of indigenous innovation and "local knowledge" hides the history of colonialism and negates the scope of this kind of knowledge. Nevertheless, in this chapter we will not enter the diplomatic or the theoretical debates about the differences among these categories. Theoretically, those differences are not clearly stabilised in the academic literature, and even less in the international context, where they are most often confounded. In the rest of the chapter, we will refer to *traditional knowledge*, because it is the easiest and broadest category.

2 These broadly shared ideal-types tend to place the following in opposition: locality to globality, particularity to universality, embeddedness to the "view from nowhere" (Shapin 1998), tangibility and emotions to abstraction, experience to speculation, actionability to inefficiency, situatedness to generality, marginalisation to domination, tradition to modernity, and even spirituality to materiality, among other contrasts.

3 This expression refers to the Weberian terminology painting bureaucratic rationalisation as a historical process of disenchantment. Climate negotiations have experienced a process of bureaucratisation and epistemic dominance (see earlier), as well as a kind of breakdown after the "failure" of Copenhagen. Various authors have proposed the concept of re-enchantment to describe the process that opposes the disenchantment (Landy and Saler 2009), as we do in this chapter.

4 Striking point: while indigenous land rights were ultimately *not* kept in the Paris Agreement, they nevertheless became an important issue of the climatisation process because various new global initiatives support these rights as one solution for forest/carbon conservation (see Ecuador Prize by UNDP, Indigenous Peoples Global Fund by Norway and the LandMark initiative).

5 References to IPCC assessments and other scientific reports are sometimes quoted in indigenous claims, but references are more used as a mark of legitimacy, in the same way that the list of indigenous rights international norms is used.

6 See for example the minutes of different meetings during 2015, in particular the one in Bonn in October.

7 Evo Morales was the first head of state to address the UN Permanent Forum on Indigenous Issues in April 2008, expressing the indianist/anti-capitalist views that also inspire his famous discourses at COP13 in Bali and at COP21. Also see the Global Alliance for Rights of Nature (http://therightsofnature.org/) and its members.

8 Cf. risk reduction and natural hazard (i.e. early warning systems), traditional agriculture or forest management (i.e. REDD+ programmes).

9 Ford et al. (2012) affirm that only 2.9% of authors have published on indigenous issues or related matters; in addition to this low participation of experts in chapters' authorship, very few external reviewers' comments are addressing this issue (0.3% for AR4).

10 In 2007 and 2008, Tebtebba organised different participatory case studies in indigenous territories in Asia and Africa about adaptation strategies. This study has resulted in a publication of reference titled *Knowledge, Innovation and Resilience* (Loretto Tamayo and Alangi 2012) and then has contributed to the articulation of traditional knowledge with resilience.

11 Nevertheless, the framing of their situation in terms of "climate justice" is not that explicit (Roosvall and Tegelberg 2015), including during COP21.

12 This event also received support from the French Ministry of Foreign Affairs, Sorbonne University, the Swedish International Development Cooperation Agency, the United Nations Development Programme (UNDP), Japanese funds-in-trust to UNESCO, the National Research Agency of France and Conservation International.

13  For a presentation of the Kawsak Sacha initiative, see: https://comunitariapress.wordpress.com/2015/11/17/kawsak-sacha-selva-viviente-propuesta-de-los-pueblos-originarios-frente-al-cambio-climatico.

14  This interview with channel TV5 Monde is accessible at http://information.tv5monde.com/terriennes/tchad-les-femmes-peules-au-coeur-de-la-lutte-contre-le-changement-climatique-25552. For an analysis of a dialogue about knowledge between meteorologists and indigenous people in Kenya, see Guthiga and Newsham (2011).

15  Ben Orlove, anthropologist at Columbia University, is a pioneer in the study of the perception of climate change among indigenous peoples; Alejandro Argumedo, a Quechua ethnobotanist, is one of the founders of the famous Potato Park in Peru; and Yiching Song belongs to the Chinese Center for Agricultural Policy, China.

16  For more details, see the IPCCA website: http://ipcca.info.

17  http://www.aidesep.org.pe/aidesep-presenta-su-propuesta-de-vigilancia-territorial-indigena-denominada-mrv-i.

18  What impacts traditional knowledge will have on climate change politics on the ground (and vice versa) is another problem that will deserve a set of empirical, ethnographic field studies.

## Bibliography

Agrawal, Arun. "Dismantling the divide between indigenous and scientific knowledge." *Development and Change* 26 (1995): 413–439.

Agrawal, Arun. "Indigenous knowledge and the politics of classification." *International Social Science Journal* 54, no. 173 (2002): 287–297.

Albert, Bruce. "L'Or cannibale et la chute du ciel. Une critique chamanique de l'économie politique de la nature (Yanomani Brésil)." *L'Homme* 33, no. 126 (1993): 349–378.

Alexiades, Miguel, N. "The cultural and economic globalisation of traditional environmental knowledge systems." In *Landscape, Process and Power: Re-evaluating Traditional Environmental Knowledge*, by S. Heckler, 68–98. Oxford: Berghan, 2009.

Aykut, Stefan C., and Amy Dahan. "La gouvernance du changement climatique: Anatomie d'un schisme de réalité." In *Gouverner le progrès et ses dégats*, by Dominique Pestre, 97–132. Paris: La Découverte, 2015.

Beck, Silke, Maud Borie, Jason Chilvers, Alejandro Esguerra, Katja Heubach, Mike Hulme, Rolf Lidskog, et al. "Towards a reflexive turn in the gouvernance of global environmental expertise: The cases of the IPCC and the IPBES." *Gaia* 23 (2014): 80–87.

Bellier, Irène. "'We indigenous peoples . . .' Global activism and the emergence of a new collective subject at the United Nations." In *The Gloss of Harmony: The Politics of Policy-Making in Multilateral Organizations*, by B. Müller, 177–201. London: Pluto Press, 2013.

Blaser, Mario. "Political ontology: Cultural studies without 'cultures'?" *Cultural Studies* 23, no. 5–6 (2009): 873–896.

Bohensky, Erin, and Yiheyis Mahru. "Indigenous knowledge, science and resilience: What have we learned from a decade of international literature on 'integration'." *Ecology and Society* 16, no. 4 (2011): 6.

Bourdieu, Pierre. *Raisons Pratiques*. Paris: Le Seuil, 1994.

Brosius, J. Peter. "What counts as local knowledge in global environmental assessments and conventions?" In *Bringing Scales and Knowledge Systems: Concepts and Applications in Ecosystem Assessment*, by M. W. Reid, F. Berkes, T. J. Wilbanks, D. Capistrano and editors, 129–144. Washington, DC: Island Press, 2006.

Cannon, Terry, and Detlef Müller-Mahn. "Vulnerability, resilience and development discourse in context of climate change." *Natural Hazards* 55, no. 3 (2010): 621–635.

Carneiro da Cunha, Manuela. *"Culture" and Culture: Traditional Knowledge and Intellectual Rights*. Chicago: Prickly Paradigm Press. 2009.

Dumoulin, David. "Local knowledge in the hands of transnational NGO networks: A Mexican viewpoint." *International Social Sciences Journal* 178 (2003): 593–605.

Ellen, Roy, Peter Parkes, and Alan Bicker. *Indigenous Environmental Knowledge and Its Transformation: Critical Anthropological Perspectives*. Amsterdam: Harwood Academic, 2000.

Folke, Carl. "Resilience: The emergence of a perspective for social-ecological systems analyses." *Global Environmental Change* 16, no. 3 (2006): 253–267.

Ford, James, Laura Cameron, Jennifer Rubis, Michelle Maillet, Douglas Nakashima, Ashlee Cunsolo Willox, and Tristan Pearce. "Including indigenous knowledge and experience in IPCC assessment reports." *Nature Climate Change* 6, no. 4 (2016): 349–353.

Ford, James, Will Vanderbilt, and Lea Berrang-Ford. "Authorship in IPCC AR5 and its implications for content: Climate change and indigenous populations in WGII." *Climatic Change* 113, no. 2 (2012): 201–213.

Goffman, Erving. *Stigma: Notes on the Management of Spoiled Identity*. New York: Simon and Schuster, 1963.

Goldman, Mara, Paul Nadasdy, Matthew Turner (eds). *Knowing Nature: Conversations at the Intersection of Political Ecology and Science Studies*. Chicago: University of Chicago Press, 2011.

Guthiga, Paul, and Andrew Newsham. "Meteorologists meeting rainmakers: Indigenous knowledge and climate policy processes in Kenya." *IDS Bulletin* 42 (2011): 104–109.

Haas, Peter, M. "Introduction: Epistemic communities and international policy coordination." *International Organization*, 46, no. 1 (1992): 1–35.

Hajer, Maarten. *The Politics of Environmental Discourse: Ecological Modernization and the Policy Process*. New York, NY: Oxford University Press, 1995.

Hastrup, Kirsten, and Martin Skrydstrup. *The Social Life of Climate Change Models: Anticipating Nature*. London: Routledge, 2015.

Hayden, Cori. *When Nature Goes Public, the Making and Unmaking of Bioprospecting in Mexico*. Princeton: Princeton University Press, 2003.

Hulme, Mike. "Problems with making and governing global kinds of knowledge." *Global Environmental Change – Human and Policy Dimensions* 20 (2010): 558–564.

Jasanoff, Sheila. "A new climate for society." *Theory, Culture & Society* 27 (2010): 233–253.

Jasanoff, Sheila. *States of Knowledge: The Co-production of Science and Social Order*. London: Routledge, 2004.

Landy, Joshua, and Michael Saler. *The Re-enchantment of the World: Secular Magic in a Rational Age*. Stanford: Stanford University Press, 2009.

Latour, Bruno. *Reassembling the Social: An Introduction to Actor-Network-Theory*. Oxford: Oxford UP, 2005.

Loretto Tamayo, Ann, and Wilfredo Alangi. *Knowledge, Innovation and Resilience*. Baguio City: TEBTEBBA Foundation, 2012.

Macchi, Mirjam, Gonzalo Oviedo, Sarah Gotheil, Katharine Cross, Agni Boedhihartono, Caterina Wolfangel, and Matthew Howell. *Indigenous and Traditional Peoples and Climate Change*. Issues Paper, Gland: IUCN, 2008.

Maillet, Micchelle, and James Ford. "Climate change adaptation, indigenous peoples and the United Nations Framework Convention on Climate Change (UNFCCC)." *Health Diplomacy Monitor* 4 (2013): 10–14.

Miller, Clark. "Climate science and the making of a global political order." In *States of Knowledge*, by S. Jasanoff, 46–66. New York: Routledge, 2004.

Müller, Birgit. *The Gloss of Harmony: The Politics of Policy-Making in Multilateral Organisations*. London: Pluto Press, 2013.

Nadasdy, Paul. "The anti-politics of TEK: The institutionalization of co-management discourse and practice." *Anthropologica* 47, no. 2 (2005): 215–232.

Nadasdy, Paul. "The politics of TEK: Power and the 'integration' of knowledge." *Arctic Anthropology* 36 (1999): 1–18.

Nakashima, Douglas, Kirsty Galloway McLean, Hans Thulstrup, Ameyali Ramos Castillo, and Jennifer Rubis. *Weathering Uncertainty: Traditional Knowledge for Climate Change Assessment and Adaptation*. UNESCO and UNU, Paris & Darwin: UNESCO and United Nations University Traditional Knowledge Initiative, 2012.

Pielke, Roger, and Daniel Sarewitz. "Bringing society back into the climate debate." *Population Environment* 26 (2005): 255–268.

Roosvall, Anna, and Matthew Tegelberg. "Framing climate change and indigenous peoples: Intermediaries of urgency, spirituality and de-nationalization." *The International Communication Gazette* 75, no. 4 (2013): 392–409.

Roosvall, Anna, and Matthew Tegelberg. "Media and the geographies of climate justice: Indigenous peoples, nature and the geopolitics of climate change." *Triple C* 13 (2015): 39–54.

Salick, Jan, and Anja Byg. *Indigenous Peoples and Climate Change*. Oxford: Tyndall Centre for Climate Change Research, 2007.

Salick, Jan, and Nancy Ross. "Traditional peoples and climate change introduction." *Global Environmental Change-Human and Policy Dimensions* 19 (2009): 137–139.

Schroeder, Heike. "Agency in international climate negotiations: The case of indigenous peoples and avoided deforestation." *International Environment Agreements* 10 (2010): 317–332.

Scott, James. *Seeing Like a State: How Certain Schemes to Improve the Human Condition Have Failed*. Yale: Yale University Press, 1998.

Shapin, Steven. "Placing the view from nowhere: Historical and sociological problems in the location of science." *Transactions of the Institute of British Geographers* 23 (1998): 5–12.

UNESCO. "Resilience in a Time of Uncertainty: Indigenous Peoples and Climate Change." 2015. http://www.unesco.org/new/en/unesco/events/natural-sciences-events/?tx_browser_pil[showUid]=30813&cHash=6537a47cb8 (accessed November 21, 2016).

Vadrot, Alice. *The Politics of Knowledge and Global Biodiversity*. London: Routledge, 2014.

# 9 The end of fossil fuels?

## Understanding the partial climatisation of global energy debates

*Stefan C. Aykut and Monica Castro*

> If 150 nations are taking it seriously and setting targets, even if they don't make them, that will generate massive investment and a huge amount of private-sector activity [. . .] And then you have to hope that somebody comes up with clean-energy technology, which makes it competitive with fossil fuel, and then, boom, you get your low-carbon economy.
>
> (John Kerry, US Secretary of State[1])

## Introduction

Fossil fuels are at the heart of the climate problem. They account for over 80% of global energy consumption, constitute the main source (~69%) of global greenhouse gas emissions and are responsible for about 78% of emission increases in the first decade of this new century. Thus, the Paris Agreement objective of holding global warming to below 2° has radical implications for fossil fuel production. Recent analyses suggest that about two-thirds of known fossil fuel reserves would have to be left unexploited to have a fair chance of reaching that goal (McGlade and Ekins 2015). Unsurprisingly then, issues of fossil fuel production, trade and use are at the centre of climate debates: economists call for "internalising" environmental costs associated with the combustion of fossil fuels, via (global) carbon taxes or carbon markets; civil society movements run campaigns against fossil fuel industries and press governments to stop fossil fuel exploration and extraction; global organisations like the OECD, World Bank and G7 call for phasing out fossil subsidies; and an increasing number of national governments initiate policies to support energy production from renewable sources and transform energy systems towards more sustainable modes of production and consumption. In parallel, and partly as a consequence of such discussions, major changes in global energy markets are underway, especially in the electricity sector: in 2014 and 2015, renewables accounted for over half of global investments and new electricity production capacities (REN21 2016).

Despite this global activism, the status of energy questions in climate governance is paradoxical: while energy debates in general, and debates on fossil fuels in particular, are in many respects "hyper-climatised", they are strangely absent from the core of the climate regime and its basic treaties. Building on this observation, the chapter reflects on modes of "climatisation" and "declimatisation" of fossil fuels. In using *climatisation*, we subsume attempts to frame questions on the production, trade and use of fossil fuels as issues of climate policy, and attempts to enable the climate regime to tackle those questions within its own organisational routines. On the contrary, *declimatisation* refers to counter-strategies and institutional dynamics that conspire to maintain existing separations between climate governance and fossil fuel regulation, factors that prevent the latter from entering formal climate talks.

This also sheds new light on ongoing debates about the "fragmentation" of global governance (Biermann, Pattberg, Asselt and Zelli 2009). Amid a context of increasing institutional density and complexity, scholars of international relations have shifted their analytical focus in recent years, from the development of individual regimes to "interactions" (Oberthür and Schram Stokke 2011) and "functional differentiation" among international institutions (Zürn and Faude 2013). This echoes research on the sectorialisation or compartmentalisation of national policymaking.[2] Our chapter makes two main contributions to this literature: first, we show that the sectorialisation of global governance does not automatically follow macro processes like functional differentiation, but results at least as much from "strategic selectivities" (Brunnengräber 2013) – namely organised resistance by public and private actors to uphold separations among international regimes or regime complexes. Second, we show how energy-related issues that do enter the climate arena become transformed in the process, as they are "translated"[3] into the dominant discursive framings and institutional logics of the climate regime.

These arguments are developed in two sections. In the first, we identify four framings that target fossil fuel production, trade and use, as well as the discourse coalitions that promote them. The second section extends this analysis to negotiations under the Climate Convention, to examine processes that make the climate regime relatively impermeable to energy questions. We conclude by building on this analysis to question and qualify frequent claims that the Paris Agreement signifies the end of the fossil fuel era.

## Climatising fossil fuels: four framings

Debates about climate and energy policy have a long, intertwined common history highlighted by early assessments of what was then called "the $CO_2$ problem" (National Academy of Sciences 1977). Despite these early linkages, international efforts to combat climate change through regulations of energy production and markets – let alone the creation of an integrated regime for both issues – have proven unsuccessful, and climate and energy governance have evolved separately (Van de Graaf 2013). This separation is questioned by recent debates that criticise fossil fuel extraction and combustion on climate grounds. Four distinct ways of targeting fossil fuels can be distinguished. These framings emerged at distinct moments of the common discursive history of climate and energy debates; they are supported by different, albeit sometimes overlapping, actor coalitions. The choice and delimitation of these framings are somewhat arbitrary, necessarily.

We view this as justified on analytical grounds, based on two principles: on one hand, we limited the scope of our analysis by excluding debates that do not target fossil fuels directly, such as those relating more broadly to energy transitions or alternative energy sources. On the other hand, we focused only on framings with a high visibility and importance in current climate debates.

## Putting a price on carbon

It might have surprised some observers when a new platform, the Carbon Pricing Leadership Coalition,[4] was launched publicly during the climate summit on 10 December 2015, diverting attention from the negotiations towards specific policy instruments. The stated aim of the structure is to strengthen existing carbon pricing initiatives and enhance cooperation among them. It unites national and subnational governments, international organisations, businesses, including mainly European oil majors and energy utilities, and international NGOs and think tanks, like the World Resources Institute, the Environmental Defense Fund and WWF.

The initiative revived a debate that began in the 1980s. Northern European environmental economists then proposed a paradigm shift in fiscal policy (Binswanger, Bonus and Timmermann 1981), arguing that the dominant labour-based taxation system of industrialised societies was out of phase with a world where automation and robotisation were replacing the human workforce, and where concerns grew about the ecological consequences of energy production and the increasing dependency of Western democracies on imported oil. They suggested a common solution to these problems: alleviate taxation on labour and shift the burden to energy consumption. This "ecological tax reform" became one of the backbones of ecological modernisation theory[5] and was promoted in early climate negotiations by European and American policymakers and international institutions (Hourcade 2001).

The idea failed, however, to make it into the Kyoto Protocol, and ecological tax reforms both in the United States and the EU nosedived during the 1990s. Instead, so-called market-based approaches inspired by American neoclassical economists were advocated as another way to integrate ecological concerns into the calculations of economic actors (Aykut 2014). The Kyoto Protocol followed this line of thinking by establishing three "flexibility mechanisms": the Clean Development Mechanism (CDM) created the possibility for firms in developed countries to invest in carbon abatement projects in developing countries (Art. 12 of the Protocol); the Joint Implementation scheme applied this approach to investments in economies in transition (Art. 6); and the international carbon market allowed for trading of emission reduction units between countries that have overachieved their Kyoto objectives and those that have fallen short (Art. 17). Supported by international bodies like the OECD and World Bank, carbon markets were also created at national and regional levels. The EU Emissions Trading Scheme (ETS) is the largest to date; similar markets exist in several other countries, such as New Zealand and Switzerland, and at subnational levels in China, Canada and the United States. This led to the emergence of a "carbon market industry" (Voß and Simons 2014) of think tanks, policy advisors, investors and international organisations that vocally defend carbon markets in climate talks.

Carbon taxes – a diplomatic non-starter in the 2000s – had a sort of renaissance in recent climate debates that was fuelled by growing dissatisfaction with existing trading schemes, especially the European carbon market that proved incapable of providing a stable economic signal to investors. Several economic reports and analyses advocated carbon taxes, including the Stern Review on the Economics of Climate Change (Stern 2006). While both debates – on taxes and markets – were largely disconnected until Copenhagen, a common debate on "carbon pricing" emerged before the Paris summit, favoured by the new bottom-up approach to climate policy that provided an opportunity for cooperative efforts outside of official climate talks. A central actor in the emerging network around carbon pricing is the World Bank, whose important historical role as a knowledge broker and lobbying institution for carbon markets was recently extended to include carbon taxing schemes (World Bank 2014). Distinctly, the carbon pricing debate has been able to attract major economic actors, some of which view moderate carbon prices as an opportunity to develop new business models based on energy production from renewables or natural gas (see Benabou, Moussu and Müller, this volume).

### Phasing out fossil fuel subsidies

On the first day of COP21, representatives of thirty-five governments and hundreds of businesses and civil society organisations issued a joint call for countries to take action against fossil fuel subsidies[6] (FFFsR 2015). The declaration was accompanied by an aggressive campaign, via traditional media outlets and social media, with the hashtag #stopfundingfossilfuels coined to publicise the issue (see Figure 9.1). This built on a broad campaign leading up to the conference: 600,000+ people signed a petition asking G20 governments to end subsidies,[7] culminating in a "day of action" on 14 November 2015. Accompanying reports noted that fossil fuel subsidies are not only environmentally harmful but also economically inefficient and socially regressive, as they disproportionally benefit upper and middle-class households (Bast, Doukas, Pickard, Burg and Whitley 2015).

Interestingly, the longer history of this debate is rooted not so much in climate politics but in structural adjustment programmes of the 1980s and 1990s, imposed in third-world countries by the International Monetary Fund (IMF) and the World Bank.[8] In the neoclassical and market liberal view of these institutions, energy subsidies constitute market distortions that must be eliminated for their detrimental macroeconomic effects. That idea gained momentum when the economic argument was extended to include environmental arguments after adoption of the Kyoto Protocol in 1997, which called for reducing fossil fuel subsidies as a means to curb global greenhouse gas emissions. This was supported by the United Nations Environment Programme (UNEP), which partnered with the International Energy Agency (IEA) for a series of workshops on reforming energy

*Figure 9.1* StopFundingFossils activist inside the "blue zone" at COP21.

Source: Climacop Collective.

subsidies in 2000 and 2001. The report of those discussions stated that energy subsidies cause environmental degradations, impose a heavy financial burden on governments, negatively impact investments in the energy sector, favour technological lock-in and constitute a socially unfair transfer of wealth to affluent socioeconomic classes (UNEP and United Nations Foundation 2003). Since then, this list of negative side effects of energy subsidies has become the core of arguments for fossil fuel reform.

Subsidy reform was also discussed in other international fora, such as the 2002 World Summit on Sustainable Development in Johannesburg and the 2009 G20 meeting in Pittsburgh, United States, where governments first committed to phasing out "inefficient" fossil fuel subsidies "in the medium term".[9] This international activism was accompanied by a series of reports from international organisations that examined past experiences with fossil fuel subsidy reform, analysed the G20 commitments and made suggestions for their implementation, and established a global inventory on fossil fuel subsidies.[10]

Civil society organisations joined the ongoing debate at the Johannesburg conference. In 2005, Oil Change International (a think tank and activist network that formed to combat human rights abuses related to oil extraction in the Global South) launched a campaign based on a set of arguments similar to UNEP's of a few years earlier. The NGO also added a distinct voice to the debate by distinguishing between *production* subsidies of fossil fuel exploration, development, extraction and transportation – those it suggested should be targeted first – and *consumption* subsidies, which it deemed more difficult to reduce in the short term (Oil Change International 2007). By the 2012 Rio+20 Conference on Sustainable Development, a growing number of NGOs interested in the topic cooperated on a joint submission for phasing out fossil fuel subsidies.[11]

Developments have accelerated in recent years: a significant number of pre-Paris national mitigation pledges include proposals for fossil fuel subsidy reform (Merrill, Bassi, Bridle and Christensen 2015, 27–29) and the 2016 G7 meeting in Japan fixed, for the first time, a deadline (2025) for ending most subsidies. As a result, the discursive positions of international organisations and NGOs aligned further, with the latter taking the role of "watchdogs" that critically accompany international efforts to reduce subsidies and scrutinise whether individual countries live up to their commitments (Bast et al. 2015).

### Challenging extractivism

A more radical approach to climate mitigation that demands ceasing the extraction of fossil fuels gained wide media attention in May 2016 when, within a few days, a global activist group managed to temporarily block the world's largest coal port in Newcastle, Australia, and one of the biggest lignite power plants in Europe, *Schwarze Pumpe* in East Germany (see Figure 9.2). These high-profile actions were accompanied by multiple smaller acts of civil disobedience and protest around the world.[12] Together, they constituted the culmination of an ongoing campaign against the fossil fuel industry.

While these actions mostly concentrated on developed countries, anti-extractivist critique originated in the Global South, amid the decade-long struggle of social

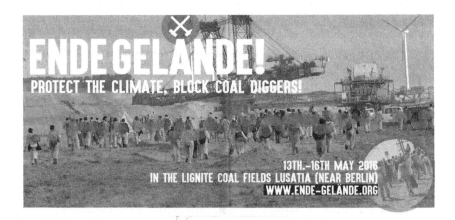

*Figure 9.2* Activist leaflet presenting an action by the social movement EndeGelaende.

Source: Climacop Collective.

movements against local environmental impacts, social disruptions and human rights violations caused by resource extraction, especially by Western oil companies.[13] Well-documented cases include the struggle of the Ogoni in Nigeria against Shell, and of indigenous peoples and *campesinos* in Ecuador, Brazil and other Latin American countries against resource extraction and oil development in the Amazonian rainforest. These local struggles internationalised during the 1980s and 1990s: they established transnational activist networks, such as Oil-watch (founded in 1996), and linked with Northern NGOs, like Friends of the Earth and Human Rights Watch. During that process of internationalisation, climate change emerged as a supplementary argument to justify its underlying cause.

In the latter 1990s, calls grew for a global moratorium on new oil exploration in pristine and frontier areas. The issue also entered the climate debate during a side event of the Kyoto conference organised by Oilwatch and other international NGOs (Temper, Yánez, Sharife, Ojo and Martinez-Alier 2013, 13). During this period it gained public visibility with the arrival of a new actor, Greenpeace International. Having just "won" the Brent Spar case against Shell, the NGO decided to launch a full campaign against the oil industry (Pulver 2007, 10–11), which focused on the link between resource extraction and climate change. In reports like *Fossil Fuels and Climate Protection: The Carbon Logic* (Hare 1997), it introduced a new argument into the debate, building on the idea of a global "carbon budget" based on long-term climate policy objectives. Comparing that budget to estimated reserves of oil and other fossil fuels, the report argued the need to limit fossil fuel use well before technical scarcity (i.e. oil peak) would pose material constraints to resource extraction. This became the quantitative underpinning of anti-extractivist activism.

The debate was reinvigorated at the end of the 2000s, due to three relatively unconnected events. First, the call for a moratorium was supported by Ecuadorian president Rafael Correa in 2007, when he proposed to refrain from exploiting new oil reserves in the Yasuní National Park in exchange for financial compensation by developed countries. While the idea failed in climate talks, it put the issue of fossil fuel extraction on the global agenda until being abandoned in 2013. Second, an exceptional boom in the extraction of unconventional fossil fuel reserves during the 2000s (mainly shale gas and tight oil in the United States, and tar sands in Canada) spurred a strong anti-extractivist movement in the Global North. Public visibility grew as the issue evolved from being viewed solely as a concern of third-world activists and indigenous peoples. Third, increasing institutionalisation of the 2°C target, and its official adoption as an objective in Copenhagen in 2009, gave scientists a solid benchmark for calculating a global carbon budget and quantifying the "gap" between the international community's long-term commitment versus the climate policies of individual countries (Meinshausen et al. 2009).

Those developments changed the campaign's form in the early 2010s. NGOs and activists rallied around the slogan "Leave it in the ground" at COP17 in Durban, South Africa.[14] In the run-up to COP21, the IPCC's fifth assessment report concluded that known fossil fuel reserves are four to seven times higher than the remaining carbon budget (IPCC 2014), and a surge of scientific studies made detailed estimates of various fossil fuel reserves that would have to be left unexploited to achieve a 2°C world.[15] These estimates in turn formed the basis for a broadening of the anti-extractivist campaign. With a slightly modified slogan ("Keep it in the ground"), a broad network of organisations worked to put the issue on the agenda in Paris. The movement was spearheaded by the NGO 350.org, involved many other NGOs, governments of vulnerable countries and even religious associations, and was backed by the UK newspaper the *Guardian*, which had decided to focus on the issue in the year before Paris. Built on the solid ground of scientific expertise, these campaigns gained unprecedented visibility and support. However, this came at a cost, as it also sidelined some of the social and local environmental issues that had been central to early activists against extractivism.

### Targeting investment

"Divestment" is another approach to climate mitigation that gained ground recently. It builds on some arguments of the anti-extractivism movement, and is supported by some of the same actors, yet it represents a distinct framing that has developed its own dynamic. Instead of fossil fuel companies, divestment targets private wealth owners, such as university endowments, public pension funds and institutional investors, and aims at convincing them to withdraw their capital from fossil fuel assets. This strategy has an important ethical dimension dating back to historic campaigns against tobacco, arms and munitions, and especially the oft-cited campaign against investments in apartheid-era South Africa in the 1980s. More so than the other framings, divestment thus appears as a "moral crusade" (Gusfield 1963) against the financial infrastructure that supports fossil fuel production and use.

Like anti-extractivism, fossil fuel divestment has its roots in local environmental and social struggles, but its origins are more recent, in the Global North. In 2009 and 2010, initiatives at US colleges opposed university investments in onsite coal plants and nearby coal extraction sites, via the Sierra Student Coalition's *Campuses beyond Coal* campaign and the *Swarthmore Mountain Justice* campaign, among others. The new type of action spread quickly and was taken up by climate activists in search of alternative strategies to lobbying inside climate talks, an approach that had shown its limits when global climate talks broke down in Copenhagen in 2009. As follows, two initiatives in 2011 helped to establish divestment as such an alternative strategy.

First in June 2011, the Wallace Global Fund (a liberal foundation with a social justice and environmental protection agenda, created in 1995 by Robert B. Wallace, son of former US vice-president Henry A. Wallace) hosted a meeting in Washington, DC, to discuss coal divestment with college students and environmental activists. The Fund also supported the publication of the "Coal Divestment Toolkit" a year later (Bendersky et al. 2012), a report by eleven NGOs that asked students to help turn coal into a "pariah industry" and further shaped the idea of using anti-apartheid–like campaigning to tackle fossil fuel investment. The Wallace grantee 350.org and its founder Bill McKibben seized the opportunity to rally a rather disparate climate movement around a common idea and launched a global "FossilFree" campaign in 2012, urging public and private organisations to divest from direct or indirect ownership of fossil fuel companies or fossil fuel–based assets. In parallel, McKibben wrote the article "Global Warming's Terrifying New Math" for *Rolling Stone* magazine, a highly influential piece in the climate debate, and undertook a nationwide speaking tour, "Do the Math". Interestingly, he acknowledges himself that the rationale behind divestment is not so much economic – it will not work "by directly affecting share prices" – but moral, because it aims at weakening the fossil fuel industry's political power by "revoke[ing] the[ir] social license" (McKibben 2013).

Second, a report by Carbon Tracker Initiative (2011), a London-based think tank founded by climate activists and consultants for the finance industry, posited that climate change is a threat to global financial stability. Like Greenpeace a few years earlier, the report highlighted the discrepancy between the carbon budget resulting from the long-term goal of holding global warming below 2°C and the carbon contained in proven fossil fuel reserves. Based on actualised figures, it called a significant amount of current fossil fuels "stranded assets", as the resources upon which they are based are literally unburnable. It then translated the arguments of the divest movement into the logic of financial investors: rather than calling for divestment based on moral grounds, it depicts the bleak picture of a "carbon bubble" ready to implode when investors realise that their assets are overrated. The solution proposed by the think tank is to establish a transparent framework to unveil the "transition risks" in investors' portfolios. International institutions proved to be sensitive to this new framing. The OECD included the topic in its roundtable on sustainable development (Fischer and Baron 2015), and the governor of the Bank of England, Mike Carney, gave a widely quoted speech called the "Tragedy of the Horizon", in which he identified climate-related risks for global financial stability and called for financial policy reforms to ensure a smooth transition to a low-carbon world.[16] Those initiatives resulted in the creation of the Task Force on Climate-Related Financial Disclosures in 2015. Launched during COP21, the industry-led structure is chaired by billionaire and former New York mayor Mike Bloomberg; it published its first report on climate-related financial reporting shortly after (TCFD 2016).

Both initiatives – the NGO-led divestment campaign and the disclosure scheme supported by institutional and business actors – gained steam in the run-up to Paris, as large public and private funds promised to divest, and investor alliances pledged greater transparency of their portfolios. Despite their common focus on investments, however, it is important to recall that the two initiatives are based on different rationales and institutional logic. In sum, as the debate on fossil fuel divestment institutionalised and internationalised, it diversified from an issue of local social justice to a global moral imperative and a problem of managing systemic financial risk.

## "Not an energy treaty": fossil fuels in climate governance

Despite being ubiquitous in climate debates, energy issues have rarely been included in official climate talks. The basic treaty and negotiation texts of the climate regime either omit talking about energy issues altogether or frame them in very specific and limited ways, in stark contrast to the way that such issues are discussed by civil society actors and even international organisations. In this section, we identify three processes that help us to better understand the treatment of energy issues in climate negotiations: (1) "collateral declimatisation" refers to institutional dynamics and cognitive factors that result from the sectorialisation of global politics, and that perpetuate the separation of climate policy from fossil fuel governance. However, the persistent fragmentation of global governance cannot be understood in purely functionalist or cognitive terms. (2) We therefore introduce the notion of "strategic declimatisation", an actor-centred perspective based on strategies that aim explicitly to keep energy questions out of climate negotiations. (3) Finally, "selective climatisation" describes discursive reframings that occur in the few cases where questions of fossil fuel regulation do enter climate talks and are formalised in negotiation documents.

### A relative absence of energy in negotiation texts

A straightforward way to trace energy framings in climate governance is to compare three treaties that structure the climate regime: the Climate Convention (1992), the Kyoto Protocol (1997) and the Paris Agreement (2015). Looking at intermediate negotiation documents gives a more detailed view of processes of inclusion or exclusion of energy questions. We therefore included two recent negotiation documents that paved the way for the Paris Agreement: the Geneva draft text of February 2015 that was compiled from countries' contributions and was the basis for the Paris negotiations, and an intermediate text called "the Co-chairs negotiation tool" that was issued on 23 October 2015 for the Bonn intermediary negotiations.

For our analysis, we identified energy-related framings in these five documents by counting occurrences of the terms "energy", "fossil", "renewable(s)" and "emission(s)" (see Table 9.1). The first three terms characterise framings in terms of energy production and use. The last term points to framings in terms of greenhouse gas emissions and their reduction. In a second step, we qualitatively examined the context in which these terms appeared.

The results show that climate policy has mainly been conceived, both historically and consistently, as a question of reducing greenhouse gas emissions.

*Table 9.1* Energy framings in climate treaties and negotiation texts.

|  | Energy | Fossil | Renewable(s) | Emission(s) |
|---|---|---|---|---|
| Climate Convention | 6 | 4 | 0 | 23 |
| Kyoto Protocol | 7 | 0 | 1 | 57 |
| Geneva text | 7 | 2 | 1 | 215 |
| Bonn text | 1 | 0 | 0 | 82 |
| Paris Agreement | 3 | 0 | 1 | 48 |

Source: Authors.

Although scientists and civil society actors claim that energy is at the heart of the climate problem, that fossil fuel subsidies are a major concern and that encouraging energy production from renewable sources would be a possible (albeit partial) response to the problem, energy issues are barely mentioned in climate treaties. Further context analysis showed that "energy" is used mostly to highlight the right to development of countries in the Global South,[17] or to ensure that fossil fuel–exporting countries potentially harmed by "the adverse effects" of climate mitigation policies[18] will be compensated somehow. The remarkable stability of the dominant framing of climate policy in these documents points to the importance of the institutional and cognitive legacy of the climate regime. In other words, organisational path dependence can be an important explanatory factor for understanding why energy questions have been excluded from climate governance. Notwithstanding this general observation, the Kyoto Protocol (generally considered the basis of the dominant approach to emission reduction targets) is also a rather surprising exception regarding energy issues. Its Article 2 lays out a detailed set of "policies and measures" that countries "shall implement" to reduce emissions, such as the "enhancement of energy efficiency" and "the promotion, development and increased use of new and renewable forms of energy, carbon dioxide sequestration technologies and of advanced and innovative environmentally sound technologies".[19] The same article also alludes indirectly to fossil fuel subsidies, when it calls for "progressive reduction or phasing out of market imperfections, fiscal incentives, tax and duty exemptions and subsidies [. . .] that run counter to the objective of the Convention".

Given that the Kyoto Protocol does mention energy questions, it seems puzzling that the Paris Agreement returns almost exclusively to framing climate policy in terms of emissions. The term "energy" appears only three times in the document: one mention is a simple reference to the status of the Atomic Energy Agency as an observer organisation to the Climate Convention, and two in the COP decision's preamble acknowledge "the need to promote universal access to sustainable energy in developing countries, especially in Africa, through the enhanced deployment of renewable energy".[20] The phrase is all that remained of an initiative by African countries to establish a renewable energy and energy efficiency bond under the Convention. Excluded from final negotiation drafts, it will finally be established outside of the Convention, on a voluntary basis.[21]

This re-exclusion of energy questions not only is an intriguing step back but also runs counter to the wider climate debate that, just before COP21, was concerned increasingly with fossil fuel issues. The intermediate negotiation documents show that path dependence may not suffice to explain this omission. Neither questions about energy in general nor fossil fuels in particular were absent from the pre-Paris negotiations. The Geneva draft text contains, among others, an article that calls for establishing the aforementioned "international renewable energy and energy efficiency bond"[22] and two others that mention the "phasing down of high-carbon investments and fossil fuel subsidies".[23] Other passages refer to "a low-carbon transition", a "zero emissions" target and "full decarbonisation". Those issues were deleted from the negotiation documents between February and October 2015, when a new informal draft text was released. This thorough cleansing of the document revealed strong objections from parties to the inclusion of energy issues. We therefore have to balance the focus on organisational path dependence with an attention to actors' preferences and strategies.

### "Collateral" declimatisation: framings and institutions

As we showed previously, climate change has been framed mainly as a *global environmental problem* (Aykut and Dahan 2015). The origins of this framing can be traced back to the 1980s and 1990s, when a range of high-level international meetings and conferences propelled climate change onto the global political agenda. First, recent multilateral action had just been successful for two global environmental issues: acid rain and the hole in the ozone layer. Those solutions focused mainly on the reduction of pollutants, suggesting that such an approach could also work for climate change. Indeed, measures such as standards and emission caps, taxes, markets of tradable emission rights and burden sharing between countries were able to curb chlorofluorocarbon, sulphur dioxide and nitrogen oxide emissions, paving the way for the adoption of similar approaches to other environmental problems. Second, the physico-chemical definition of climate change as a global phenomenon, with a range of notions attached to it – global mean surface temperature, general circulation models and so forth – had a peculiar political translation: to ensure global cooperation and avoid free-riding by some nations, it was thought that the political solution had to be as global as the problem itself.

The framing of climate change as a global environmental problem had important consequences for the design of instruments and institutions chosen to address it. For *instruments*, global climate governance and most national climate policies aim at regulating GHG emissions. However, such "end-of-pipe" measures exclude important aspects of the problem, such as issues relating to infrastructure and fossil fuel extraction, trade and consumption. Despite their importance these questions are not discussed in climate negotiations; for example infrastructure, once built, may lead to long-term carbon lock-in (Unruh 2000), and fossil fuels, once extracted, are very likely to be used. Interestingly, however, that narrow focus on emissions reduction cannot be explained solely by the fact that the climate regime was modelled on other environmental regimes. As a case in point, the Montreal Protocol for the protection of the ozone layer (adopted in 1987) not only targeted emissions but also specifically banned the production and trade of ozone-depleting substances. With climate, following that approach more closely could arguably have shifted the focus away from emissions reduction objectives, to directly targeting fossil fuel production and trade (Vogler 2016, 17).

On the level of *institutions*, the climate change regime is separated from a range of other international regimes and organisations, such as those regulating global trade, development, energy security, finance and development. Maintaining the established "firewalls" (Altvater 2007, 37) between the climate regime and other international regimes increases the sectorialisation of the international scene and hinders the development of common approaches and linkages among global problems (Aykut and Dahan 2015). This has important consequences for climate governance, as the ways in which economic globalisation and financial globalisation unfold and global energy markets function are vital to the evolution of global emissions. In the words of David Victor (2011, xix), the main problem is that climate change is framed as an environmental issue, but "its root causes and solutions lie in the functioning of energy markets". This has immediate practical consequences. To give just one example, the extreme volatility of oil and coal prices has destabilising effects on policies aimed at reducing greenhouse gas emissions or at developing alternatives to fossil fuels, like the EU Emissions Trading Scheme or feed-in tariffs for renewables (Rüdinger et al. 2014). The inability of the climate regime to address energy issues therefore also renders it ineffective for coordinating efforts to diminish such detrimental effects of price volatility on fossil fuel mitigation policies. Further, a coherent global energy regime where such questions could be addressed is still lacking, and despite some recent, slow changes in the International Energy Agency, existing institutions are more concerned with questions of security of energy supply than sustainability (Van de Graaf 2013, 102).

### Strategic declimatisation: keeping energy out

The exclusion of energy issues from climate governance results not only from the power of dominant framings and organisational path dependence. It also stems from deliberate strategies by key actors in the climate regime that have actively sought to prevent discussion of energy governance issues in climate talks. Historically the most visible and arguably most important actor in this respect has been Saudi Arabia, which has consistently argued that the Climate Convention is "not an energy treaty" (Depledge 2008, 14) and has successfully blocked progress on energy-related issues.[24] In the following paragraphs, we first lay out the Saudi negotiation strategy, before assessing its alliances inside and outside of the negotiations.

In the early years of climate negotiations, a major concern of Saudi Arabia was preventing taxation-based approaches. Their opposition was stated explicitly during the negotiation sessions. In her "article-by-article textual history" of the Kyoto Protocol, Depledge (2000, 20) recalls that Saudi Arabia, together with Iran and other OPEC members, pleaded for "the identification of policies and measures that Parties should not implement, notably, '$CO_2$ and energy taxation', 'new or increased oil taxation' and 'new greenhouse gas taxes'". This strategy was pursued and extended in the aftermath of Kyoto, when Saudi negotiators opposed any debate on the agenda item "policies and measures". This relates to Paragraph 2.1(a) of the Protocol, which contained some of the more explicit language relating to energy issues. As a result of this negotiation strategy, discussions on the agenda item were delayed for years, and have not advanced substantially ever since. More recently, in the intermediate negotiations to the Paris conference, Saudi Arabia and its allies among oil-exporting countries engaged in a systematic battle against any formulations of the long-term target that contained the word "carbon", such as "decarbonisation", "carbon neutrality" or "low-carbon economies", because they felt these terms focused exclusively on carbon dioxide (Biniaz 2016, 19). This endeavour to "decarbonise" the long-term goal proved highly successful: most of the incriminated formulations had disappeared in the draft text released in October 2015, and the final agreement did not mention them.[25]

Saudi Arabia spearheaded a more or less formalised coalition comprising energy utilities, parts of the oil, gas and coal extraction industry and some of the big fossil fuel–producing and consuming states. At the core of this coalition, historically, the Gulf Cooperation Council (GCC) and most OPEC members have aligned themselves with the Saudi positions. This convergence stems from the fact that all of these states depend heavily on oil revenues for their economic and political stability. As Barnett (2008, 1) recalled, "a US$ 10 rise in the price of a barrel of oil results in a 14 percent rise in GDP in Saudi Arabia, a 17 percent rise in GDP in Oman and Kuwait, and a 22 percent rise in GDP in the United Arab Emirates". These countries have thus repeatedly argued that climate mitigation would harm their economies greatly. Although less visibly obstructionist in the negotiations, other large fossil fuel producers, like Russia, Australia and the United States, have tacitly and sometimes actively supported Saudi Arabia and its allies. Some authors have also argued that since the early years of climate negotiations, an informal alliance linked OPEC to fossil fuel interests in the United States opposed to climate policies.[26] After the official American retreat from the Kyoto Protocol under President George W. Bush, these ties have become more obvious. Finally, Saudi Arabia has often been supported or at least tolerated by the G77, of which it is an important member (Dessai 2004). This may seem rather counterintuitive, as the group includes some states most vulnerable to climate change, like the small island states, which are also among the strongest supporters of ambitious climate mitigation. This continued tacit support despite diverging – if not opposing – interests can be explained by the economic power of Saudi Arabia and the widely recognised negotiation skills of its delegation.[27] Another oft-overlooked factor is that the climate regime is not the only arena where the G77 is the voice of the Global South. As a result, G77 unity is seen by many as an objective in itself that transcends the climate regime.

### Selective climatisation: reframing fossil fuels

When energy issues have appeared in climate negotiations, their formulation reflects the dominant framings and power equilibria of the climate regime. One of the oldest and most persistent debates relating to fossil fuels in climate negotiations has been about the so-called adverse effects of response measures. Pushed by OPEC, the notion is a cynical reversal of attempts to include fossil fuels in climate governance. Again, Saudi Arabia played a leading role, claiming that stringent mitigation policies would lower the value of its oil resources and potentially prevent it from exploiting them fully (Depledge 2008, 15, 16). That motivated demands of compensation for the prospective economic losses resulting from climate regulations. Although this has clearly been unacceptable to other parties,[28] OPEC has used its de facto veto power to uphold the issue on the agenda. Thus, the issue has been present in every major negotiation round since the 1990s, and several subsequent special working groups have resulted in "complex, time consuming, and otherwise unnecessary negotiations around the issue of 'the adverse effects of response measures,' which to OPEC means 'compensation for lost oil revenue'" (Barnett 2008, 3). Ironically, the debate partly mirrors arguments brought forward by the divest movement.

A second framing in the negotiations views fossil fuel regulation through the prism of market-based approaches, especially the concept of tradable permits (Voß 2007). As we have shown earlier, the Kyoto approach that combines quantified reduction objectives (or "quotas") with flexibility mechanisms (or "carbon markets") was crafted on the ruins of earlier approaches based on internationally coordinated energy and/or carbon taxes. Adoption of the Kyoto Protocol ended that project, but opened a new possibility: the creation of an integrated global market for emission reduction certificates, and the subsequent emergence of a global carbon price. Questions of energy regulation have thus been translated, via their inclusion in climate talks, into the "market grammar" (Aykut and Dahan 2015, 154–162) dominant in the Kyoto climate regime.

Finally, energy issues also entered climate negotiations via a technological framing. This applies in particular to the debate over inclusion of carbon capture and storage (CCS) in the CDM of the Kyoto Protocol. CCS describes technologies that capture, compress and store $CO_2$ emissions in stable geological formations, such as aquifers or hydrocarbon fields. It builds on industry solutions to enhance oil and gas recovery, but its large-scale feasibility for climate mitigation is controversial on both economic and technical grounds. Inclusion of the technology in the CDM has been advocated post-Kyoto by an industry alliance of large oil and gas majors – who possess the technology – and parts of the coal industry that see CCS as a way to secure a place for "clean coal" in the future energy mix (Vormedal 2008). The Kyoto Protocol itself alludes to CCS only in a brief reference to "carbon sequestration technologies" (Article 2.1[a]), but it does not mention the option of including it in the flexibility mechanisms. The topic was then pushed by a coalition of oil-exporting states led by Norway, whose national energy company Statoil initiated the first CCS project to reduce $CO_2$ emissions (Depledge 2008, 29). The EU and other developed countries later joined the coalition, leading to intense consultations from 2005, when a first set of CCS methodologies was submitted to the CDM Executive Board, to 2011, when rules for the technology were approved officially at the climate conference in Durban.[29] Debates about CCS gained momentum after adoption of the Paris Agreement, whose Article 4 stipulates that efforts should aim to "achieve a balance between anthropogenic emissions by sources and removals by sinks of greenhouse gases in the second half of this century". This formulation of the long-term goal was viewed widely as calling for increased development of CCS technologies. Particular focus in subsequent discussions has been on "BECCS", a technology that combines bioenergy combustion with CCS to achieve "negative emissions", which some consider necessary to offset a temporary surpassing of global emission trajectories, compared to 2°C (or 1.5°C) scenarios.[30] These discussions – about the inclusion of CCS in the Kyoto mechanisms and about the long-term goal – reveal a "technical fix" framing that accompanies the inclusion of energy regulation issues in climate talks.

## Conclusion: the energy paradox and its political consequences

The last decade has seen an increasing climatisation of debates about fossil fuels. Activists, international organisations, governments and scholars of climate policy and economics have problematised the exploration and extraction of new resources, tackled combustion and use, engaged in campaigns against investors and proposed reforms of taxation and subsidy schemes. Two recent events have contributed to a new wave of fossil fuel activism. First, disappointment after the failure of climate talks at Copenhagen in 2009 has resulted in a reorientation of communication and mobilisation strategies among private and institutional actors. While civil society movements have begun to target fossil fuel industries directly, international organisations backed by a number of proactive governments have initiated a campaign against fossil fuel subsidies and relaunched the debate on carbon pricing. Second, a shale gas and tight oil revolution in the United States birthed a powerful social movement that linked a local anti-fracking agenda with concerns about global warming. To be sure, opposition against extractivism has a long history in the Global South, but the surge of such concerns in developed countries marked a turning point, as new actors entered the arena and raised public awareness on questions of fossil fuel production and financing.

Given this general trend, the climate regime's resistance to engage questions about energy in general, and fossil fuel governance in particular, is all the more disconcerting. It provides an interesting empirical case to analyse institutional dynamics and actors' strategies that contribute to declimatising energy issues in formal climate talks. It also sheds light on the politics of selective climatisation: closer to the core of the climate regime, issues of fossil fuel governance become more excluded or reformulated according to the dominant framings of the problem in the negotiations. Such reframings conceptualise fossil fuels either in terms of compensation for potential or actual losses of oil revenue, or through the lens of market-mechanisms and technological fixes.

However, assessing the concrete impacts of this partial climatisation of fossil fuels on decarbonisation strategies is not straightforward. Recent global trends suggest increasing deployment of renewables, and momentum has been building steadily for more sustainable national energy systems, indicating a growing awareness among governments that issues of energy regulation (and not just $CO_2$ abatement) are at the heart of the climate problem. One might therefore conclude that the absence of energy questions in climate treaties is not so problematic after all. Under the new "bottom-up" governance initiated in Copenhagen and formalised in Paris, international negotiations seem to be geared less towards prescribing concrete measures and instruments. Instead, they are now expected to provide a "signal" to investors and businesses, and to sketch a transformation pathway for public actors (see Aykut, this volume).

Did Paris deliver such a signal? Debate about the long-term goal enshrined in Article 4.1 of the Paris Agreement provides a starting point for answering this question. While it is probably the best outcome the international community could deliver under the existing negotiation framework, the "zero-net" objective that lurks behind the complex formulation that finally made it into the text also has a major drawback, in that it is open to a wide range of interpretations. While "the end of fossil fuels" is one such interpretation, other readings note how official emission scenarios that are compatible with the long-term goal continue to assign a central role to fossil fuels in the future energy mix, combined with CCS or offset by prospective negative emissions technologies (IEA 2015). This has far-reaching consequences for global climate politics, as the impossibility of directly addressing fossil fuel regulation or full decarbonisation in climate talks paves the way for discussions about economic and technical solutions. In other words, the Paris outcome radicalises both the implications of climate policy for energy governance *and* the already yawning gap between ambitious but abstract long-term objectives, and the inability to clearly name and instigate the necessary transformations over the short and medium term (Aykut 2016). Due to the incomplete climatisation of fossil fuels, the Paris Agreement may therefore not actually signify an end to fossil-fuelled capitalism. Rather, it might encourage the extension of a range of "solutions", like the reliance on not-so-climate-friendly natural gas,[31] and on technological chimeras that create new markets, but also perpetuate existing infrastructures and create new lock-ins that displace the problem without contributing to its resolution.

# Notes

1 Cited in Goodell (2016).
2 Among many others, see Dobry (1986) and Jordan and Schubert (1992).
3 This process is described by Lascoumes (1996) in his analysis of French environmental policy.
4 http://www.carbonpricingleadership.org.
5 For an introduction to this concept, see Mol, Sonnenfeld and Spaargaren (2009).
6 http://fffsr.org/communique.
7 https://secure.avaaz.org/en/g20_a_new_plan_to_save_the_planet_b.
8 UNEP and United Nations Foundation (2003, 24).
9 http://www.g20.utoronto.ca/2009/2009communique0925.html.
10 Among many others, see OECD (2007), IEA, OPEC, OECD and WB (2010) and Coady, Parry, Sears and Shang (2015).
11 http://www.iisd.org/gsi/sites/default/files/pb_12_pledge.pdf.
12 https://breakfree2016.org.
13 For an introduction to the debate, see Sawyer and Gomez (2012) and Bebbington and Bury (2013).
14 http://leave-it-in-the-ground.org.
15 Among others, see McGlade and Ekins (2015) and Rogelj et al. (2015).

16  http://www.bankofengland.co.uk/publications/Pages/speeches/2015/844.aspx.
17  United Nations Framework Convention on Climate Change (UNFCCC), 4.6.1992, New York: preamble.
18  Ibid., Art. 4.10. See also Kyoto Protocol to the UNFCCC, 11.12.1997, Kyoto, Article 3.14.
19  Kyoto Protocol, Art. 2.1(a).
20  Paris Agreement, 11.12.2015, Paris, FCCC/CP/2015/L.9/Rev.1: preamble.
21  http://newsroom.unfccc.int/lpaa/renewable-energy/africa-renewable-energy-initiative-increasing-renewable-energy-capacity-on-the-african-continent.
22  Ad-hoc Group on the Durban Platform (ADP), 12.02.2015, Negotiating text, Art. 53.1(c).
23  Ibid., Art. 34ter and Art. 53.1(d).
24  For Saudi Arabia's influence in climate negotiations, see Leggett (1999), Oberthür and Ott (1999), Dessai (2004), Barnett (2008) and Depledge (2008).
25  A similar exercise of linguistic cleansing was undertaken for the word "transition".
26  Leggett (1999), Barnett (2008, 4) and Depledge (2008, 16).
27  See the account that Bo Kjellén (1994), a professional diplomat, gives of chief negotiator Al Sabban.
28  The Ecuadorian Yasuní initiative builds on a similar argument, but proposes to leave oil reserves in the ground. This was never part of Saudi proposals.
29  Decision 9/CMP.7, FCCC/KP/CMP/2011/10/Add.2.
30  For a discussion of this notion, see Fuss et al. (2014).
31  New estimates suggest that methane leakage across the production chain of natural gas is largely underestimated and might even offset its comparative advantage to coal (Heath, Warner, Steinberg and Brandt 2015).

## Bibliography

Altvater, Elmar. "The social and natural environment of fossil capitalism." Socialist Register 2007 (2007): 37.

Aykut, Stefan C. "Gouverner le climat, construire l'Europe: l'histoire de la création d'un marché du carbone (ETS)." Critique Internationale 62, January–March (2014): 39–56.

Aykut, Stefan C. "Taking a wider view on climate governance: Moving beyond the 'iceberg', the 'elephant', and the 'forest'." WIREs Climate Change 7, no. 3 (2016): 318–328.

Aykut, Stefan C., and Amy Dahan. Gouverner le climat? 20 ans de négociations internationales. Paris: Presses de Sciences Po, 2015.

Barnett, Jon. "The worst of friends: OPEC and G-77 in the climate regime." Global Environmental Politics 8, no. 4 (2008): 1–8.

Bast, Elizabeth, Alex Doukas, Sam Pickard, Laurie van der Burg, and Shelagh Whitley. Empty Promises: G20 Subsidies to Oil, Gas and Coal Production. London: Overseas Development Institute and Oil Change International, 2015.

Bebbington, Anthony, and Jeffrey Bury. Subterranean Struggles: New Dynamics of Mining, Oil, and Gas in Latin America. Austin: University of Texas Press, 2013.

Bendersky, Corinne, Emily Flynn, Martin Bourqui, Joshua Frank, Amy Galland, Bob Burton, and Kim Teplitzky. "Coal-Divestment-Toolkit: Moving Endowment beyond Coal." As You Saw. 2012. http://www.sustainabilitycoalition.org/wp-content/uploads/2012/04/Coal-Divestment-Toolkit.pdf (accessed November 16, 2016).

Biermann, Frank, Philipp Pattberg, Harro Van Asselt, and Fariborz Zelli. "The fragmentation of global governance architectures: A framework for analysis." Global Environmental Politics 9, no. 4 (2009): 14–40.

Biniaz, Susan. *Comma but Differentiated Responsibilities: Punctuation and 30 Other Ways Negotiators Have Resolved Issues in the International Climate Change Regime.* Columbia Law School Working Paper, Sabin Center for Climate Change Law, 2016.

Binswanger, Hans Christoph, Holger Bonus, and Manfred Timmermann. *Wirtschaft und Umwelt. Möglichkeiten einer ökologieverträglichen Wirtschaftspolitik.* Stuttgart: Kohlhammer, 1981.

Brunnengräber, Achim. "Multi-level climate governance: Strategic selectivities in international politics." In *Climate Change Governance,* by Jörg Knieling and Walter Leal Filho, 67–83. Heidelberg: Springer, 2013.

Carbon Tracker Initiative. *Unburnable Carbon: Are the World's Financial Markets Carrying a Carbon Bubble?* 2011. http://www.carbontracker.org (accessed November 16, 2016).

Coady, David, Ian W. H. Parry, Louis Sears, and Baoping Shang. *How Large Are Global Energy Subsidies?* Working Paper No. 15/105. Washington, DC: International Monetary Fund (IMF), 2015.

Depledge, Joanna. "Striving for no: Saudi Arabia in the climate change regime." *Global Environmental Politics* 8, no. 4 (2008): 9–35.

Depledge, Joanna. *Tracing the Origins of the Kyoto Protocol: An Article-by-Article Textual History.* FCCC/TP/2000/2. 2000. http://unfccc.int/resource/docs/tp/tp0200.pdf (accessed November 16, 2016).

Dessai, Suraje. *An Analysis of the Role of OPEC as a G-77 Member at the UNFCCC.* WWF Report. 2004. http://www.wwf.org (accessed November 16, 2016).

Dobry, Michel. *Sociologie des crises politiques.* Paris: Presses de Sciences Po, 1986.

FFFsR. *Fossil-Fuel Subsidy Reform Communiqué.* Briefing Note. 2015. fffsr.org (accessed November 16, 2016): Friends of Fossil Fuel Subsidy Reform.

Fischer, David, and Richard Baron. *Divestment and Stranded Assets in the Low-Carbon Transition.* Background paper for the 32nd Round Table on Sustainable Development. 28 October. Paris: OECD, 2015.

Fuss, Sabine, Josep G. Canadell, Glen P. Peters, Massimo Tavoni, Robbie M. Andrew, Philippe Ciais, Robert B. Jackson, et al. "Betting on negative emissions." *Nature Climate Change* 4, no. 10 (2014): 850–853.

Goodell, Jeff. "Will the Paris climate deal save the world?" *Rolling Stone,* no. 1253, 28 January 2016.

Gusfield, Joseph R. *Symbolic Crusade: Status Politics and the American Temperance Movement.* Champaign: University of Illinois Press, 1963.

Hare, Bill. *Fossil Fuels & Climate Protection: The Climate Logic.* Technical Report, Greenpeace International, 1997.

Heath, Garvin, Ethan Warner, Daniel Steinberg, and Adam Brandt. *Estimating U.S. Methane Emissions from the Natural Gas Supply Chain: Approaches, Uncertainties, Current Estimates, and Future Studies.* Technical Report NREL/TP-6A50–62820, Denver, CO: Joint Institute for Strategic Energy Analysis, 2015.

Hourcade, Jean-Charles. "Le climat au risque de la négociation internationale?" *Le Débat* 113 (2001): 136–145.

IEA. *World Energy Outlook 2015.* IEA, Paris: IEA/OECD, 2015: 12.

IEA, OPEC, OECD, and WB. *Analysis of the Scope of Energy Subsidies and Suggestion for the G-20 Initiative.* Paris: IEA, OPEC, OECD, World Bank, 2010.

IPCC. *Climate Change 2014: Mitigation of Climate Change. Contribution of Working Group III to the Fifth Assessment Report of the Intergovernmental Panel on Climate Change.* Geneva: Intergovernmental Panel on Climate Change, 2014.

Jordan, Grant, and Klaus Schubert. "A preliminary ordering of policy network labels." *European Journal of Political Research* 21, no. 1–2 (1992): 7–27.

Kjellén, Bo. "A personal assessment." In *Negotiating Climate Change: The Inside Story of the Rio Convention*, by Irving M. Mintzer and J. Amber Leonard, 149–174. Cambridge, UK: Cambridge University Press, 1994.

Lascoumes, Pierre. "Rendre gouvernable: de la 'traduction' au 'transcodage'. L'analyse des processus de changement dans les réseaux d'action publique." In *La gouvernabilité*, by CURAPP, 325–338. Paris: PUF, 1996.

Leggett, Jeremy. *The Carbon War: Global Warming and the End of the Oil Era*. Harmondsworth, UK: Penguin Books, 1999.

McGlade, Christophe, and Paul Ekins. "The geographical distribution of fossil fuels unused when limiting global warming to 2°C." *Nature* 517 (2015): 187–190.

McKibben, Bill. "Is divestment an effective means of protest?" *The New York Times*, 11 February 2013. http://www.nytimes.com/roomfordebate/2013/01/27/is-divestment-an-effective-means-of-protest/turning-colleges-partners (accessed June 28, 2016).

Meinshausen, Malte, and Nicolai Meinshausen. "Greenhouse-gas emission targets for limiting global warming to 2°C." *Nature* 458 (2009): 1158–1162.

Merrill, Laura, Andrea M. Bassi, Richard Bridle, and Lasse T. Christensen. *Tackling Fossil Fuel Subsidies and Climate Change: Levelling the Energy Playing Field*. Copenhagen: Nordic Council of Ministers, 2015.

Mol, Arthur P. J., David A. Sonnenfeld, and Gert Spaargaren. *The Ecological Modernisation Reader: Environmental Reform in Theory and Practice*. London: Routledge, 2009.

National Academy of Sciences. *Energy and Climate: A Scientific Assessment*. Washington, DC: US Climate Research Board, 1977.

Oberthür, Sebastian, and Hermann E. Ott. *The Kyoto Protocol: International Climate Policy for the 21st Century*. Berlin: Springer, 1999.

Oberthür, Sebastian, and Olav Schram Stokke. *Managing Institutional Complexity: Regime Interplay and Global Environmental Change*. Cambridge, MA: MIT Press, 2011.

OECD. *Subsidy Reform and Sustainable Development: Political Economy Aspects*. Paris: OECD, 2007.

Oil Change International. *Aiding Oil, Harming the Climate: A Database of Public Funds for Fossil Fuels*. Washington, DC: Oil Change International, 2007.

Pulver, Simone. *Three Pathways to Political Liability: The Effects of Oil Industry Dynamics on Climate Change Advocacy NGOs*. Paper presented at International Studies Association Annual Convention Session on "NGOs, Civil Society, and the Environment", Thursday, March 1, 2007. http://compon.org/sites/default/files/privatefiles/library/environmentalmovements/Pulver%202007b.pdf (accessed November 16, 2016).

REN21. *Renewables 2016: Global Status Report*. Paris: REN21 Secretariat, 2016.

Rogelj, Joeri, Gunnar Luderer, Robert C. Pietzcker, Elmar Kriegler, Michiel Schaeffer, Volker Krey, and Keywan Riahi. "Energy system transformations for limiting end-of-century warming to below 1.5 °C." *Nature Climate Change* 5, no. 6 (2015): 519–527.

Rüdinger, Andreas, Thomas Spencer, Oliver Sartor, Mathilde Mathieu, Michel Colombier, and Teresa Ribera. *Getting Out of the Perfect Storm: Towards Coherence between Electricity Market Policies and EU Climate and Energy Goals*. Working Papers n°12/2014, Paris: Iddri, 2014.

Sawyer, Suzana, and Edmund Terence Gomez. *The Politics of Resource Extraction: Indigenous Peoples, Multinational Corporations and the State*. Basingstoke, UK: Palgrave, 2012.

Stern, Nicholas. *Stern Review on the Economics of Climate Change*. London: HM Treasury, 2006.

TCFD. *Phase I Report of the Task Force on Climate-Related Financial Disclosures.* Presented to the Financial Stability Board. March 31, 2016. https://www.fsb-tcfd.org/wp-content/uploads/2016/03/Phase_I_Report_v15.pdf (accessed November 16, 2016).

Temper, Leah, Ivonne Yánez, Khadija Sharife, Godwin Ojo, and Joan Martinez-Alier. *Towards a Post-Oil Civilization: Yasunization and Other Initiatives to Leave Fossil Fuels in the Soil.* Ejolt Report No. 6. 2013. ejolt.org (accessed November 16, 2016).

UNEP, and United Nations Foundation. *Energy Subsidies: Lessons Learned in Assessing Their Impact and Designing Policy Reforms.* Geneva: United Nations Environmental Programme (UNEP), 2003.

Unruh, Gregory C. "Understanding carbon lock-in." *Energy Policy* 28 (2000): 817–830.

Van de Graaf, Thijs. *The Politics and Institutions of Global Energy Governance.* Houndmills: Palgrave Macmillan, 2013.

Victor, David G. *Global Warming Gridlock: Creating More Effective Strategies for Protecting the Planet.* Cambridge, UK: Cambridge University Press, 2011.

Vogler, John. *Climate Change in World Politics.* Houndmills: Palgrave Macmillan, 2016.

Vormedal, Irja. "The influence of business and industry NGOs in the negotiation of the Kyoto mechanisms: The case of carbon capture and storage in the CDM." *Global Environmental Politics* 8, no. 4 (2008): 36–65.

Voß, Jan-Peter. "Innovation processes in governance: The development of 'emissions trading' as a new policy instrument." *Science and Public Policy* 34, no. 5 (2007): 329–343.

Voß, Jan-Peter, and Arno Simons. "Instrument constituencies and the supply side of policy innovation: The social life of emissions trading." *Environmental Politics* 23, no. 5 (2014): 735–754.

World Bank. *State and Trends of Carbon Pricing 2014.* Washington, DC: World Bank, 2014.

Zürn, Michael, and Benjamin Faude. "Commentary: On fragmentation, differentiation, and coordination." *Global Environmental Politics* 13 (2013): 119–130.

# Index

For Product Safety Concerns and Information please contact our EU
representative GPSR@taylorandfrancis.com Taylor & Francis Verlag GmbH,
Kaufingerstraße 24, 80331 München, Germany

Printed and bound by CPI Group (UK) Ltd, Croydon, CR0 4YY

01/05/2025

01858413-0001